FORCE OF GOD

Insurrections: Critical Studies in Religion, Politics, and Culture

INSURRECTIONS: CRITICAL STUDIES IN
RELIGION, POLITICS, AND CULTURE

Slavoj Žižek, Clayton Crockett, Creston Davis,
Jeffrey W. Robbins, editors

The intersection of religion, politics, and culture is one of the most discussed areas in theory today. It also has the deepest and most wide-ranging impact on the world. Insurrections: Critical Studies in Religion, Politics, and Culture will bring the tools of philosophy and critical theory to the political implications of the religious turn. The series will address a range of religious traditions and political viewpoints in the United States, Europe, and other parts of the world. Without advocating any specific religious or theological stance, the series aims nonetheless to be faithful to the radical emancipatory potential of religion.

Force of God

Political Theology and the
Crisis of Liberal Democracy

CARL A. RASCHKE

Columbia University Press   New York

Columbia University Press
Publishers Since 1893
New York   Chichester, West Sussex
cup.columbia.edu
Copyright © 2015 Columbia University Press

Library of Congress Cataloging-in-Publication Data
Raschke, Carl A.
Force of God: political theology and the crisis of
liberal democracy / Carl A. Raschke.
pages cm. — (Insurrections : critical studies
in religion, politics, and culture)
Includes bibliographical references and index.
ISBN 978-0-231-17384-1 (cloth: alk. paper) —
ISBN 978-0-231-53962-3 (e-book)
1. Political theology. 2. Democracy—Religious aspects.
3. Religion and politics. I. Title.

BT83.59.R37   2015
261.7—dc23   2014042954

Columbia University Press books are printed on
permanent and durable acid-free paper.
This book is printed on paper with recycled content.
Printed in the United States of America

c 10 9 8 7 6 5 4 3 2 1

Add cover/jacket credit information

TO MY ENTIRE FAMILY:

my son Erik,
daughter-in-law Jikke,
grandsons Kes and Casjen,
and my wife Sunny.

Contents

Preface

In 1922 Carl Schmitt wrote that "the metaphysical image that a definite epoch forges of the world has the same structure as what the world immediately understands to be appropriate as a form of its political organization." What Schmitt did not say is that often crisis arises because the metaphysical structure—Gilles Deleuze's "image of thought"—is no longer in alignment with the political form. Jacques Derrida perhaps intended something similar when in *Specters of Marx* he introduced the concept of the "messianic" in the context of his diagnosis of the present time, what Shakespeare had in mind when he wrote that "time is out of joint." Our time is out of joint because the principal political form on which Derrida began to meditate with the fall of Communism—i.e., democracy—is increasingly dislodged from its own "metaphysical structure." This metaphysical structure was forged through various historical circumstances from the seventeenth through the late nineteenth and early twentieth centuries, a metaphysical structure we know simply and perhaps too uncritically as "modernism." The political form is what we know as "liberal democracy."

As we slide onward into the newborn millennium and become increasingly cognizant that both the present and the future will be in many ways vastly different from the previous century, the daily headlines as well as a distinct but cloying feeling for the disjointedness of the times reinforce an unprecedented sense of reality. It is quite obvious that liberal democracy as we know it is in crisis. Since the end of the totalitarian era, most dramatically symbolized in the fall of the Berlin Wall in 1989, many new democracies have come and disappeared with a disturbing rhythm. At the same time, the Western democracies, both in America and in Europe, have descended into profound crises of historically unique proportions. Deepening political dysfunctions are exacerbated by economic challenges that have grown overwhelming for a variety of reasons. The sources of this crisis are multilayered: unsustainable demands on the capacity of governments to provide for the general welfare while maintaining its tax base; insatiable consumerist fantasies combined with an epidemic of narcissistic personality pathologies propagated by the substitution of pure signs for useful commodities (Jean Baudrillard's so-called hyperreality), which can best be described in Fredric Jameson's phrase "the logic of late—global—capitalism"; an explosion of ethnic and cultural identitarian politics as well as resurgent types of religious exceptionalism and zealotry that go hand in hand with the slow but steady collapse of the institutions of civil society and authority of the nation-state that, from a generic standpoint, underpins liberal democracy; what Olivier Roy has termed the "de-culturing" of worldwide religious belief, leading to the divorce of faith from politics and the many metastasized manifestations of what Mark Lilla terms "the great separation," including religious fanaticism and terrorism as well as the sort of smarmy, kitschy, mindless, pseudo-intellectual, and slyly bigoted brand of unbelief expressed in the movement known as the "new atheists."

The crisis remains imperceptible only to the most wizened ideologues and those who are historically and culturally trend-deaf. Normally the response, which reflects our own sordid and self-referential subcultural (what we mistakenly describe as "partisan") politics, is to find, assign, and embroider the countless constructs for blame. As Nietzsche himself diagnosed, generalized social *ressentiment* cannot be disentangled from an addiction to causal explanations. In the age of the social sciences with their exhaustless capacity to single out "problems," victims, and therapeutic or policy remedies, such *ressentiment* goes viral and the engines driving it become a juggernaut.

"Scientific" causal analysis failed most theatrically with the global economic meltdown of 2008, a failure that in many ways can traced to a certain deficit in the professional disciplines themselves, which many contemporary theorists have lamented for well over a generation. Aside from the "great" separation of the political from the religious, a more telling rupture has been the separation of political theory from economic thinking—in short, the default of what was once known as "political economy." It can be said that Karl Marx—or at least the Marx of the 1830s and 1840s—was the last great political economist in the omnibus sense, and it is the raw economism and intellectual dogmatism of later, "orthodox" Marxism-Leninism, from which the subtleties of communal interaction along with the inscription of social life within some sort of wider, far more nuanced, ontological matrix are completely absent, that commentators have only surmised as the leading factor in the elaboration of its darker totalitarian legacy as well as in its eventual historical demise. A more supple and genuinely "humanized" Marxism could easily have provided a warning of the economic disaster of 2008. The question of capital is not at all dead, and it will take a bona fide political economy of the future to chart its vicissitudes and anticipate its crises to come.

But the default of political economy, particularly in the twentieth century, has had hitherto undetected side consequences that go a long way toward accounting for the crisis of liberal democracy in the main. In the forthcoming pages we shall explore at length the nature, indications, and social-theoretical intricacies of the default by seeking to conduct, à la Nietzsche and Foucault among others, a *genealogical* investigation into the crisis of liberal democracy, conceptually as well as historically. In short, we will seek to revive the angle of classical political economy by deploying the genealogical perspective, if not its exacting method.

Yet, as we shall discover, any political economy *redivivus* remains impossible without some approach that accounts once more for the *authorization* of the political as a whole. The authorization of the political has been the persistent preoccupation of so much twentieth-century social thought, amounting to what Jürgen Habermas once dubbed a "legitimation crisis." The end of Marxism has served to deprive political economy of its putative "historical-materialist" justification. Certainly we have seen even the wannest ghosts of natural rights reasoning, except perhaps in some revanchist corners, fly off into

the great historical night. The late twentieth-century phenomenon—
perhaps the word *insurgency* would be more apt—Derrida has named
the "return of the religious" has filled the void in a certain measure,
generating a dynamic comeback in the twenty-first century of a certain once highly discredited form of political thinking that Schmitt
christened "political theology." Political theology has partnered both
directly and indirectly with a reenergized discipline of the theory of
religion (or "religious theory"), distinctively within the new globalized, multicultural, and multidisciplinary frame of analysis. What do
we mean for the purposes of this book by "political theology?"

There are many different ways of construing the expression these
days, but briefly we will summarize what it signifies for the strategic
and operative purposes of our undertaking. Political theology is never
political theory, of course. Nor is it ever *sensu stricto* what commonly
passes for "theology." Political theology is only conceivable and plau-
sible at a time where we have witnessed, and are continuing to witness,
the *end of theology*.

Political theology is *not* a theology of the political. Instead it aims
to inquire into the grounds—or perhaps we should say the *ontological
grounding*—of the political as we know it. It inquires into the *apparition* of the political, which has its origins in Greece and has evolved,
drawing on the "metaphysical" superstructure of that inaugural formation or representation, into modern liberal democracy. Understanding this grounding—in German we would choose along with Marx
the term *Grundrisse*—is what Nietzsche meant by genealogy, and it
is back to Nietzsche's understanding we are compelled to turn. With
his critique of "moral-Christian" (i.e., Platonic) metaphysics as well as
the politics of the democratic "herd," which he pursued with a genealogical scalpel that laid bare the secret of all cognitive certainty as
valuation, Nietzsche genuinely discerned political theology as genealogy. The "out-of-jointedness" of today can be laid at the feet of the
very forces Nietzsche divined. It is impossible to arrive at a sense of
crisis without a commitment to a genealogical adventure, which one
must forthwith undertake. It is no longer a question of the Owl of
Minerva taking flight, but of the mongoose going for the coiled cobra,
the cobra that is the senescent metaphysico-political order in its dying
gesture of defiance.

We say "divine" here not merely as a trope, because in his own *deep politics* of the Dionysian Nietzsche recognized something that placed him prophetically ahead of his time, something that perhaps can be compared to Einstein's insight into the ontological equivalence of mass and energy. *Dio-nisus* is the "drive of the divine," the *Trieb* that forges value domains as Krishna in the Bhagavad Gita manufactures worlds. Every genealogical foray ends up staring in the face of the Dionysian, the occasion for Nietzsche's own apocalyptic madness. But we must go there despite the risks. What Nietzsche grasped, and Deleuze in his use of Nietzsche so well articulated, is that genealogy leads us to an intuition of the deeper *play of forces* behind the deep politics of not only our era but also previous ones. The play is at the same time a *Wechselspiel,* an "interplay," which both in its origins and in its outtake can be deciphered as "divine" in an authentic political theological entailment of all its inferential possibilities. It is what we will designate as the *force of God.*

The first four chapters of part 1 lay the philosophical groundwork for this genealogical foray into the concept of the political by exploring the different ramifications of the question Nietzsche himself raised in problematizing the Western philosophical tradition overall, the question of force—specifically, the relationship between force and value. These chapters aim to show how the principle I have termed the "force of God" emerges within the Hegelian dialectic and crystallizes in radical and avante-garde thinking, including the arts, in the late nineteenth and early twentieth century, coming to the fore finally in the political philosophy of Jacques Derrida. Chapter 5 investigates the nature and background of the crisis of liberal democracy by using the genealogical terms and tools developed in part 1. Following a thread of analysis implicit in the thought of Nietzsche, it explores how the crisis of representation is in effect a crisis of valuation driven by the hollowing out of the "relations of production" into pure "symbolic economies" that no longer have any real, only a "hyperreal," character. Chapter 6 frames the crisis of liberal democracy in terms of the new era of globalization and "postnationalism," pursuing how the thought of Carl Schmitt, who invented the term *political theology,* can be reappropriated in a new way to comprehend the breakdown of modern representative democracy into irreconcilable claims of "identity politics." Chapter 7 demonstrates how the legitimation crisis of liberal democracy results not from the failure of liberal institutions to "represent" the generic will or interests of their constituents, but from the "metaphysics" of representation itself. Chapters 8 and 9 look at the collapse of the political within the growing "economy of resentment" and the overrunning of political life by the metastasis of the state.

The book does not pose an articulated solution to the crisis any more than Nietzsche himself posed a "solution" to the death of God. The death of God and the crisis of liberal democracy, in fact, consist in different facets of the same epochal "event" delineating the late modern period. But, like Augustine's vision of the city of God that lies beyond and grows almost indistiguishably within the frenzy of history on the whole, it summons us to realize that the force of God outstrips the death of God. This force is the force of both "resurrection" and "insurrection," which etymologically have much the same meaning.

The book undertakes a project framed slightly earlier by Jeffrey Robbins's fine work *Radical Democracy and Political Theology*. Robbins argues that what political theology, following Schmitt, "brings is a sustained focus on the nature of sovereign power." However, Robbins makes it clear that Schmittian sovereignty must be turned upside down in the present era and radically recast in terms of the diffusion of decision within the panoply of democractic practice and pluralism, rather than as unimpeachable executive authority. Sovereign power manifests no longer as the classical God-king prerogative, but in a "radically immanent" form of secular distribution of "generative potential" within the *demos* itself. Such a "political potency" turns out to be "radical democracy's resistance to all forms of hegemony . . . not by way of a transcendent authority . . . but by way of an exodus emanating within."[1] This "exodus" in my estimation—and in light of my analysis of the capture of democratic desires by the corporate consumerist state apparatus—emanates, as I show in conclusion, from the "revolutionary" religious potentialities that are first evident in the early modern era.

Finally, *Force of God* seeks neither to offer a scholarly review of the relationship between political theology and political economy nor a risky, bathyspheric venture into the genealogical abyss that Nietzsche himself undertook. Nietzsche is the pioneer and perfecter of our political faith. Ours is but probing exegesis and cautionary commentary. It is understandable that after completing this exercise, we—especially we impatient, pragmatic Anglophone readers—feel compelled to ask the perennial question of "what is to be done?" But what is to be done will become slowly evident as we begin to absorb why we are where we are. That is the task of *real politics*, not political theology. As Alain Badiou reminds us, the only real politics is a militant politics, a politics of the truth that can best be glimpsed far into the depths, the "truth" that generates the event, the truth that Nietzsche, in his *Thus Spoke Zarathustra,* wanted to marry by offering the "nuptial ring" of *Ewigkeit*, "endlessness." A real, militant politics rides on the great, eschatological steed of political genealogy. But the final battle is yet to come. That is for when we sit down and write next time.

Acknowledgments

Many factors enter into the long and complex process whereby a book progresses from original inspiration through early gestation to completion. The conception and progress through the early stages of this book would not have been possible without sabbatical time off from the University of Denver in 2009 and a briefer, minisabbatical two years later. I would also like to especially thank Creston Davis for his encouragement and guidance of this manuscript through the final stages as well as his advice on how to configure it specifically for the Insurrections series. Finally, I would like to thank the following colleagues and graduate students for their input, suggestions, and consultation at various stages: Victor Taylor at York College of Pennsylvania, David True of Wilson College, David Hale at Colorado Mesa University, and Luis Leon at the University of Denver; Tyler Akers, Jason Alvis, Joshua Ramos, Timothy Isaacson, Donnie Featherston, and Zachary Settle. Last but not least, I want to express my love and appreciation for my wife Sunny, without whose daily support, admiration, and inspiration I could hardly find the focus and persistence to carry such a project through.

FORCE OF GOD

Part 1

HISTORICAL AND THEORETICAL CONSIDERATIONS

I

Liberal Democracy and the Crisis of Representation

Qui définit le moment où j'écris?
—MICHEL FOUCAULT

The crisis today of liberal democracy in the West may have roots that run far deeper than what the prevailing theories consistently suggest. Innumerable causes and factors have been cited to question the long haul viability of liberal democracy. Yet in certain respects these "reasons" are simply excuses diverting our attention to an underlying structural shift—we might even invoke the rather clichéd descriptor *seismic*—in what Michel Foucault, analyzing almost half a century ago the precipitous transition from the modern to the postmodern, elegantly termed the present-day *episteme*. Foucault rightly and insightfully recognized that the fatal crisis of modernity was fundamentally a *crisis of representation*.

The crisis was precipitated, Foucault observed, when modernism after Immanuel Kant rejected the classical theory of representation as reflective analogy and offered instead the dual strategy of replacing the idea of knowledge as representation with either a formalized system of quasi-mathematical tokens, as in the case of symbolic logic, or the "transcendental" investigation of the nature of the subject in its variable guises. Postmodern philosophy took an entirely different course in seeking to resolve the crisis by demystifying the subject entirely and returning to the Renaissance focus on interconnections among signs. Foucault's own "discourse analysis"—the emphasis on broad, linguistic procedures whereby knowledge is produced and power relations maintained—was one major staple of this "semiotic" revolution in which the peculiar postmodern era of thought emerged.[1]

The crisis of representation, however, has had an especially corrosive effect on political thought and practice, and in the sociocultural macrocosm that is the present-day order of things has undermined the very order of legitimacy on which liberal democracy was always based. The conventional idea of liberal democracy as "representative democracy" strongly implicates such a close correlation. In liberal democracy both legislative and executive institutions in a wide range of degrees represent the "will"—more specifically the aggregate *interests*—of the populace. But representative democracy as a set of institutions, or Foucault's *praxes* of "power/knowledge," has ultimately foundered on the crisis of representation itself, which is in truth an *epistemic crisis*. Different epistemic strategies have been brought to bear in aiming to resolve it, or to go beyond it, for several centuries.

As the English political philosopher C. B. McPherson noted, about the same time Foucault published his major theoretical work in France known as *Les Mots et les choses* (translated into English as *The Order of Things*), the very anchoring principles of liberal democracy were forged in, and are peculiar in both their language and historical relevance to, the situation in England in the seventeenth century.[2] MacPherson helps us understand how the situational idiosyncrasies of the discourse of the "rights of Englishmen," to which the American colonists appealed a century later, cannot be separated from a theory of political sovereignty bound up uniquely with that period's tendency to "deconstruct," as we would say nowadays, previous natural law theory in order to operationalize once and for all the identification of sovereignty with *subjectivity*—subjectivity *as ownership* or the *appropriation* of everything that was distinctively *not human* in nature.

The definition of "humanity" in original liberal theory thus was based on a pure limit-concept, the abstraction of the possessive individual for whom all instances of *otherness* are never real or concrete, but theoretical bounding principles utilized for the defense of property. Even the state is no longer envisioned as a corporate *persona*, as it was in the Roman context. Its alterity belongs to this limit-concept as well.

Even if "rights" nowadays have been abstracted to include such intangible *propria* as privacy, freedom of speech and mobility, etc., this essential "representational" model—the governing function as the protection of what is uniquely one's "own"—remains. As MacPherson observes, "the difficulties of modern liberal-democratic theory lie deeper than had been thought, that the original seventeenth-century theory of individualism contained the central difficulty, which lay in its possessive quality. Its possessive quality is found in its conception of the individual as essentially the proprietor of his own person or capacities, owing nothing to society for them."[3]

The abstract individual, therefore, remains at the same time merely, as Marx would have phrased it, an *abstract human being*. Classical liberal political doctrine abstracts from the concretized formality of *homo historicus*—the unique social, relational, and technological creature who has developed and been transformed over time, metamorphosing from a mere ligament in the primitive collective to modern participant in civil society. These progressive transmutations are what confer genuine content upon the subject matter of all post-Enlightenment anthropologies. The contentless formalism of "possessive individualism"—a not-so-disguised homology for *humanitas* as redefined by modern capitalism according to such a theory—is deployed nominally to support the ideal of human emancipation, but paradoxically becomes the operational principle of *enslavement*.

Such servitude is the outgrowth a fundamentally defective theory of human nature, a truncated characterization of the species itself that, according to Marx, substitutes mere "acquisitive" desire (which in itself results from the self-alienation of labor value as monetized, and hence abstract, surplus value) for the full, "natural" ensemble of productive, reciprocal, and inextricably *social* connections and commitments. But the political theory of possessive individualism, as first articulated in the early twentieth century by R. H. Tawney and enshrined in the early 1960s with the publication of McPherson's *chef d'oeuvre* by the same title, can no longer be sustained in the post-Marxist era as the groundwork for a critique of liberal democracy. The failure of such a theory has less to do with the collapse of Marxism itself as a global motivating force for historical change as with the growing recognition that the current world crisis stems from an even more profound failure to discern something in the human reality that has hitherto gone unnoticed. Moreover, the crisis of representation in political thought itself is simply an adjunct of this failure to discern. It stems not so much from a system of foundational oversights within the ambit of anthropology as from a necessity to retool the basis of political theory itself. It arises from not only a hollowing out of the conception of human, but from a reductionism that makes sclerotic, or even "zombifies," the very embodiment of sovereign authority we have understood since Aristotle's time as the *politeia,* the notion of a certain community from which we derive the words *politics* and *political.*

Sovereignty and Subjectivity

In this respect the crisis of representation proves itself to be intertwined with a crisis in the theory of sovereignty. The question of sovereignty, which lies at the heart of all modern political thought, was given a curious spin in the writings of Carl Schmitt after World War I and has often been blamed, rightly or wrongly, as an ingenious strategy of legitimation for the lethal antidemocratic movements in the last century, especially fascism. The seemingly indistinguishable boundary between the democratic maxim of "we the people" and its complete negation in the totalitarian *Führerprinzip* has been attributed to Schmitt's own theoretical innovations, particularly his identification of sovereignty with a kind of absolute religious monarchism that suspends the classical association of *politeia* with *nomos*, of political life with citizenship.

We are not by any means the first, of course, to be concerned with the dissolution of the political in our time or to begin to conceive its possible rescue through its reformulation on "theological" grounds. Like Schmitt, the German Catholic whose influence has been immense, we have Leo Strauss, the Jew, whose works has had an outsize impact on recent political thought. Both Schmitt and Strauss were passionately preoccupied with the disintegration of liberal democracy in the lengthy period since the European Enlightenment. At the same time, Strauss and Schmitt's reputations have been tarnished over the years because they have been associated for different reasons with now suspect, or discredited, historical movements. Schmitt was long dismissed as a proto-ideologue of National Socialism. More recently, Strauss has been typecast as the intellectual inspiration for neoconservatism and the Bush administration's military adventures in the Middle East. Schmitt turns out to be more historically culpable because of his actual flirtation with the Nazis. Strauss's fall from favor unfortunately is more a matter of guilt by association insofar as the neocons were always citing him in their academic justifications of policies after 2001.

We raise the question of Schmitt and Strauss here only because each in his own way had certain provocative, if not somewhat eccentric, insights into problems with modern democracy that Western "liberalism" in general has too long ignored and is currently in danger of ignoring at all our peril. Their insight, broadly speaking, was that any form of democracy that seeks to marginalize the religious is bound to shatter against its own internal contradictions.[4]

Furthermore, both figures, like Nietzsche in the nineteenth century—and Heidegger, Lacan, and Žižek in the following one—frame the question of the political in terms of the modern metaphysics of subjectivity—what Heidegger dubbed "subjectism." It has been the distinctive insight of so much of modern "political theology" that subjectism and the political are intrinsically incompatible with each other. The philosophical postulate of the transcendental subject reigned supreme for three hundred years from Descartes forward, but ultimately collapsed in the twentieth century with the realization that all subjectivity is *intersubjectivity*. The thesis of intersubjectivity was first advanced in Hegel's dialectic of master and slave, but refined considerably in the thought of Jacques Lacan and Emmanuel Levinas. Concomitantly, the political theory of the possessive individual fractures with the recognition that property is inherently unrepresentable, mainly because it has no real "interests" to represent. It is no more than a transcendental condition of the right to appropriate, which outside the state of nature amounts, as Marx presciently saw, to the infinite right to *expropriate*. What is expropriated is not the bounty of the state of nature, but the productivity of labor.

Whereas seventeenth-century liberalism had used the theory of appropriation to justify the rights of traders and the landed gentry against the encroachments of the monarchy, nineteenth-century industrial capitalism employed the same model to legitimate the wage servitude of the landless urban proletariat with "nothing to lose but their chains." With the rise of social democracy and the transformation of the working class into property owners in the twentieth century, the theory of possessive individualism became the pure, antistatist libertarianism we see, particularly in America, today. However, it is also equally manifested in the latter-day phenomenon of what *New York Times* columnist David Brooks once identified as the "bohemian bourgeoisie," the assetless and fashionably indebted consumer of culture and knowledge who believes he or she is entitled to the largess of the economically productive classes through government subsidies and taxation of "the rich."

The "right" to expropriate in pursuit of some ultimately abstract, unrepresentable construct of self-identity has been the preoccupation of both postwar left and right, as social philosopher Christopher Lasch acidly opined during the late 1970s in his best-selling book *The Culture of Narcissism*. Lasch also made the point that liberal democracy is impossible without a commitment within the culture to building strong personal character, which in turn requires a consensual obligation to common, clearly articulated values as well as a general deferral to the guiding role of religion and the family. The idea harks back all the way to Jefferson and even beyond that to the Enlightenment assumption that effective self-governance was ineluctably founded on the maintenance of "virtue" throughout society.[5]

The crisis of representation, however, as Nietzsche discerned, is not merely a problem of the degeneracy of a civilization. It can be attributed to the innate autocorrosive properties of the modern *episteme* itself in which the theory of representation is rooted. Nietzsche's well-known prophecy of the advent of modern nihilism was not some proto-Spenglerian identification of a "decline of the West" syndrome.

Nihilism stood "at the door," according to Nietzsche, because of the hollowing out of the very Platonic architecture of thought that sustained the entire *episteme* itself, the architecture he dubbed the "moral view of the world" where "scientific" concepts and values remained indistinguishable from each other across the landscape of a metaphysical lotusland rife with idealist illusions. The virtuosity—the indigenous "excellence," or what the Greeks termed the *arête,* of the peoples of the West—had not simply succumbed to the inevitable civilizational cycles of decay and disarray, as Plato had predicted. "The highest values devalue themselves."[6] Why?

Nietzsche, like Freud, Marx, and the other great critics of "ideology" in the nineteenth century, was convinced that an answer to such a question required a clinical diagnosis rather than an explanation. A diagnosis is focused on symptoms, not causal connections. And Deleuze's innovative redescription of philosophical transparency as *symptomatology* rather than as phenomenology owes a direct debt to Nietzsche, who was his most telling, lifelong source of inspiration. Unlike phenomenology, a symptomatology does not seek to bring the deeper essentials of a situation to light. It seeks to show how a certain confluence of actions, artifices, and indexes are interrelated in such a way that the general condition in which we find ourselves becomes merely more intelligible. A symptomatology, as Deleuze pointed out, is concerned with surfaces rather than underlying realities. The diagnosis comes from the careful coordination of observations regarding transient effects, even if at some point the obvious "causal" factor becomes apparent. Despite the philosophical theory of causation, which he considered a spectral afterglow of God language, what mattered most for Nietzsche was the way in which both synchronic (cultural) and diachronic (historical) patterns of signs and meanings coalesced into a kind of critical language that would set in motion wholly new vistas of interpretation. Nietzsche's "gay science" was, therefore, a hermeneutics of lightness, an emancipation of thought from the clunky, factitious posturings of metaphysical explanation and allowing it to "dance" with the liberated movements of what he called "free spirits." Postmodern philosophy, mistakenly dismissed as antiphilosophy, is the progeny of Nietzsche's mythic free spirit.

NIETZSCHE'S METHOD OF GENEALOGY

Nietzsche's named his method of correlating the fluid, surface metrics of his ironic observations "genealogy." Nietzsche's notion was modeled on the common practice of family genealogy as a tracing of both genetic connections and social contexts backward through a branching system that becomes more complex as it moves ever further backward in time. Nietzsche's aversion to causation in the scientific realm was mirrored in his skepticism of a search for "origins," not to mention direct lineages, in the historical disciplines. As in all "sciences," including what the Germans in the nineteenth century dubbed *Geisteswissenschaften*, the operative protocol for unearthing significance should be "interpretation."

But genealogy as interpretation must be distinguished from hermeneutics, or hermeneutical theory, which focuses on texts and artifacts. Genealogy is not a "fusion" of interpretative horizons, as Hans-Georg Gadamer's famous definition of the hermeneutical process implies. Genealogy is preoccupied not with meaning but with value (*Wert*)— or, more precisely, valuation (*Bewertung*), which he characterized as an activity or agency rather than a state of affairs. Nietzsche's well-known concept of the "transvaluation [*Umwertung*] of all values" implies such an agential reformatting of what we mean by the term *Wert* itself (cognate with the English "worth"). The procedure of genealogy is part and parcel of this *Umwertung*.

The act of transvaluation is, therefore, at the same time a moment of "reinterpretation" in a more technical sense that it normally entails. It is not so much "historical" as belonging to what Nietzsche referred to as the "higher history" of the human race, for which the eschatology of the "overman" (*Übermensch*) was the anchoring trope. The vision of a higher history, or "future philosophy," is impossible without the transvaluing role of the genealogical approach.

Nietzsche's *Zur Genealogie der Moral* (*On the Genealogy of Morals*), first published in 1887, deployed this method in a formidable manner that distinctly colors every later aphoristic comment on Christianity, Platonism, modern philosophy, and European culture. However, his collection of essays on history entitled *Unzeitgemässe Betrachtungen* (translated in various ways, most commonly as "Untimely Meditations"), completed in 1876, over a decade earlier, provides the theoretical key to Nietzsche's understanding of genealogy.

Particularly in the essay *Vom Nutzen und Nachteil der Historie für das Leben* ("On the Use and Disadvantage of History for Life"), Nietzsche attacked contemporary German historicism and its obsession with "understanding" historical events as the clue to the present. Many biographers of Nietzsche have cited his disgust with the self-congratulatory rhetoric in the new unified Reich following its victory in the Franco-Prussian War and its pseudo-appeal to German cultural superiority as the motivating factor behind his criticism. But Nietzsche was less compelled by his signature distaste for Teutonic chauvinism than by the insight that historical criticism could either "serve life" or serve the degenerate tendencies of an increasingly "philistine" bourgeois civilization. The latter indeed had bought into a pervasive cheap form of neo-Kantianism, which made "truth" indistinguishable from morality. Kant himself had encouraged this popular German view of truth in the *Critique of Practical Reason* and the *Groundwork of the Metaphysics of Morals* when he went beyond his earlier efforts to demonstrate the limits of scientific rationality and argued that supersensible, or "noumenal," reality (i.e., the Platonic *eidos* or "idea") can be correlated with the human mind if it is a "representation" (*Vorstellung*) of our consciousness of the universally valid moral law.[7]

For Nietzsche, this popular manner of thinking constituted the ultimate mongrelization of Western ontology, far more than had been the case even with Plato. In essence, Kantianism itself was clear evidence that the crisis of representation could be seen as the inexorable culmination of the Platonic identification of being with value. Historicism and scientism, used in the service of mass propaganda, amounted to the same kind of degeneracy. What were taken smugly as "facts" supporting the new democratic ideals of nationalism and the sovereignty of the Volk were in actuality covert valuations that did not serve "life" but *decadence*.

History as opposed to historicism, therefore, must concern itself with reshaping the present. "History belongs . . . to the man of deeds and power, to him who fights a great fight."[8] The transformative element—which is also a "transvaluative" element—in the pursuit of history is comprised of what Nietzsche calls a "plastic force" that can be found in persons as well as cultures. Out of this plastic force grows "distinctively" the power to "replace what is lost" and to reform (*nach-formen*) the "broken forms" from past cultures.[9] Nietzsche would later name this "plastic force" the "will to power" (*Wille zur Macht*). It is the stunting of the plastic force that has produced the decadence and hypocrisy of Western culture by channeling it into an obsession with the transcendent "reality" behind what is merely given, by locating the essence masked by the appearance, by insisting on a "formal" system of evidentiary correspondences between representations and mere sense presentations, by seeking to ground the "noumenal" in the force of reason itself.

The *force* "behind" phenomena is, instead, a creative force that must be mastered, structured, morphed into one's own *command* rather than simply reacting, as in Kant's moral epistemology, to the dictates of "pure reason" (*reine Vernunft*). These dictates, Kant insisted, must be "represented" as a "command," because to recognize them required not simply our conscious assent but our active obedience. Whereas for Kant one defers to the force, in Nietzsche one takes the reins over it. The historian hence becomes a genealogist. A genealogist, as Deleuze observes, "evaluates the origins of forces from the point of view of their nobility, or baseness, since it discovers their ancestry in the will to power and the quality of the will."[10]

Nietzsche's genealogical approach, therefore, relies on historical discernment that serves the plastic force. Foucault's subsequent use of the term *genealogy* to analyze discursive practices as the interplay of language and power adopts many of Nietzsche's tactics. A genealogist, according to Foucault's reading of Nietzsche, is not concerned with "origin" (*Ursprung*) but "emergence" (*Enstehung*), which is always "produced through a particular stage of forces."[11] What Nietzsche termed "effective history" (*wirkliche Historie*) is an interpretative "dissociation" of seemingly coherent processes, themes, and principles that brings to light this confluence of forces. History is not a question of understanding (*Verstehen*), as it was for Wilhelm Dilthey's historicism, or of divining deeper significations and applications, but of the articulation of these forces for which events are but "masks." Nietzsche's celebrated aphorism—*alles, was tief ist, liebt die Maske* ("what is profound loves masks")—testifies to this *antimetaphysical* assemblage of forces with phenomena as what we would term the "events of history."[12] A "mask" does not hide something in the background as it serves as a metaphor for the intractable opacity of events as they occur. We cannot, and should not, seek what is "behind" the mask. We should seize these forces as we find ourselves enmeshed in them and redirect them, make each one a tour de force.

THE GENEALOGY OF THE POLITICAL

Furthermore, Nietzsche's genealogical strategy has a genuine bearing on what we would call the political, even though Nietzsche should never be considered a *political thinker* in the usual connotation of the phrase. Our thesis is simply that the crisis of liberal democracy, stemming from the crisis of representation, requires a genealogy focused on the forces immanent within modern history, an opening to seize the momentary configuration of what lies at hand in the new, globalized world and bring about a transformation of values. Politics is ultimately about values. But values are not lucidly inscribed within the order of things. Values are neither discovered nor selected, but—as Nietzsche understood—"willed."

The classic problem of expressing "will" in its political formulation —whether we are talking about Plato's philosopher kings, the baroque absolute monarchs, liberal democracy, or the twentieth-century totalitarian state—comes down to what scholars have noted is the critical untranslatability of the word from which "political" eminently derives, i.e., *politeia*. *Politeia* was the word Aristotle himself employed in his *Politics*, which most experts regard as a designation of the formal and theorizable structure of the city, or *polis*.[13] *Politeia* is also the actual Greek title of Plato's *Republic*, which draws on Cicero's translation of the same Greek word. Why Cicero invented the expression *res publica* ("matters public") to render *politeia* remains something of a mystery among classicists. Perhaps it reflected the Roman "republican" emphasis on civic service as opposed to the Hellenic preoccupation with human nature and the cultivation of virtue.

But the question of the "best" form of *politeia*, which is at bottom the question of political theory, cannot be seriously engaged without an assessment of the decisional components in the form of organization itself. Plato was suspicious of democracy because he had recent historical memories of the disastrous results of the Peloponnesian War and the thirty tyrants who had manipulated the *demos* for their dictatorial ends. Aristotle, on the other hand, laid the groundwork for later notions of "representative" democracy with his favoring of a "mixed" *politeia* that combined the democratic, aristocratic, and oligarchic forms. The issue of *authority*, or who "authors" the decisions made in governance, is the key to what is meant by *politeia*, and it has been since ancient Greek times.

All these ancillary issues coalesce centrally in Nietzsche's question, which Foucault framed, of "who speaks"? Perhaps a better way of framing the question, "genealogically speaking," would be "who wills?" As Alan Schrift has commented in his penetrating study of the influence of Nietzsche on French poststructuralism in the 1960s and 1970s, the former's "recognition that the faith in the representational accuracy of language had been eclipsed led Nietzsche to shift the focus of his critical attention away from *what* was said, turning this attention instead toward a genealogical critique of *who* said what was said, and what the *reasons* were which had given rise to what was said."[14] Nietzsche himself regarded what the French poststructuralists, such as Lacan and Foucault, deemed the "creation of the subject" as an act of *interpretation*, which is at the same time an act of *affirmation*. In this "yea-saying" the *Wille zur Macht*, drawing on its "plastic power," both forms itself and commands others, and thus transvalues the passive "slave values" of the political masses.

Poststructuralism has routinely been accused of contributing fatefully to the crisis of representation and, by implication, of contributing to the undermining of liberal democracy. But the record clearly shows that the opposite is the case. The crisis of representation was astutely recognized, not only by Nietzsche but also by Heidegger, as the condition of modern nihilism, for which poststructuralism sought an answer. Using different styles, the different post-structuralists performed their own "genealogical" investigation as the route to a new philosophy of both the affirmative and the *singular* as opposed to the generic or universal.

The torchbearer for this post-Nietzschean project was actually Jacques Derrida, especially in his later "political" and "religious" phases. The Derridean backdrop and contribution to the effort first undertaken by Plato in *The Republic* has still not been appreciated with any real subtlety to this date. For both Plato and Derrida, the secret of the *politeia* is the establishment of "justice." But for both Plato and Derrida as well the secret lies not in an economy of relations among those who make up the "political" community, but in the very *eschatological* question, the question of how to evaluate these relationships as one approaches the finite limits of human life, knowledge, and achievement.

The problem of justice at the outset of *The Republic* is introduced as an obsession of the wealthy Athenian Cephalus, who is "filled with apprehensions and concern about matters that before did not occur to him."[15] Cephalus wants clarity on how his wealth and behavior has affected others, both positively and negatively, and what he can look forward to in the afterworld. As *The Republic* winds through its ten books and numerous pages, it meanders from Cephalus's concern with the status of his own soul in the afterworld through various discussions about how the meaning of the term *dike* in ordinary language transitions to the well-known portrayal of an ideal state, finally coming full circle to the initial conundrum of what happens in the hereafter, as portrayed in the Myth of Er.

In Derrida the eschatological question is revived once more; it relates to what he terms the "messianic," not the hereafter but the *avenir*, the "to come," which makes justice at once "impossible" and "undeconstructible." In Derrida's work we have the riddle of justice as the overarching theme in any inquiry into the unsearchable mystery of what is not yet, which throws any consideration of the "political" back on to outer limits of representation itself—something standard political "theory" has always resisted. The proper ordering of human relationships that "politics" subtends therefore diffuses into the region of not merely the supersensible, but the form of transcendence we recognize as the "religious." Recognition of the boundaries of representation within the realm of the political cannot be attributed solely to the Hebraic magnitude of Western thought as it has endured for two millennia in tension with the Hellenic, the tension Derrida identifies as our "Jew-Greek" dilemma. It is found in Plato himself, the architect of the very Western theory of representation.

Thus a genuine genealogy of the crisis of representation belongs to a general "deconstructive" reading of philosophy as a whole, something on which Derrida cannily embarked in his later years. Nietzsche's charted "reversal of Platonism" is far less than meets the eye, insofar as the matter of nihilism perhaps is seated within a fateful misreading all along of the theoretical project of describing "justice" as the proper symmetry of human relationships within a "state." Indeed, the problem of the state has little to do with Plato's baseline problem of the *politeia*.

Nietzsche's concept of the will to power may constitute little more than a decisive and radical rereading of the actual tendencies to subordinate justice, the binding principle of the *politeia* in Aristotle's view, to forces or influences that are not so much supersensible as *suprarepresentational*. The paradigm of political thought as a type of sought-after eidetic clarity concerning the ordering of subjective dispositions within a given polis—an epistemological bias that does not have its antecedents in Plato as much as in Descartes—is appropriate only to the modern—and by extension only to the different modern schematisms of "representative government." If modern political theory banished the mystics, they have returned today with a vengeance through the historical failure of the theory of representation itself.

FORCE OF LAW

Nietzsche's true "political" heir is Derrida, which first becomes apparent in his keynote address to a major conference titled "Deconstruction and the Possibility of Justice" at Cornell University Law School in 1989, which was later captioned in a set of collected essays as "Force of Law: The 'Mystical Foundation of Authority.'"[16] Until he was invited to give such an address, Derrida had not explicitly tied the "demand" of justice with his already famous concept of deconstruction. Even though the address itself is complicated, it signifies the first, major fracture in the kind of textualist-enclosed armature of Derrida's earlier writings, opening the way for what is in a regular, overly simplistic manner depicted as his later concerns with ethics, politics, and religion. Derrida never proceeded topically with his particular interests, only strategically with respect to ever more sophisticated "deconstructions" of important classical and contemporary texts. So this opening amounts less to a "turn" away from pure deconstruction to matters ethico-political and religious than a kind of epochal elucidation of what has been tacit but not apparent in his philosophical enterprise all along.

Early on in the talk, Derrida makes it clear that he is not for the first time simply "addressing" the consummate issue of the political. It is the issue of how the *politeia* is to be constituted, the same as Plato's challenge of establishing the proper connotations of *dike*, or justice. His address is not really "addressing" the affinity between deconstruction and justice. The affinity has been there all along. Deconstruction, like Kierkegaard's "authorship," always takes on tasks *obliquely*. "At this very moment," Derrida asserts, "I am preparing to demonstrate that one cannot speak *directly* about justice, thematize or objectify justice, say 'this is just,' and even less 'I am just,' without immediately betraying justice, if not law" (231).

If justice is not a predicate, as Kant said of "existence," or a state or condition that might be defined, characterized, or teased out in its intricate extensions, then what is it? Deconstruction makes "possible" both law and justice. Both law and justice as schema, operations, or procedures—how in a practical sense they in fact become concrete and meaningful—only remain viable or successful in the measure that they are "enforceable." The theory of enforcement belongs, Derrida says in citing the German philosophical tradition of both law and justice as derivative forms of "right" (*Recht*), has everything to do with an understanding of the jurisprudential as "force" (*Gewalt*). In the German language *Gewalt*, which can also be translated as "violence," is normally used in the case of "law enforcement" and is distinguished from *Kraft*, the other word for force, which Nietzsche used routinely. "There is no law (*loi*) without enforceability and no applicability or enforceability of the law (*loi*) without force" (233).

The question of justice, therefore, curiously boils down to a "force that can be just." And the larger question of the "just" type of *politeia*—the "political" question—hinges not so much on its form of organization as on *the forces that converge to realize its formal makeup*. Derrida moves immediately into his own "genealogy" of the relationship between force and justice through an exegesis of a familiar, but brief, essay by Walter Benjamin in the 1920s, "Zur Kritik der Gewalt." Derrida points out that the normal translation into English (and also for the French) is "Critique of Violence," but he makes the salient observation that *Gewalt* in this context really means "force." The translation "violence" automatically suggests the force is unjust. But he argues that *Gewalt*, as Benjamin contextualized it, implies also "legitimate power, justified authority." The association of justice with the "justifying" role of *Gewalt* in the creation of the state and the enforcement of its law goes to the heart of "deconstruction."

In his own deconstructing of related texts "the word 'force' is both very frequent and, in strategic places, I would even say decisive" (234). Although Derrida does not use the example, we could cite the common phrase in German *Gerechtigkeit walten lassen* ("let justice prevail"), where *Gewalt* is the noun substantive of the relatively archaic word *walten* ("to work forcefully"). In Old German *walten* was often used to describe the workings of God. Thus *Gewalt* suggests a divine force that, even though inscrutable or repugnant from the finite point of view, is mysteriously "just."

Indeed, as Derrida's subtitle "The Mystical Foundation of Authority" hints, there is both a genealogical and substantial linkage between a *politeia* that is "justly" founded *and* the force of the religious or, more technically, a faith-based or "fiduciary" bonding. "The very emergence of justice and law, the instituting, founding, and justifying moment of law implies a performative force, that is to say always an interpretative force and a call to faith" (241). It is this performative quality of the language of law that makes it "mystical," according to Derrida.

It is a deeper question than Nietzsche's about "who speaks"? *Who founds?* And how can this *founding be justified*. It is not accidental that even in ancient times it was the gods who founded states. Today, for the most part, especially in today's globalized, increasingly "religious," world, the state is "under God." Secularists are effectively speechless, Derrida suggests, because they cannot give an acceptable account for the "establishing" of justice, only of its ongoing rationale and administration.

Derrida's crucial axiom in "Force of Law" is as follows: *laws are deconstructible, justice is not.* Derrida explains this asymmetry in the following quotation: "it is this deconstructible structure of law or, if you prefer, of justice as law, that also ensures the possibility of deconstruction. Justice in itself, if such a thing exists, outside or beyond law, is not deconstructible. No more than deconstruction itself, if such a thing exists. *Deconstruction is justice*" (243). The curious aspect of this seminal statement on Derrida's part is what significance can be attached to the locution "itself" or "in itself." Both deconstruction and justice have this strange *an sich* quality. Derrida naturally is not somehow reviving the German idealist construal of the "in itself" as either pure givenness (*Gegebenheit*) or mere perceptual inaccessibility (as in Kant's *Ding an sich*).

The *in itself* ostensibly indicates a temporal element—what Derrida elsewhere names *avenir*, "to come." But it also refers to what Derrida names the "impossibility" of justice itself. This impossibility is intimately bound up with the fact that justice remains *unpredicatable*. To predicate is to establish an authorizable signifying connection between a universal concept and a particular instance, and in legal theory the specific case must be subsumed under a general rule. Thus we have in a nutshell Kant's infamous problem of "judgment."

But justice has nothing to do with judgment in either the epistemological or the juridical sense so far as Derrida is concerned. Justice is not the subordination, as in Kant, of the specific datum to a principle with universal validity, but follows what I have elsewhere called the *grammar of address*.[17] Justice turns inexorably on the "aporia" of two subjects encountering one another. "One must know that this justice always addresses itself to singularity, to the singularity of the other, despite or even because it pretends to universality" (248). Justice often demands an on-the-spot decision, a response to the infinite claim of those who in themselves also require justice, as Levinas might say. The impossibility of justice is inseparable from its "heteronomy" or, more pointedly, its *heterology*. There is always an "excess" of justice when measured against "law and calculation," hence its alteration with "deconstruction."

In order to enforce these themes, Derrida turns to Benjamin's essay. Benjamin, in a rather coy, but convoluted fashion, radically frames the crisis of representation—and historically of course the ineffectuality and disenchantment of "representative" democracy during the Weimar Republic—by underscoring the genetic correlation between violence and the *politeia,* both in its beginnings and in its preservation. Benjamin thus performs a genealogy of the political with a disarming incisiveness of which even Nietzsche was incapable. The crisis of representation that underlies the modern dysfunction of the *politeia* stems from the Jew-Greek aporia itself. As Derrida notes, *"Zur Kritik der Gewalt* is also inscribed in a Judaic perspective that opposes just, divine (Jewish) violence, which would destroy the law, to mythical violence (of Greek tradition), which would install and preserve the law" (259). Derrida concludes by citing Benjamin's remark at the end of the essay that such "divine violence" (*die göttliche Gewalt*) in fact is, or "may be called sovereign" (262).

Derrida is leveraging Benjamin as a wedge to exercise his own genealogy of liberal democracy with an eye to such subsequent notions as messianism, cosmopolitanism, and, of course, "friendship." Benjamin's essay amounts to a distinctive "philosophy of history," according to Derrida, that recognizes how history is "on the side of . . . divine violence," a violence that "destroys the law, we could even venture to say, deconstructs the law" (290).

Benjamin's *göttliche Gewalt*—and by extension Derrida's as well—is what is really at stake here. The singularity of justice mirrors the singularity of *Gewalt* itself, both the singular violence of a God who says "[just] vengeance is mine" and the inscrutable and justiceless, singular force/violence that erases God's justice, as Derrida describes the Holocaust. "Force of Law" is more a sober meditation on the unrepresentability of divine *Gewalt* and its meaning, which makes all "democracies" seemingly impossible, than it is a prolegomenon to his later "prophetic" musings on a future democracy to come. Could it be that the force of God in Benjamin and Derrida has something to do with Nietzsche's *Wille zur Macht*? To answer that question, we need to do our own genealogy of Derrida and "deconstruction" itself.

2

Force of Thought

> The elements set up as independent pass over
> into their unity, and their unity directly into its
> explicit diversity, and the latter back once again
> into the reduction to unity. This process is what is
> called Force.
>
> —G. W. F. Hegel, *Phenomenology of Spirit*

Deconstruction was always in its own right a *force*, if not a force of
"truthfulness," as Nietzsche would say. Truth in the Nietzschean context always has a genealogy. This modus operandi, which Nietzsche
himself birthed, over the years has been alternately characterized as
"deconstruction" or "postmodern thinking." However, a genealogy of
deconstruction has not yet been written. We can begin to track it, to
discern the traces of such a genealogy in Derrida's early work. The writings of the young Derrida have a consistent intentionality about them.
They radiate the preoccupation of that generation of intellectuals in
France, and slightly later in England and America, with appropriat-
ing and deploying Alexandre Kojève's "humanist" and "revolutionary"
reading of Hegel, which, more than any other book,[1] subtly and indirectly shaped all of avant-garde Western thought from the late 1960s
onward. Kojève was the nephew of Wassily Kandinsky, the incarnate
spirit of modernism in the arts. He was also the architect for the

European Union and, more obliquely, the prophet of the collapse of the Soviet Union. Although a self-proclaimed "Stalinist"/Marxist utopian, Kojève was more responsible for the hubris of globalist neoliberalism, with its end-of-history triumphalism, than for any perfection of the socialist vision.

To his last days, Derrida remained a radical utopian in his own right, a political as well as a philosophical visionary cut from Kojèvean cloth. His later political and religious writings reflect this radical sensibility, although they are distinguished by the manner in which they thoroughly move beyond—as had history itself at their moment of conception—the stock-in-trade Marxism of the European left in the late twentieth century as well as the Hegelianized Marxism of Kojève himself. Derrida's political and religious radicalism can be attributed indirectly to an *implicit,* radical Hegelianism that stalks like the very specters, about which he wrote so copiously from 1989 onward, but is *explicitly* foregone by his own lifelong project of "deconstruction."

Deconstruction was always about *force,* the force of language in action, the force of the creative and the artistic process, the force of history and the passion for a history that remains yet "to come."[2] But, at the same time, is *always coming about (venant),* because it tenses in a grand and urgent movement what is at once *revenant* ("ghost" of what has come), *eventement* (present "event" that consistently comes by surprise), and *l'avènement* of what is *avenir,* "advent" arriving, "to come" (i.e., the "messianic future" that draws past and present far beyond itself in the direction not of what is simply imaginatively and breathtakingly possible but also of the *impossible*). This force is also the key to Hegel, though not the Hegel with which we are familiar.[3]

PLASTICITY AND THOUGHT

The Hegel with which we are familiar is the Hegel of the concept (*Begriff*) and of the dialectic. It is the mature Hegel that has dominated Marxism, though not the Hegel that inspired Kojève to chart a different trajectory for future renderings of Marx and Hegel. Derrida has a different take. His Hegel is of the future. In his preface to Catherine Malabou's *The Future of Hegel: Plasticity, Temporality, and Dialectic,* published in 2004, about the time of his death, Derrida writes that

"Hegel is a thinker of the future." Indeed, he is the thinker, Derrida adds, of the *avenir*, what is "to come."[4] Malabou's book, according to Derrida, is not just a book, but an "event" that radically revisions everything that we have come to assume about Hegel. At "its turbulent and paradoxical heart," the book "projects nothing less than an unheard history," Derrida adds, a history of time as a 'history of the future' and hence as a 'history of the event.'"[5] The event is past, present, and future; it is the "surprise *in* what is coming."

Derrida commends Malabou for downplaying the "speculative" side of the Hegelian dialectic—the reversals or upturnings that constitute the power of negation—in favor of what she calls "plasticity" of the movement of Spirit, the secret of the event. The future "Hegelian" project amounts to "rethinking precisely what constititutes the *eventality* of the event, what comes in the event, what comes forth or comes again in the event, what can be seen as coming in what comes, and what can be seen as coming in the future itself."[6]

Such an *eventuality*, an event-actuality, constitutes a historicization of Kant's principle of judgment as outlined in his third *Critique*, of what he dubbed *hypotoposis*, or making a concept "sensuous" through the schematization of the imagination. The being of the concept is the becoming-sensuous of the concept, which accounts for its history. It also accounts for why all concepts have a historicity, a mobilizing and multiplication of their signifying momenta. Such a realization is behind the well-known remark of Gilles Deleuze and Félix Guattari that "the concept is not an object but a territory . . . it has a past form, a present form and, perhaps, a form to come."[7] This temporalized "formalism," if such a paradoxical notion is possible, relies on the "formative" process of thought itself that Kant recognized as the cipher for the connection between *theoria*, or "seeing," and knowledge. It is not the "imagination" per se, but "the power of imagination" (*Einbildungskraft*). Such a power is realized less as a "faculty" (as in Kant) than as a *force* in Hegel. This force Malabou identifies in Hegel as "plasticity," the temporal-transformative element in all thought. Plasticity temporally "extends" the indefinite assemblage of significations "through ordered transformations" of the concept. "Plasticity, is, therefore, the point around which all the transformations of Hegelian thought revolve, the center of its metamorphoses."[8]

Malabou wants to go even further and open the gates for an eminently deconstructible Hegel. The plasticity of the Hegelian dialectic
stems from the "deconstructive reading" that is inherent in his transformation of the propositional logic of the Aristotelian, and by implication the entire philosophical, tradition into the "speculative sentence."
For Derrida, the "work" of deconstruction is always at work within
the work. It is not so much a *Werk* as a *Wirkung*, an ongoing effectua-
tion of the force of the work. The speculative sentence is not so much
the reflection of the work in itself and upon itself, but the "working
out" of the virtual semiology of the proposition. This interpretation
has some bearing on Deleuze's ideal of the "donation of sense" and his
remark that "the Event is actualized in diverse manners at once."[9] As
Malabou argues, "the coming of the event takes place in the proposition, revealed as the scene of the advent (*lieu d'avènement*). Hence the
proposition in which the subject develops its own self-differentiation
is the very place that promises the future."[10]

This insight into Hegel is clearly what drives Derrida in a not-so-
Hegelian modus operandi, even from the start. In his protodeconstruc-
tionist essay "Force and Signification" published in 1963, Derrida sal-
lies forth with the "poststructuralist" rendering of Hegel's speculative
sentence in his suggestion that writing is "inaugural." Inaugural writing is "dangerous and anguishing. It does not know where it is going,
no knowledge can keep it from the essential precipitation toward the
meaning that it constitutes and that is, primarily, its future."[11] There is
no "interior design" to writing. Writing does not "create" because of
its "freedom to bring forth the already-there as a sign of the freedom
to augur." It is a "freedom of response which acknowledges as its only
horizon the world as history and the speech which can only say: Being
has already begun."[12] The work, or the text, is *being-in-force,* which is
(as it was for Hegel) being as temporalization, as differentiation, as
coming-into-being. In the essay Derrida applauds and cites Hegel. "To
say that force is the origin of the phenomenon is to say nothing. By its
very articulation force becomes a phenomenon. Hegel demonstrated
convincingly that the explication of a phenomenon by a force is a
tautology. But in saying this, one must refer to language's peculiar
inability to emerge from itself in order to articulate its origin, and not
to the *thought* of force."[13] Force is what forces thought, and writing for

that matter, into its mobility, into its "session" and its supersession. "Force is the *other of language without which language would not be what it is*."[14]

But the force of word and, *mutatis mutandis,* the force of thought derive from the "duplicity," which Hegel recognized in the dialectical thrust of discursivity itself, Derrida sights in the transition of the sign, and Ferdinand de Saussure, in inaugurating both "structural" and "post-structural" linguistics, understood as "difference." For Hegel, force is always dividing itself and "forcing" itself *back upon itself*—hence the dialectical return of the proposition back to itself. Hegel's somewhat opaque discussion of "force and the understanding" in the early pages of the *Phenomenology of Spirit* is routinely given short shrift by apostles of Hegelian "idealism." And it was also scanted by Kojève himself as a somewhat arcane run-up to the heart of what he considered genuine, post-Stalinist Marxian-Hegelianism—the master and slave dialectic. It may be irrelevant to Marxism, but it is the turnkey antecedent for deconstruction.

Hegel introduces the notion of "force" (*Kraft*) in subsection 3 of the opening portion of the *Phenomenology*. It is the bridge notion that joins his initial analysis of "sense certainty" and the primitive determination by the mind of what is meaningful to the fuller exploration of self-consciousness. Force is what shapes or lends a "plasticity" to the roiling diversity of elements (*Materien*) in the process of conceptual construction—and "deconstruction," for that matter. These sundry *Materien* "mutually interpenetrate," but it is only because of the workings of "force" that they come together in an anticipation of Spirit becoming conscious itself in the specification of the "concrete universal." "The [*Materien*] posited as independent directly pass over into their unity, and their unity directly unfolds its diversity, and this once again reduces itself to unity. But this movement is what is called *Force*." Force "expresses" itself. Yet force remains "within itself in the expression."[15] Force is what draws and holds together every constituent and its alterity, or "other." Expression is the "materialization" of this force, its shaping and configuring. "Force is rather itself this universal medium in which the moments subsist as [*Materien*]." But it is also the force that drives the formative concept beyond these momentary configurations. "In fact Force is *itself* this reflectedness-into-self, or this supersession of the expression. The oneness, in the form in which it appeared, viz. as an 'other,' vanishes. Force is this 'other' itself, is Force driven back into itself" (83).

THE PHYSICS OF FORCE

Although Hegel, on writing the *Phenomenology*, did not have at his disposal the common language of physics that is quite familiar by now, he is obviously seeking to draw an analogy between the movement of thought and the elaboration of the elements in a "force field." Prior to the early 1800s, the model of force that prevailed in scientific circles was largely what had been advanced by Sir Isaac Newton two hundred years earlier. Force always manifests itself in "action and reaction" dyads. Newtonian physics is intrinsically suspicious of what would later be termed *fields of force*, which in his day were considered either mysterious or superstitious. Newtonianism resisted the picture of force regarded as "action at a distance." Force was conceived as monadic, not dyadic. It was the discovery of electricity in the eighteenth century, its investigation by the French physicist Charles-Augustin de Coulomb, and its eventual codification of "electro-magnetism" as a branch of science by British scientist Michael Faraday within a generation after the *Phenomenology* that gave us the popular, and often "sci-fi," image of the force field.

At the same time, Hegel in the *Phenomenology* was on to something that would only be established as truly "scientific" toward the end of his lifetime and has now become a commonplace in what Deleuze would call the "image" of modern thought. Prior to Faraday, there were both lay efforts and somewhat stumbling attempts by "natural philosophers" of the Napoleonic period to explain "action at a distance" by various *occult* theories. The chemical paradigm of "elective affinities," common in the late eighteenth century and pushed by Johann Wolfgang von Goethe to account for many human interactions, is such a notion. The paradigm was later refined experimentally in the nineteenth century to lay the foundation for the now long-established theory of chemical bonding, which relies on the electric properties of molecules.

Hegel found himself between two thought worlds (both temporally and intellectually), Goethe's and Faraday's. It is in this context that we can begin to understand not only what Hegel really had in mind by the idea of "force," at least in the *Phenomenology*, but also how the origins of the Hegelian dialectic can be rethought along the lines that Malabou suggests and that Derrida commends. In the paragraph succeeding the one in which Hegel characterizes force as "driven back upon itself" he talks, rather curiously from our vantage point today, about the splitting of "force" into a dyad and of one force "soliciting the other." "What appears as an 'other' and solicits Force, both to expression and to a return into itself, directly proves to be the *itself Force . . .* Force, in that there is an 'other' for it, and it is for an 'other'" (83–84). This "second Force is essentially an alternation" of the two moments of force "and is itself Force; it is likewise the universal medium only through its being solicited to be such; and, similarly too, it is a negative unity." Force is "transformed into the same reciprocal interchange of the determinateness [*die selbe Austauschung der Bestimmtheit gegen einander*]" (84).

The word *solicitation*, familiar in English but problematic in this context, is a direct translation of the German *sollicitieren*, which belongs to Middle High German and has been out of use completely in the modern era. Its etymology, even in German, is obscure, but it appears to be a transliteration of the Latin *sollicitare*. In the late medieval and early modern setting, to which the young Hegel belongs, it seems to have the general meaning of "to rouse," to "shake violently," or to "stir up." The recognition that the agitation of objects caught up in a force field could be the result of the action of the field itself rather than a push and pull of antagonistic agencies (though admittedly the negative and positive polarities of such fields give this impression) was not evident to Hegel. But Hegel is proposing a root metaphor for the dialectic itself, not a scientific hypothesis in its empirical guise. The emergence of determinate objects, or "predications" in a linguistic sense, rests on the action of a field of countervailing influences, which we may dub the *force of thought*. The agitation of the "thought field" through the force of thought is what propels the dialectic, according to Hegel.

The dialectic is not so much "negation" (other than as differentiation), therefore, as it is a kind of "plastic," *formative* dynamism that is at times gritty, chaotic, and violent. It is not as "inexorable" as the metaphysical reading of Hegel, which mythologizes as a kind of divine juggernaut the deductive logicism of Greek philosophy—Aristotelean syllogisms on steroids, Derrida's much-rebuked "logocentrism" in its monstrous incarnation. According to Hegel, "science sets forth this formative process [*bildende Bewegung*]" of the dialectic as *plasticity* "in all its detail and necessity, exposing the mature configurations of everything which has already been reduced to a moment and property of Spirit" (17). In the following pages Hegel characterizes the odyssey of Spirit as movement of shaping and historical life formation, which is why the *Phenomenology* itself has often been depicted as a philosophical *Bildungsroman*, a story of the "self-development" of *Geist*.

Tarrying with the Negative

Following Kant, Hegel describes the process of conceptual analysis as the movement of dissolution, constitution, and specification, parrying the transcendental thrust of metaphysical reason. The understanding breaks the "idea into its original moments." Understanding relies on "the tremendous power of the negative," the "most astonishing and mightiest of powers, or rather the absolute power" (18). But the imagination is no match for the "life of the Spirit." Such a life "is not the life that shrinks from death and keeps itself untouched by devastation. It wins its truth only when, in utter dismemberment, it finds itself. . . . Spirit is the power only by looking the negative in the face, and tarrying with it. This tarrying [*Verweilen*] with the negative is the magical power [*Zauberkraft*] that converts it into being" (19).

This oft-quoted passage in Hegel is much richer in its overtones than Hegel scholarship has given it credit for to date. It is an allusion, of course, to Goethe's *Faust*, in which Mephistopheles makes a "demonic pact" with the aged scholar. Mephistopholes, as the "spirit that denies," is the power of the negative in the Marxist sense. But the spirit that "tarries" with that very power, ultimately disclosed in the power of death, takes death into itself, grasps it, and reshapes it. Ultimately, thought is not "understanding" (*Verstehen*) but artistic figuration (*Bildung*). In Goethe's famous drama, Faust is granted the "elixir" of life by the devil as restless creativity and self-transformation. But he is warned not to "tarry" at the moment of true inspiration and in the sight of beauty. *Verweile doch! du bist so schön!* That would forfeit creativity for eternity. But for Hegel the "creativity" that constitutes the "self-reflecting" *force* of Spirit has the power to tarry and to transfigure even death! This passage prefigures the triumph of Absolute Spirit at the end of the *Phenomenology*, which of course is the triumph of the incarnate *logos* over the seemingly "final" negation of the Cross. The Devil, who once held the keys of death, is defeated in the cosmic battle by philosophy itself.

Derrida's "force of language" is closely akin to Hegel's "force" of persistent conceptual genesis, the venture of Spirit. It is the "other" that keeps impinging, that both backgrounds and foregrounds, that rouses, disturbs, and penetrates all configurations of thought, which might otherwise stagnate. Indeed, force is constantly "soliciting." To date, so much of the effort at deciphering Derrida has concentrated on the semiotic exfoliation of texts. But this exfoliation is animated and sustained by the force that runs throughout, though remains invisible within, the semiotic process. There is a "Mephistophelean" restlessness to the proposition itself.

Derrida does not name such a "force. But *not-naming* is not the same as a *negative* naming, a deconstructive apophaticism or negative theology. Derrida does not really "name" the force until somewhat late in his career, and at that point it becomes more problematic than the "name" itself that is putatively named—*religion*. It is the best name under the circumstances and at that juncture that he can come up with. But by naming it he cannot circumscribe it. If religion is the *force* of religion, then there is more to force itself than meets the eye, especially when one is pondering something known as "the religious." His "not-naming" of this force, which early on becomes evident as a *force of deconstruction*, is contained in his generative reading of Hegel in the essay "The Pit and the Pyramid, Introduction to Hegel's Semiology." Derrida challenges in a subtle yet determined manner the received wisdom concerning the Hegelian dialectic.[16]

HEGELIAN SEMIOLOGY

In "Hegelian Semiology" Derrida performs a close reading of what is normally considered the "dialectic" by a thorough analysis of the sign-function in the play of difference. "Why is the metaphysical concept of truth in solidarity with a concept of the sign, and with a concept of the sign determined as a lack of full truth?" Derrida asks. If indeed Hegelianism, as conventionally held, is "the ultimate reassembling of metaphysics," why does it defer the meaning of the sign as only an "orientation" toward truth-in-progress, as "the lack and remainder in the process of navigation?" (80–81). Hegel, according to Derrida, notes a "kind of separation, a disjointing" between the intuition of presence and the movement of signification. The sign is not a representation, but a "fantastic" deposition of the intuition, a "representation . . . of a representation." It becomes *etwas anderes vorstellend,* "something other the representing." In this setting "*Vorstellen* and *represent* release and reassemble all their meanings at once" (81). Derrida terms this second-order representation "a strange intuition" (Hegel dubs it *einen ganz anderen Inhalt*), because it remains highly questionable what it "represents," if it represents anything at all. In other words, the production of the sign in the dialectical movement of consciousness, for Hegel, is part and parcel of the generation of what Derrida calls the trace. This process of "tracing" in Hegel is at the same time *self-generating.* It arises from the temporalizing of thought, which reading and writing ultimately certify in accordance with the "marking" of the text. "The production of arbitrary signs manifests the freedom of the spirit," Derrida observes (86).

In subsequent pages Derrida leverages these same passages in Hegel to expose the incestuous union between phonics and metaphysics (his essential argument against "logocentrism"). The relation of "relevance" between signs, whereby signs signify, is not based on the simple *differential* that de Saussure indicated. *Différance,* in Derrida, constitues a "different" kind of differential that runs throughout the kinetic ensemble of inscriptions, sounds, and significations. But it is more the formal differential between speech, writing, and phenomenon that reveals the mechanism whereby ontology remains the ghost of presence than it is an indicator of how signification itself actually works. Here Derrida ties "relevance" to the Hegelian moment of *Aufhebung* in the dialectic, translated into the French as *relève,* the "relifting" of the sign into "sight" through sound whereby it becomes permanent presence: whereby it "cannot be eaten," Derrida says, quoting Hegel himself. The sign that is *relevé* becomes an ideal object for thought, a mode of "temporal interiority." Such ideal objects are such matter for "phenomenology" in the Husserlian, not the Hegelian, sense. But they remain impassive. They "resist the *Aufhebung*" and they "hold back the work of dialectics" (92).

Derrida goes on to show how any genuine *Aufhebung* requires the kind of work that deconstructs the work, which writing accomplishes. But what Derrida fails to mention in "Hegel's Semiology" is that the theory of a "grammatology" is already apparent, if not somewhat inchoate, in the latter's own account of the nature of "spirit." Written languages push the pure "contingency" (*Zufälligkeit*) of phonic utterances into a grammatical formality, whereby historical languages truly become possible, Hegel writes in the *Encylopedia*. Citing Wilhelm von Humboldt, who at the time was forging the principles of comparative linguistics through the study of various living languages, Hegel draws a comparison between the philosophical "intelligence" inherent in languages with a structured, linear grammar and those, such as Chinese, that are purely pictorial and representational. "The imperfections of spoken Chinese are familiar. Plenty of their words have multiple, entirely different meanings, sometimes from ten to twenty, so that in enunciating bare differences a subtle emphasis, intensity, inflection, or cry is made."[17]

In the same section of the *Encylopedia* where Derrida discusses Hegel he directly ties the operation of the sign to written language. The significance within a text of "mere signs" (*einfache Zeichen*), consisting of "multiple letters and syllables" in which they seem on the surface to be "dismembered" (*zergleidet*), according Hegel, is that they are able to collate and to foster an alliance (*Verbindung*) of numerous representations. That allows for the possibility of many kinds of logical inference and accounts for the superior value of written languages.[18] Several pages earlier, Hegel attributes the creation of this "alliance" to the force of language itself. It is a "force of attraction" (among similar imagined objects), a force that "forces" the sign toward a unity of representations and consequently allows for the unity of thinking.

Whereas Kant had assigned this tendency toward *Verbindung* in the form of subjective consciousness in the so-called transcendental unity of apperception, the *I think* that conditions the coalescence of thoughts, Hegel explains the force of thought as a kind of "parergon" to the force of language along with the differentiation and reciprocal coherence of signs that comes about with the advent of a written language, a *Grammatik*.[19] Hegelian semiology amounts to analysis of the *intragrammatical* field of force in which Hegel himself, long before Derrida and without the precedents of structural linguistics, discovered the "power" (*Macht*) of the negative we understand as the dialectic. Deconstruction is in many ways the "subsumption" of the text by itself, its "Golgotha" (in Hegel's sense at the end of the *Phenomenology*) as an *Anschauung,* that is, the death of God put into writing.

If there is no Easter morning in deconstruction, however, there is yet the "promise" that deconstruction conceals, a force that augurs the advent of what is "to come," the force of the religious, the messianic. Where does this force come from? Is it only possible after God's "death"? The death of God in Nietzsche's sense—and in the sense suggested earlier—is not so much a condition as an "event." As Nietzsche's madman puts it, this "tremendous event is still on its way, still wandering [*ist noch unterwegs und wandert*]; it has not yet reached the ears of men."[20]

The event of God's death, is "tremendous" (*ungeheurer*). What makes it truly "tremendous" is the realization that it has somehow been known from the beginning—known but not acknowledged. Hegel drives this point home in his own way in the *Encylopedia.* The "subsumption" of the singular under the general, as Hegel points out in a parroting of Kant, depends on an "association of representations" (*Assoziation der Vorstellungen*). But this associating process, critical to reflective thought, requires the intuition of self-consciousness, a "transcendental unity" of subjective contents, as Kant would have it. However, "the intelligence" (*die Intelligenz*) is the force of this "interiority" that operates from such an intuition. It "is *in itself determinate, concrete* subjectivity with its own contents." This concrete subjectivity is the "reserve" (*Vorrat*) of speech, Hegel argues in accordance with the logocentric dictum. "The intelligence is the power over the reserve of its affiliated imaginative data (*Bilder*) and representations, and thus freely conjoins and subsumes the contents of this reserve under its own structure."[21] Hegel identifies these forms of raw data as "fantastic, symbolical, allegorical, or poetic" elements of the imagination. They are material for thought.

Thus, it seems, Hegel has not moved much beyond Kant. Yet these shadowy figurations of the imagination—the "picture thought" that belongs specifically, as Hegel insists elsewhere, to religion—are driven out of the reserve by the force of language, which is at the same time the force of writing, as we have already noted. They are not overcome and "subsumed" by any predeterminate, "transcendental logic" that makes judgment possible in the first place, as Kant maintained. The act of "intelligence" is identical with the imaginative interiority in which the reserve is situated. A *Vor-rat* literally is a prior (an "a priori") counsel or mechanism of judgment. Hegel calls language a "curious" (*eigentümlich*) product of the intelligence. It is curious because it does not proceed from the intelligence. Language has its own strange "excess" (*Überfluss*) of "the sensical and non-sensical" because of its tendency to pictorialization.

This excess can be explained to the extent that "its peculiar elements rest not only upon self-referring outer objects but on inward symbolization."[22] As writing refines the process of inward symbolization, so that the interior/exterior oscillation in the connecting and erasure of signs is made more complex, meaning grows more expansive. This expansion of signification, and its disclosure as an infinite process of indications and erasures, through textualization, which includes both reading and writing, amounts to the secret of both the Hegelian dialectic and deconstruction. *Spirit itself in Hegel is a movement of deconstruction.* If communism, as Lenin once quipped is "soviet power plus the electrification of the whole country," deconstruction is *Spirit plus structural linguistics.*

THE HEGELIAN GENESIS OF DECONSTRUCTION

If we reconsider what we can characterize as a tacit Hegelian genesis for deconstruction, we discover one that demonstrates itself by way of metonymy in the concept of force. The force of deconstruction can be seen as stemming not merely from the Hegelian "tarrying with the negative" and the pressure on the temporal structures of signification from the presence of the Other, as Derrida himself underscores, but from the very "divine" *questioning* of the propositional form of language that is indigenous to the *world-historical* movement of Spirit. Derrida begins to take up the "question of questioning" in his 1987 lectures on Heidegger gathered in the volume *Of Spirit*. It is one of the

first times that Derrida introduces the construct of the *revenant*, what
returns, the "ghost." Heidegger, even more than Hegel, is the *revenant*
perhaps for all deconstruction.

In the introduction Derrida writes that the task of the book is to
inquire into Heidegger's notorious "avoiding" (*Vermeiden*) of the
venerable philosophical and theological theme of spirit. It is not simply a matter of neglect or omission. Heidegger himself, Derrida notes,
counseled in the period when he composed *Being and Time* against
using those words that have anything smacking of the "spiritual"—
e.g., *Geist, geistig,* or *geistlich*. And the warning persisted throughout
his career. Moreover, Derrida notes, Heideggerians of all stripes continue to enforce the taboo. Spirit in Heidegger, and the Heideggerian
heritage, does not belong simply to what remains "unsaid," but to
the *deliberately unspoken*, what one refuses to say. At the same time,
Derrida opines, Heidegger's "silence" on the subject "is not without
significance." Even though "the lexicon of spirit is more copious in
Heidegger than is thought, Heidegger "never made it the title or the
principal theme of an extended meditation, a book, a seminar, or
even a lecture."[23]

It is here that Derrida, as a propaedeutic to taking on the question of
Heidegger—at a time when the controversy over Heidegger's Nazism
was raging in both Europe and the United States—explicitly ties force
to Spirit. In deconstructing Heideggerian texts Derrida promises to
drill to the core of what is involved in any genuine "secret" of deconstruction. Derrida asks, in effect, if Heidegger did not suppress the
question of Spirit in preference to the question of Being (*die Seinsfrage*), because the latter's call for an "overcoming" (*Überwendung*) of
metaphysics is grounded in the recognition that the coming-to-being
of Being is in truth the *force of force*. "What thereby remains unques-
tioned in the invention of *Geist* by Heidegger is, more than a coup de
force, force *itself* in its most out of the ordinary manifestation."[24] The
overwhelming "authority" of Spirit in the German philosophical tradition is due to the priority of the very force of Spirit. The intimate
relationship between force and authority as not so much a political as
an ontological issue, is something Derrida elaborates in deconstructing
Carl Schmitt in his seminal essay "Force of Law." "Force of Law," published in 1989, is generally regarded as Derrida's overture to his later

writings on the "religious."[25] Spirit as force is the *revenant* of modern and postmodern philosophy in both their continuity and rupture.

But in his 1987 lectures, which seek to unlock something not yet ascertained in Heidegger, the force of Spirit is the force of questioning. Heidegger's question of being (*Seinsfrage*) becomes the question of Spirit (*Geistesfrage*), which in turn becomes a question of the question (*Fragerfrage*), so far as Derrida is concerned, or in our reading the *question of force* (*Kraftsfrage*). Derrida insists that he is posing not just a question to Heidegger but a question "to the 'beyond' and to the possibility of any question, to the unquestionable itself in any question." There is an "interlacing" of this question through Heidegger's whole project of fundamental ontology. *Geist* in Heidegger, according to Derrida, "is another name for the One and the *Versammlung* [the effective assembling of the elements or "beings" of Being], one of the names of collective and gathering."[26] Thus the unquestionable in the question "forces" the ingathering of what comes together as *logos*, one of Heidegger's other very important names for what is. The force of Spirit is what makes "Being be" in the originary sense. The power of the negative is what propels difference, but it is the force of Spirit that propels Being's self-unveiling. The force of Spirit is the force of the question.

The "spiritual" of Spirit, therefore, is in its *creative force*. To create, as Nietzsche's Zarathustra proclaims, is to *make be*. Nietzsche's oft-misunderstood "will to power" (*Wille zur Mache*) is in reality a force, as Deleuze argues in his epoch-making book on Nietzsche; as a creative force it is an *active force*. But Derrida takes a noticeably different path in his departure from Nietzsche than does Deleuze. Force does not belong to the singularity of the event, as it does for Deleuze, to the "univocity" of the element that becomes or comes to be. In Derrida's view, force is not a *coup*, as indicated in the passage already quoted, or a thrust, an impulse, but a round or circulation, a "tour," literally a *tour de force*, an expression that applies to all truly "creative" works and workings. The circulation of force in the production of both the novel and the intelligible, as Hegel himself suggests, is the meaning of Spirit.

Yet here is where the question of the question arises. In the circulation of force the "unquestionable" forces itself into the circulation. It is not clear from even a casual reading of Hegel whether the Romantic "infinite" (*das Unendliche*) could in any permissible manner be assimilated somehow to the unquestionable. But the movement of the Spirit to overcome the "bad infinite" of abstract infinity and concretize it suggests that the force of what Heidegger terms "questioning" is indeed operating below radar in the Hegelian dialectic. The force of the unquestionable drives the Spirit to "realize" itself in the mediated, discursive connectivity of that which has been sundered in thought by the negative. Yet the force of the unquestionable, for Derrida, has an entirely different vector than Hegel's dialectic per se. Whereas the Hegelian dialectic "drives" toward successive, spiraling moments of *alteritization* and self-return or resolution (*Aufhebung*), the deconstructive process attains its instances of rupture and engagement with the *tout autre*. Questioning is not necessary, commensurate with reflection. Questioning has its moments when it reaches an impasse within the moment, the Derridean undecidable or *aporia*. Deconstruction is a "broken circuit," not a closed one as in the dialectic.

But this moment of the undecidable has nothing to do with any simple erasure (*rature*), vanishing without a "trace," let alone a simple exhaustion of the potentialities of language. The Derridean undecidable amounts to an engagement with the *force* of the other, the other to whom one is thereby "respons-ible" in Levinas's terms. But what remains not so transparent is the reason for Derrida's own distinctive "turning," which can be said to result from a special reading of Heidegger's even more famous *Kehre*, in accordance with which the question of the meaning of Being is not so much a project as *a response to a call*.[27]

THE QUESTION OF THE QUESTION

Speaking religiously, in a way, which Derrida himself "avoids," we can say that the "pledge," an affirmation of the moment, is the foundation of the Hebraic covenant between Yahweh and his chosen, to whom he makes an enduring *promise*. Thus "covenantal" language disrupts the entirety of Greco-European propositional language, radically putting in question an assertion about what is through an affirmation of what is now as well as what is *to come*. The *Zusage* redirects the question and puts it in question as a question of the task of questioning itself. The "grant" of language is no longer merely a force from within language, as in both the dialectic and deconstruction as it was understood prior to Derrida's *Of Spirit*, but rather a force that intervenes in and provides a new momentum to language. One is no longer simply "signifying" (*besagen*), but addressing or saying something "to" (*zu*) a *significant other*, whether that other be an equal, a superior, or an underling. It is the force of the ethical, which serves to deconstruct the propositional texture of all textuality, interpretation, and reflection. The *zu* of the *Zusage*, as far as philosophy is concerned, is similar to the *a* of *adieu*, a gesture to the other that Derrida incorporates in his testimony to Levinas, which turns out to be as momentous in the long run as the *a* of *différance*. It is the *a* of address.

The "question of the question" is adumbrated especially in Derrida's meditations in 1964 on Edmond Jabès. Derrida inverts Jabès's *Le Livre des questions* (*The Book of Questions*) to take on what would become the focal theme of his writings on textual deconstruction, *la question du livre* ("the question of the book"). The question of the book is what happens when God no longer speaks. "He has interrupted himself: we must take words upon ourselves."[28] The Jew, for Jabès, writes from a place of exile, says Derrida. The secret of the entire Greco-Christian, ontotheological tradition that comprises Western philosophy and metaphysics takes its "literary" form from Judaism, that is, the book, which also comes from this place of exile. Derrida quotes Jabès that God is "in the book." The book is "before" Being. "Being is a Grammar," and "the world is in all its parts a cryptogram."[29] Hence the cipher of ontology is grammatology.[30]

But what, Derrida asks, if "Being were radically outside the book, outside its letter?"[31] Hence Jabès's God is a "questioning of God," a God that no longer speaks but becomes the question of the question itself and implies that the deconstruction—or what Derrida here dubs the "dissipation"—of the book drives us beyond any *Seinsfrage* to a sense of being that is not *avant la lettre* but *hors de la lettre*, that is, not simply *autre* but *outré*, impossibly exterior to it. Both the ontological questions of origin and fulfillment (Heidegger's *parousia* of Being) are circumscribed by a "question" that is in no way ontological. The question is *orthogonal;* it drives into the spacings of the text and the silences of the *logos* as a force from "right angles," from a dimensionality that is totally severed from the systematics of signification. It says not *ein* but *zu*, not *in* but *a*. The "question" addresses, pledges, and promises.

There can be no "clearing" in which Being opens itself as language for Derrida, the Jew. The "saying" of Being in Heidegger is an oracle at a location for ecstatic communication with the god, a location that is fixed. A Heideggerian *Geist* in this regard leads to Nazism. But what if this *Geist* were not bound to any place? What if the "site" of the "beyond being" that intervenes as an *extradimensional* force to interrupt the cycle of force and linguistic formulation turned out to be only episodic, the trace of the impossible place—the burning bush on the mountain or atop Sinai—where the pledge was made? "The thinking of Being," Derrida writes in his subsequent meditation on Levinas, "thus is not a pagan cult of the *Site*, because the Site is never given a proximity but a promised one." Levinas's "infinite exteriority of the other" poses the question of the "unsayable transcendence of the other."[32] The "language that asks this question" can only account for "the historical coupling of Judaism and Hellenism," where "Jewgreek is greekjew. Extremes meet." Echoing Levinas in the same essay, Derrida concludes that "we live in the difference between the Jew and the Greek, which is perhaps the unity of what we call history."[33]

Hegelian history as *Geist*, an unfolding of the "speculative sentence" in the form it takes in Genesis, as *God said*, therefore meets up with Derridean history, also as *Geist*, in its aporetic—or perhaps even its Lurianic—form: *God questioned God, God deferred*. The deferral of God in *Writing and Difference*, however, is not a sufficient theme to carry through the genuine problem that haunts Derrida from inception to end. The silence of God as what might really be at stake in the question of the question. What is at stake, Derrida insists, years later, what can be located at that site of indecision we know as history, is a secret, the *secret of responsibility*. The secret of responsibility is a "deferred response."

Oftentimes, when the "secret" is a necessary response to the force of God in one's life, one's responsibility is silence, as when Abraham was commanded to take his son Isaac up Mount Moriah and sacrifice him. In *The Gift of Death* Derrida deconstructs Kierkegaard's pivotal text *Fear and Trembling* to show that the secret of responsibility is "the secret truth of faith as absolute responsibility and absolute passion, the 'highest passion,' as Kierkegaard will say."[34] The secret has "no history," yet it is the secret of history, as Derrida argues in the opening essay

"Secrets of European Responsibility." It is the secret of history as "the difference between the Jew and the Greek," as can be discerned in the Christian break in the formation of European consciousness with the religion of orgiastic rites that underlies Greek thought and transforms the "mysteries" into the responsibility to the other. What is unveiled in this "mystery" is not the secret of the hidden tellurian deity, but the secret of the other. The "good" is no longer "a transcendental objective, a relation between objective things, but the relation to the other, a response to the other; an experience of personal goodness and a movement of intention."[35] Interpersonal relationality carries the force of the secret itself. That has been the secret of the Jew all along—not election or exile, but relationality. The Jew bears the awesome secret of responsibility, the secret, in fact, of all ethics.

But the European version that we call Christianity *enforces* the secret to the extent that it has profound political ramifications. It is founded on a presumed once-and-for-all instantiation of this infinite relationality and responsibility in what Christians call the "gift" of God's son, the gift of a divine death for the sake of eternal life.

Christianity is the ultimate secret of European responsibility, and it is here that Derrida seems to give some clue of what he ultimately means by the messianic and the democracy to come. Derrida implies that Kierkegaard was the first to unlock this secret in the invisible passion of the knight of faith. The political ultimately comes down to the "structure of invisible interiority" and the passion of the infinite, the infinite responsibility to God and, on behalf of God, to the other. "That is the history of God and of the name of God as the history of secrecy, a history that is at the same time secret and without any secrets. Such a history is also an economy."[36]

Derrida's "political economy," therefore, is something far more challenging and interesting than can be fathomed through its conventionalized association with Western-style left-wing secular politics and a suspicion of authoritarian ideologies. Derridean deconstruction operates within the syntax of the "impossible." But its impossibility rests on its own secret force, which is much different than those naturalistic "forces" Czech writer Jan Patočka attributes to Heideggerian, and by extension Nazi and Stalinist, politics. The secret is *freedom*, a secret "that is not phenomenalizable," as Kant understood, yet unlike Kant

is "neither phenomenal nor noumenal."[37] Such a lack of either phenomenality or noumenality can be attributed to the relationship to the
other, which cannot be reduced to a matter of experience or sight.

In the three essays of 1993 that have been collected and published
in English as *On the Name*, Derrida identifies the "secret" with *khora*,
"foreign to every history." *Khora* is the secret as "that in speech which
is foreign to speech." It is found at a site that "is no longer time nor
place."[38] *Khora* is the secret place where the secret force of what is to
come, the *avenir*, can indeed be experienced. Like Nietzsche's mountain perch at Sils Maria, it is the vantage point for an abysmal glimpse
at the forces that carve and shape the grand chasms of the future.

3

Force of Art

He who will one day teach mean to fly will have
moved all boundary stones; the boundary stones
themselves will fly up into the air before him, and
he will rebaptize the earth—the "light one."

—NIETZSCHE, *THUS SPOKE ZARATHUSTRA*

Derrida's "question of the question," therefore, leads us to the *force of the question* itself. And in "forcing" this question we arrive at the juncture in modern thought that left Nietzsche perplexed perhaps at where in his philosophical radicalism he had actually arrived and Heidegger preoccupied with the *Seinsfrage* in a guise that stood in the way for at least a generation of bringing to fruition what Derrida was all about in the first place. The force of the question is expressed figuratively by Nietzsche's Zarathustra in the section from book 1 of *Also Sprach Zarathustra* entitled "The Flies of the Marketplace": "In the world even the best things amount to nothing without someone to make a show of them: great men the people call these showmen. Little do the people comprehend the great—that is, the creating. But they have a mind for all showmen and actors of great things."[1] Though Nietzsche cannot be said to have picked any bones directly with Hegel, and for the most part completely ignores the "Hegelianism" already established at his time in German culture, the aphoristic observation here is quite—and in a most revolutionary manner—*counter-Hegelian*.

The key words are those translated by Kaufmann as "mind" (*Sinne*) and "show" (*aufführen*). The common are restricted in their understanding of "greatness" (*das Grosse*) to what remains a presentation of sense or pure sensibility (*Sinn*). They rely on showmen and "performers" (*Schauspieler*), literally those who "play" (*spielen*) with what we see, who are the wonderworkers of the visible. Their experience of greatness is limited by what is masterfully manipulated in the magic theater of representation. Little do they know that true "greatness" is not in the manifest, but in the force of manifestation, in creativity itself (*das Schaffende*). To present or perform something is a kind of "leading up" (*Auf-führen*) onto the stage or in a context that is at a distance from us, as something to behold; it is a putting out there, the crafting of a "spectacle" as opposed to an intimate view. In the Hegelian dialectic, the fostering of the spectacle is necessary for self-reflection, for the cycle of *Geist*, for the event that we call the *speculative*.

But, as we have seen, what drives this circulation is a force that emerges in pure sense-representation, while remaining anterior to all sense-representation, and that continues to be exerted through the spiraling circulation of Spirit on its way to absolute knowledge. Nietzsche's Zarathustra is saying it is the *creative force* that serves as the key to all thought, all "mind," all sense. The creative force Nietzsche quite elliptically named the *will to power* (*Wille zur Macht*), following the nineteenth-century German convention that begins with Kant of identifying the protological impulse of all consciousness as "will." It is evident in Nietzsche's later writings that he considered the will to power a kind of cryptogram for most of his thought. In *Zarathustra* Nietzsche closely associates the "will" with self-conscious, self-motivated, and self-disciplined affirmative determination of *what is*. "The will is a creator." The will is the creative force that has been harnessed and orchestrated by the power of the "creator" himself.

ART AND TRUTHFULNESS

In Nietzsche's idiom the creator is one who can raise force to the level of art itself. The weight of language, tradition, and what is *represented* within the temporal storehouse we regard as memory comes to be transformed by art into what Milan Kundera famously termed the "unbearable lightness of being." "All 'it was' is a fragment, a riddle, a dreadful accident—until the creative will says to it, 'But thus I willed it.' Until the creative will says to it, 'But this I will it; thus shall I will it.'" The will as the creative force cannot be constrained by any "reconciliation" (*Versöhnung*) with what already been sedimented by memory as representation—whether those representations persist as elements of "objective" knowledge or principles of moral law. The will smashes all of the "old tablets." It is a force that constantly *overcomes*. "For that which is the will to power must will something higher than any reconciliation."[2] In short, the will to power is the "will to a truthfulness," as Nietzsche dubs it, that pierces through everything that wants to "tarry," turn to sediment, or materialize into some sort of cloying verity. The will to power is the will to art—purely and simply.

But the will to art as *the force of art* has nothing to do with the iteration of artistic indicators, artistic signifiers, artistic figurations, and, of course, artistic representations. Art is not about what is produced in art. Art is not about "pictures," or representations, in any sense of the word. *Art is about the artist*, about creation itself and its expression through the creator. "I feel only my will's joy in begetting and becoming," Zarathustra rhapsodizes.[3] In one of his most important posthumously published aphorisms, all of which are collected in the volume *The Will to Power*, Nietzsche directly tags *die Wille zur Macht* with the idea of force. "The victorious concept 'force,' by means of which our physicists have created God and the world, still needs to be completed: an inner will must be ascribed to it, which I designate as 'will to power,' i.e., as an insatiable desire to manifest power; or as the employment and the exercise of power, as a creative drive." Nietzsche goes on to say that "one is obliged to understand all motion, all 'appearances,' all 'laws,' only as symptoms of an *inner event* and to employ man as an analogy to this end." Nietzsche's continues in the following aphorism with a polemic against the Newtonian—and Kantian—account of force as the phenomenal correlation of cause and effect. "Has a *force* ever been demonstrated? No, only *effects* translated into a completely foreign language."[4]

This particular set of passages proved to be a turnkey one for Deleuze, with his epochal introduction during the early 1960s in France of the "new Nietzsche" who would later become the former's own *éminence grise*. In the second chapter of *Nietzsche and Philosophy*, Deleuze appropriated this "symptological" reading of the effects of force. "The will to power," Deleuze insists, "is thus ascribed to force, but in a very special way: it is both a complement of force and something internal to it. It is not ascribed to it as a predicate."[5] Each force, according to Deleuze, "has an essential relation to other forces." Furthermore, "the essence of force is its quantitative difference from other forces," and "this difference is expressed as the force's quality."

The will to power, therefore, "is the element from which derive both the quantitative difference of related forces and the quality that devolves into each force in this relation." Deleuze adds that the will to power is "the genealogical element of force, both differential and genetic."[6] Deleuze of course is here laying the groundwork for his understanding of Nietzsche's "eternal recurrence" as a key to his mature conception of a noncircular "dialectic" of differentiation, which applies to all modes of semiology—what he, writing with Guattari, will dub a "difference engine."

It is dubious how much of Nietzsche himself can be ascertained in Deleuze's Nietzsche, but that is not really the point. Deleuze recognized in Nietzsche, as Derrida would in Hegel, that impelling the forward mobility of all critical thinking, from dialectics to structural linguistics to cultural semiotics, is *a unique, inward configuration of force*, or *forces*, that are not apparent in their phenomenalized or representational interconnections. What is force for Deleuze is the force of art for Nietzsche. And art has its own privileged interiority because it is the *pure expression* of the will to power. What music was to the metaphysical will for Nietzsche's own "educator," Schopenhauer, art, in its multidimensional exhibition, is to the *will to power* in Nietzsche. And whatever we understand by the "apparent" world, the world we experience in its raw and beguiling phenomenality, according to Nietzsche, amounts to this exfoliation of the will to power. Even science is subservient to it. "*This world is the will to power—and nothing besides!* And you yourselves are also this will to power—and nothing besides."[7]

These "concluding" lines of Nietzsche in the published version of this literary remains have major significance. Another more idiomatic way, according to Kaufmann, of translating the words *und nichts außerdem* ("and nothing besides") would be "and nothing plus." Hence, what Nietzsche could very well be saying is, as Schopenhauer himself did, that "world" and "will" are inwardly one and the same. But Nietzsche is not really a metaphysician, despite Heidegger's attempt to typecast him as the figure who precipitates the "end" of metaphysics.[8] The "inner" will, world, event, etc. that constitutes the will to power in all its dynamism and ambiguity is sufficient to account for any philosophy, metaphysics, morality, natural science, or religion, as far as Nietzsche is concerned. In the preceding sentences Nietzsche talks about this "world" as follows: it is, he says, "my *Dionysian* world of the eternally self-creating, the eternally self-destroying, this mystery world of the twofold voluptuous delight, my 'beyond good and evil,' without goal, unless the joy of the circle is itself a goal; without will, unless a ring feels good will toward itself—do you want a *name* for this world?"[9] The name, of course, is *der Wille zur Macht.*

Like Derrida's "name," which can paradoxically be both God and *khora,* and therefore has to be "saved" in the space of an "exception" (*sauf le nom*), Nietzsche is naming a singularity that does not admit of generality, iteration, or repeatability. It is not pure difference so much as the singular force of creative differentiality. This name too is exceptional, for "beside" it there is "nothing" (*nichts*). That is what the word Dionysus means—the pure divine (*dios*) force of penetration. The original Greek word *nyssos,* whence the name Dionyssos, has the connotation of "to pierce or penetrate." It implied the fertile marsh waters in which life teemed and from which both fecundity and death seemed to emanate. It has some of the sense of Plato's—if not exactly Derrida's—*khora,* though the two come from entirely different contexts.

It has often been asserted that Nietzsche was trying to "reduce" everything to what the Germans in the nineteenth century habitually termed *Lebenskraft,* or "life force," from which everything from certain benign mystical philosophies of "vitalism" to the sinister politics of Nazism can be said to stem. Yet this thoroughly *inner force* that is within but independent of appearances is central to Nietzsche's thought of the will to power. What makes Nietzsche entirely different from the vitalists and the fascists, however, is his adulation not so much of creativity as the *creator,* the one who through the creative act performs a "transvaluation" (*Umwertung*). Indeed, the German subtitle of the *Will to*

Power is *Versuch einer Umwertung aller Werte* ("An Experiment in a Transvaluation of All Value"). This "experiment," "essay," or "attempt" (*Versuch*) is itself an act of will, a tour de force where the undisciplined Dionysian force of life is transformed into a creative artistic exhibition. It is force mastered as art, as will, as power, as the force of art.

ART AS THE CREATION OF VALUE

Art is not expression so much as it is "value creation." The role of the creator is "to create new value" (*schafft neue Werte*).[10] This creation of values is in itself a transformation, or "transvaluing," of those values supplied to us as the representations (the "old tablets"), the givenness (*Vorstellungen*) of a moral legacy; it takes us "to the other side of" (*jenseits*) values and amounts to their "overcoming," as the "overman" overcomes man himself, what Nietzsche characterizes metonymically as "beyond good and evil." This kind of *art* itself is "experimental." Philosophy in Nietzsche becomes an *experimental art of the impossible*.

Michel Henry has traced the emergence of virtually the same project in the abstractionist painting of Wassily Kandinsky. Kandinsky (1866–1944), who was one of the great architects, enablers, and theoreticians of modernism in painting, lived a life that spans the great antirepresentational revolution of the previous century and a half. One of the distinctive features of Kandinsky's work was his radical effort to synthesize the musical and visual planes of artistic expression. Influenced heavily by Wagner and his towering concept of the *Gesamtkunstwerk* ("total artwork"), Kandinsky sought to reveal what he called the "inner necessity" of the aesthetic event. As Henry emphasizes, what historians and art critics conventionally designated as "abstract art" is not what Kandinsky, who sketched the intellectual framework for the reception of such art, undertook with his program of *pure abstractionism*. Abstractionism is more than the "disappearance of the object." Cubism as practiced by Pablo Picasso, Georges Braque, and Juan Gris pioneered geometric abstraction in painting as a way of penetrating, as Husserl did with his phenomenological reduction, to the "essence" of the object. Piet Mondrian, taking a cue from Kandinsky, did the same with lines and color. But abstractionism, according to Henry, is the opposite of any kind of painterly essentialism.

"Abstract" painting in this regard does not amount to a break with classical standards of art, which focuses ultimately on the formality of the visible, the perfection of what we see. Abstract art remains object dependent. In cubism even "the object dictates the rules of its deconstruction as well as its reconstruction to the artist."[11] But Kandinsky's abstraction consists not in a vanishing but in a "sudden failure of the object." Its content turns out to be indefinable. It "no longer refers to what is derived from the world at the end of a process," but to "what was prior to the world and does not need the world in order to exist."[12] What Kandinsky "painted" was akin in many ways to Nietzsche's Dionysian, prephilosophical, and ultimately *nonphilosophical*, universe— one that, of course, we realize in reading Nietzsche's early works, especially *The Birth of Tragedy* as an exploration of *Geist* in early Greek poetry and music.

Both Kandinsky's and Nietzsche's pictures of the universe entail a shocking form of alternate reality; they comprise accounts that aim to penetrate profoundly beyond what is coded in our languages as well as our recognizable thought patterns and images. What they push us to accept is a pure *arepresentational* universe that can be summed up as an *indivisible, pure temporality*. A genuine vision of this universe has the capacity utterly to transfigure art and thought as a whole. If Nietzsche discovered the force of art in philosophy, Kandinsky located it in art itself.

In his 1911 manifesto *Concerning the Spiritual in Art (Über das Geistige in der Kunst)*, Kandinsky described what he called a "new harmony" and a "new art" in the realm of painting. The new harmony is something quite unprecedented because it breaks with the classical canon of unity of form, representation, line, and color. "The new harmony demands that the inner value of a picture should remain unified whatever the variations or contrasts of outward form and color. The elements of the new art are to be found, therefore, in the inner and not the outer qualities of nature."[13] Kandinsky's new harmony was a thesis he transplanted to painting from music. Not only was art to be made musical and therefore *interiorized,* in keeping with the the metaphysics of Schopenhauer, the aesthetics of Wagner, and the philosophical "musicology" of the early Nietzsche, it was designed to function as a kind of *painted vibration*; ultimately it was not to be seen but "heard."

Only in this sense can Kandinsky's work be considered an act of making the invisible "visible" on the canvas. The "harmony" to be manifested through painting was not to be associated with what is "pleasant," as it was in Kant's aesthetics, but with what grates, jars, and thereby pushes itself into our frame of attention, creating a "force field."[14]

The force field that is the painting creates a coherence of what we see that remains independent of form and the abstract recognizability of pictorial representation. Kandinsky compares viewing a painting to the act of listening to an interesting personality. "We do not bother about the words he uses, nor the spelling of those words.... We realize that these things, though interesting and important, are not the main things of the moment, but that the meaning and idea is what concerns us." It is not what makes words, but the *force of the words* that impress upon us an "idea and meaning." The same holds with the components of a painting, including its pictorial representations and resemblances. They do not count; it is the consonance of internal force and impact on us that matters. When art is recognized as the impact of its internal force field rather than the associations it produces in our mind with certain familiar experiences, memories, and explanations, "the artist will be able to dispense with natural form and colour and speak in purely artistic language."[15]

The thoroughly interior art of Kandinsky can be considered, like poststructuralism itself, an early declaration of independence from the tyranny of representation and an acknowledgment that an understanding of the "force" behind phenomenality, as opposed to the presence of the phenomenon, is where the future of both art and thought lies. Art, as Plato and the Greeks understood it, is a pure presentation of the phenomenon. The phenomenon is what *appears*. It is what crystallizes as what Kant understood as a "synthesis" via the imagination of the field of sensible data in tandem with a second-order assemblage through the "power of judgment" (*Urteilskraft*) of the structure of thought.

In order to grasp what Kandinsky is advancing, we must nevertheless reference Kant. In Kant the completely empty abstraction of the noumenal is contrasted with the layered and interstitched "manifoldness" of both sense experience and conceptual understanding, which yields "objective" knowledge. But Kandinsky wants to propose a different sort of "synthesis" that leads to a higher manifoldness of experience in the production and contemplation of paintings them-selves. This synthesis is not contingent on perception per se. Its "abstractness" is fully concrete to the extent that it generates an intu-ition of the forces necessary to the creation of art.

Perception synthesizes elements of a painting—color, shading, line, form, plane, brushstrokes, etc.—in what art pedagogy terms the "composition" of a canvas. Yet, in Kandinsky, according to Henry, "the unity of the elements is nothing besides the unity of the painting. It is the unity of the composition, or more precisely, it is this composi-tion."[16] From the standpoint of the painting, unity is always a singular-ity. Each painting has its own "order and spatiality." But this order is not the order of elaboration, but the *order of creative genesis*. "Art is the becoming of life," Henry says, "the way in which this becoming is carried out."[17] That sentiment, of course, encapsulates Nietzsche's own Dionysian philosophy.

THE HYPERPOWER OF ART

But Kandinsky is not doing philosophy under the cover of art theory. The unique property of authentic art is its *pathos*, its capacity to com-pel feeling and emotion. Such pathos cannot itself be theorized; it can only be *revealed*. And what drives the revelation that is *art is the force of art*. "Force is affective not due to the vicissitudes of its history, its failures or successes, but due to its experience of itself in the embrace in which it grows from its own power . . . it is the *hyper-power* through which force takes hold of itself in order to be what it is and to do what it does."[18]

In a significant respect Henry seems to be describing with his trope of hyperpower Nietzsche's will to power. Every force empowers its own "form"—the triangle, the circle, the color blue, etc. And the composi-tional unity of these forces adds up to the force of the singular painting. *Der Blaue Reiter* ("The Blue Rider"), the cryptic painting of the young Kandinsky after which a very important transitional movement in modern art was named, embodies this particular principle. The paint-ing of 1903 centers on a mysterious dark blue horseman without much detail engaged in an odd gallop across a green landscape. Although there has been much debate over the meaning of the painting and why it was chosen as the actual name for an influential movement that included other celebrated German modernists such as Franz Marc and Paul Klee, an interpretation is not that difficult to come by. Kandinsky, in his writings and teachings, singled out blue as the primary "spiritual" color. Marc was infatuated with horses, but these noble animals were always a symbol in modern art and literature of untamed *force*. Indeed, *form follows force*.[19]

Again, we have an aesthetic resonance in Kandinsky of Nietzsche's notion of the *Umwertung*. Both art and philosophy are manifestations of the creative force itself. But this creative force requires a creator to materialize it, at which point it becomes a "valuation." The role of the creator, or artist, in creation lies in the principle of composition, which is an outgrowth of the visible materials and elements of a painting.[20] Composition signifies the strategic creation of values in painting, which are not merely "aesthetic values," but ultimate *spiritual* values, *values per se*.

Neither philosophers such as Nietzsche or Derrida are able to directly "name" what poses a mystery from the standpoint of discourse itself in the manifestation of the forces that bisect the plane of writing and being. Only tentative sorts of trace labelings, such as "specter" or "will to power," and mnemonic associations—for example, "mourning," "gift," etc.—become possible. But the artist or, more concretely, the painter is endowed with the ability to see and to limn with brushstrokes, colorations, textures, and so forth what words can only leave as an open question. Art can make visible what simply appears an ineffable void in posing the question of the question. Paintings are not only signs of force, but *the force of signs* themselves.

Kandinsky had a major influence on Dadaism, which is not necessarily obvious to conventional students of art history. He had a profound impact, for example, on the German artist and poet Hugo Ball, who in his relatively short life came to be recognized largely for having originated the name Dada. Giving a radical spin to the symbolist dictum that all aesthetic productions must articulate a visual idiom of interiority, Ball considered the fusion of poetry and painting to be a form of modernist incarnationalism. "Poetry and composing poetry belong together. Christ is image and word. The word and image are crucified." The word itself as poetry in the new Dadaist expressionism has "developed a plasticity" that "can hardly be surpassed. The result was achieved at the price of the logically constructed."

Affirming that expressionism and Dadaism provide a pure voice for Kandinsky's inner necessity, Ball writes: "we have changed the word with forces and energies which make it possible for us to rediscover the evangelical concept of the 'word' logos as a magical complex of images." In the "age of total disruption" that was time of war, "the new art . . . has conserved the will-to-the-image, because it is inclined to force the image, even though the means and part be antagonistic."[21]

German expressionism as an artistic movement had several different vectors, of which *Der Blaue Reiter* was only one trajectory. The other influence, of course, was the group formed in Dresden in 1905 known as Die Brücke ("The Bridge"), consisting mainly of Fritz Bleyl, Erich Heckel, Ernst Kirchner, Karl Schmitt-Rottluff, Otto Mueller, and Emil Nolde. The history of art has sometimes treated Die Brücke as a transitional movement between traditional German art and modernism as well as a Bohemian variant on the aesthetic German nationalism that played into both the popularization of Nietzsche's work and the later rise of the National Socialist movement. But this portrayal is seriously misleading. Heavily influenced by the thought of Nietzsche, Die Brücke saw itself as the new "philosophy of the future," a kind of messianic future shaped by the impulse of the arts themselves.[22] For the sake of public consumption, the group supposedly named itself as the putative "bridge" between old and "new" German culture and spirit that would play a decisive role in contemporary European history. But its more esoteric vision drew from the famous line in Nietzsche's *Zarathustra* concerning the *Übermensch*, or "overman."[23]

NIETZSCHE AND EXPRESSIONISM

The Nietzschean emphasis on *overcoming* was at the core of the expressionist project. The primary theme was the demand to outstrip what had already been affirmed and established, a *psycho-esthesis of the excessive*. "Not your sin but your thrift [*Genügsamkeit*] cries to heaven; your meanness [*Geiz*] even in your sin cries to heaven. Where is the lightning," Nietzsche asked, "to lick you with its tongue? Where is the frenzy with which you should be inoculated? Behold, I teach you the overman: he is this lightning, he is this frenzy."[24] The vision of the overman is "frenzy," literally "madness" (*Wahnsinn*). It is the visionary madness of the madman who announces God's death, the end of predicative thought, the rule-boundedness of inferential as well as speculative reasoning and metaphysical grandiosity. The "lightning" signifies the deep, interior, and eruptive energy of thinking itself, which such a vision both summons and arouses. Just as the strength of a lightning flash requires a transient, but extreme, polarity, so the "frenzy" of the overman requires the radical disjunction of the "all too human" and the *Übermensch*. The lightning is *that ultimate force inscribed as art*.

Deleuze's own reconsideration of Nietzsche in the early 1960s should give us an indication of what is critically at stake here. Deleuze argued quite extensively that what the Nietzschean oracular and aphoristic style succeeds in "overcoming" is the Platonic concept of the "essence" of the thing. In pioneering what Deleuze named "the new image of thought," Nietzsche redescribed the Aristotelian *to ti on*, the specificity or "whatness" of something, as a convergence of forces. "Essence is determined by the forces with affinity for the thing and by the will with affinity for these forces."[25] Deleuze himself renders Nietzsche's key concept of "valuation" as the instrumentality for making something ontologically determinate as a "logic of sense." Sense, as opposed to essence, is what brings these forces to bear in a given situation, in a particular *site* of active valuation or meaning.[26]

Deleuze has grasped the implications for philosophical thinking in Nietzsche's experimentation, yet the real drive of Nietzsche "frenzy" was in the direction of art. The highest subjective valuation is that of the pure *creator*. Hence in certain respects we can regard Nietzsche's vision as a *radical semiotics of force* in its crystallization as a moment of experienced immediacy, as *plasticity*. This plasticity applies as much to tangible and visual signs as to a verbal semiotics. If art is the *expression* of force, then the signifying praxis of those who are "overcomers," bridge performers, consists in making such an expressivity intelligible in countless circumstances and media contexts. Hence both philosophy and art consist, according to Nietzsche, not in construction, but in *genealogy*. Genealogy is not a laborious process of tracing back historical connections from a present vantage point so much as it is an intuition of the generative force of the event itself. "Genealogy," as Deleuze says, "means both the value of origin and the origin of values."[27]

The difference between these two expressions—"value of origin" and "origin of value"—is what *philosophy as genealogy* seeks to discern and in the process opens up an interval at a site of experience that is neither conceptual nor purely "aesthetic." We may call this interval the *space of the experience of art*, which allows us to intuit both the force that gives rise to the experience and the *event* of its formation that illumines in its plasticity. Holding together in tension the force and its visual articulation as its *expressive moment* is the job of the philosopher as genealogist. The creative act in Nietzsche of "valuing" remains inseparable from this moment, thereby necessitating a conflation of the meanings of valuation (*Bewertung*) and origin (*Ursprung*). But in recognizing this moment of valuation, genealogy goes even one step further. It arrives at the threshold of establishing how force sets in motion the kind of complex value structures and value assemblages that inform the collective life of humanity. In short, it seeks to ascertain the force that constitutes the political.

4

Force of the Political

All efforts to render politics aesthetic culminate
in one thing: war.
—WALTER BENJAMIN

But if the force of art converges with the force of the political, do we
not know what this strange union begets, as was frighteningly evident
throughout the twentieth century? Does it not give birth to *fascism*?
At the same time Derrida was conducting his own odd archaeology
of the religio-political, starting in the 1980s, the controversy over
Heidegger's Nazism was gathering full force in France and spilled
relentlessly onto American shores. In retrospect there are a number of
factors in the virulence of the controversy. The controversy itself was
triggered by the French publication in 1987 of Victor Farías's *Heidegger
et le Nazisme*, translated into English in 1987.[1] But, as Richard Wolin
observes, the hullabaloo was most intense in Gallic climes because, first,
early Heidegger had permeated the French intellectual tradition since
the 1930s, leaving its mammoth imprint on figures such as Jean-Paul
Sartre and Maurice Merleau-Ponty, and, second, the Heideggerian critique of ontology had been the persistent background noise of the then

ascendant and globally influential poststructuralist movement. Wolin asserts that "Paris was the logical staging ground" for debate about Heidegger's Nazism if one takes seriously the oft-quoted maxim 'Today, Heidegger lives in France.'"[2]

But we find far more in the Heidegger controversy, especially as it played out in France, than meets the eye. While in Anglophone letters the invective against Heidegger has largely been bundled into an ongoing contempt for the putative obscurantism of Teutonic thinking, allegedly fueling fascism, in France it has sometimes taken on a more subtle style of Gallic nationalistic insinuations that duplicate what anti-German rhetoric since perhaps the time of Napoleon has routinely engaged in.

Thus we have Philippe Lacoue-Labarthe's contention that Heidegger's Nazism follows almost by necessity from his fundamental philosophical agenda. At its core Heidegger's "project" is "theopolitical," says Lacoue-Labarthe. "It is a formidable project, in that it tries to deepen and insists on verifying fascism."[3] Lacoue-Labarthe claims that Heidegger's entire prospectus of thinking the "originary," and thus too his ontological quest for the *archai*-convergence of poetry, language, and the *Seinsfrage*, is a not-so-veiled rehabilitation of Romantic mythology, which itself can be viewed as a kind of *concretized metaphysical theatrics* in its own right. The peril of remythologizing, Lacoue-Labarthes implies, lies in its tendency to transmute the Being of the predicate within Greek ontology into performance, and that celebration of the performance principle through art—Wagner's *Gesamtkunstwerk* is a good illustration—conjures up a "theopolitics" that culminated, for example, in the pageantry of the Third Reich and the Nuremburg rallies.

Lacoue-Labarthes goes way too far in indicting the entire Heideggerian enterprise as a subterfuge for the purely political advancement of the Hitlerian agenda of a German "peopledom," a *deutsches Volkstum*. He fails miserably in his efforts to tie directly the Nazi use of neo-Romantic culture for its totalitarian program. Lacoue-Labarthes, who admires Alain Badiou, does not see the irony in winking at the "romantic" politics of Maoist, collectivist totalitarianism while reviling German totalitarianism. The totalitarian temptation of philosophy, given the right historical conditions, is as applicable for the French—

we tend to forget that Pol Pot was a disciple of Sartre—as it has been for the Germans.

MYTH AND CONSTITUTIVE FORCE

But, polemics aside, Lacoue-Labarthes raises an issue that the horrific era of Nazism to this day has left unresolved. That is the issue of how the seemingly "originary" question of *constitutive force*, which Derrida through his reading of Benjamin sees as the key to a new democratic, albeit "messianic," futuricity can skirt the temptation of the totalitarian. Derrida suggests, following Benjamin, that the divine "violence" of Yahweh and his eschatological demand for justice is only formally cognate with the "founding violence" of the *mythic* state. The former deconstructs all statist polities, which in themselves resist the heterological mandate of the Hebraic "I am that I am" and hence manifests itself as the true type of justice that is ultimately and *infinitely* "undeconstructible."

As the case of Nietzsche shows us, what we have termed the "force of God," coming to disclosure through a genealogy of the political, does not simply come down to a decision over whether we prefer to be Greeks or Jews. The mythic imagination, especially as it is found in Schelling in his quest for the origin of the "gods" and human, is the controlling dynamic of a philosophical genealogy. Ever since Žižek began his rehabilitation of Schelling in Continental philosophy via Lacan two decades ago, a sense that origin (*Ursprung*) is not necessarily the same as inauguration (*Entstehung*), as Foucault first discerned in his reading of Nietzsche, has been gathering steam. This *differentiating distance*—Žižek's "parallax" factor—between the two seemingly cognate renderings of "first things" can be traced, as Žižek makes us obliquely aware, back to Schelling. Schelling's postulate of a primordial "abyss" (*Abgrund*) of freedom out of which both God and subjectivity arise, can only be approached, as far as Schelling is concerned, through mythologemes, which are metaphysical ideas in germination.

Contrary to Lacoue-Labarthes charge that Heidegger appropriated the "mythological" as a stratagem for an ideology of neopagan power politics, we know enough about Heidegger's self-declared indebtedness to Schelling to acknowledge that he most likely and quite consciously absorbed the many resonances of his nineteenth-century predecessor's rejection of all idealist ontologies, even the Kantian one. Heidegger's principle of "difference" between Being and beings is a second-generation variant on Schelling's epochal discovery. The so-called ontological difference arises from a kind of protological fissure in Being itself. "Mythology says or seems to say something different than is meant," Schelling says in *Historical-Critical Introduction to the Philosophy of Mythology*" (German title in translation).[4]

Mythology in many ways can be considered a first-order genealogy, because the "gods are not just present abstractly and outside these historical relations: as mythological, they are by their nature, from the very beginning, historical beings." If such a quote sounds like eighteenth-century "euhemerism," the ancient thesis that the gods are but heroic but forgotten mortals in disguise, it is not at all. The historicity of the gods is tied in indispensably with the historicism of language. They are *archaeological* placeholders for semantic and grammatical structures of signification.

Thus philosophy can only decode its own discourse when it delves into the mythemes that both gave rise to, sustain, and have inspired it. In the presence of the gods "we face the peculiar whole of human ideas [*Vorstellungen*], and the true nature of the whole is to be found and mediated and grounded in" this *deep historical* set of conditions.[5] Schelling's brief against Hegel toward the end of his life, according to Joseph Lawrence, revolved primarily around his resistance to the "totalitarianism of reason," which he saw as the critical danger of the dialectic. Schelling worked out this resistance through his own philosophical mythology in the *System der Weltalter* ("System of the Ages of the World"), in which metaphysical abstractions such as God and self are generated in a timeless but "evolutionary," matter from the autogenerative chaos that subsists in the primordial dark night that is both Abyss (*Abgrund*) and the *Absolute*.[6] There can ultimately be no sovereign, willful God—either in a religious or a metaphysical sense—because even God, in a rather strange *façon parler*, for Schelling, "comes to be." There is indeed a divine theogony, which makes metaphysics possible.

It is no accident that Schelling's revival has corresponded to the age of poststructuralism with its struggle against Hegel and all totalitarianisms of language and *logos*. Derrida's logocentrist philosophy is incarnate in Hegel. Mythology, however, suggests that language is not being, as in most idealisms but, as Heidegger would say, the "opening" with its finite system of self-limiting, signifying relations to a disclosure of Being that seizes, but does not *freeze* in, linguistic constellations. But behind the *theogenesis* of language there is also a *play of forces,* a productive *Wirbel* ("maelstrom") that makes what we "theologically" mistake as the directed handiwork of a creator God. In the beginning there is a Platonic *khora*, Derrida's pregnant negative, yet there is no demiurge or "craftsman" to guide it with intelligent design.

In "Ages of the World"—or what part of the intended manuscript we actually have at our disposal—Schelling suggests that the historicity of the gods and the historicism of language cloaked in myths somehow mirror this primordial state, which following modern physics we might term a *dynamic archaeo-cosmic indeterminacy*. It is going too far perhaps, as Žižek does, to Lacanize and make God a fit subject for the analyst's couch. But Schelling's own strange theogony in the *Weltalter*, where he probably took an immediate cue from his own interpretation of myth, provides a genealogical marker for Derrida's much later venture into the "mystical foundation of authority." In the German version of the text Schelling employs extensively the word *force*—both as *Kraft* and as *Gewalt.* The former seems to be more routinely used in reference to those forces that play against each other, a motif we find pervasive in Nietzsche, as Deleuze reminds us. The latter is used in that kind of syntax where the play results in a singular act of constituting, founding, or "authorizing"—as Derrida notes in Benjamin's own text and Schelling intimates becomes the basis of God's actual creative sovereignty.[7] The "force of God" thus is subordinate to the force of the coming into being of the "representations" (*Vorstellungen*) of language. The primeval struggles and conflicts among the gods portrayed in mythology are similar to the ancient mythical *gigantomachy*, of which Plato speaks in *The Sophist* and that Heidegger cites in *Being and Time* as the source of the *Seinsfrage*. Heidegger and Plato recognized something (as did Kant in certain measure) of which ferocious critics of the ancient philosophical tendency to resort to myth remain ignorant—the inability of "pure reason" either to master or to replace the strife, or discord (*eris*), that lies at the heart of what *logos* seeks to engage. Both mythology and rationalism have historically launched their own "totalitarianisms,"[8] but the drive to totalization stems from other sources.[9]

In the *Weltalter* Schelling ascribes an "irrational principle" to the beginning of the world that is lodged within the divine itself. "Without this principle which resists thinking, the world would actually already be dissolved into nothing." This principle is "the real might (*Macht*) in God." It is not only *Macht* but also *Gewalt*, whereby Being becomes determination, whereby God's *forceful singularity* establishes the world in its specificity and particularities. But this authorization remains as well behind its governance and administration. "It is necessary to acknowledge this as the personality of God, as the Being in itself and for itself of God." Ontology is inseparable from *kratology*, the *logos* of authorizing force, which is what "theology" ultimate implies. Furthermore, this principle as "an active principle . . . precedes the principle of the existing God." However, Schelling laments, "many do not want to acknowledge that ancient and holy force of Being and they would like to banish it straightaway from the beginning."[10]

When it comes to a genealogy of the political, Schelling's *Weltalter* has multifaceted implications. Western political thought in general, and political philosophy in particular (including the current strand that has come to be known as "political theology"), has resisted, or been impervious to, the kind of genealogical treatment that has been routine in the last 150 years for other forms of thought. The effort to relativize Western political thinking through different kinds of supposedly "heterological" critiques such as intercultural, postcolonial, or other fashions, which could all be lumped together as an attack on Enlightenment universalism, through the myriad strategies of "identity politics" (feminist, disability, African American, Latino, LGBT, etc.), are nothing more than ideological axes that have adopted their respective customized discourses of critical theory. But they do not amount to either genealogy or even political theory in the deeper sense. Theory as the handmaiden of any political theology requires genealogical subtlety, and one must *read* behind the familiar conceptual waddles of idealist and crypto-idealist "philosophies of history" that have been passed on through Marxism—and neo-Marxism—since Hegel in order to reestablish what Nietzsche would term a certain "perspectivalism," whereby we can follow the intricacies of political thinking, and the kind of anti-ideological historical sensibility that is its correlative field of inquiry, that enable us to confront the crisis.

As Foucault makes us aware, Nietzschean genealogy was invariably an exposure of the lie that poses as "truth." Nietzschean genealogy, therefore, was a much more complex project than the mere reversal of Platonism, which had identified truth with the "good" (*to kalon*), a perverse crossbreeding of a theory of knowledge with the production of values. Foucault draws a careful distinction between what he sees as the deliberate, finely tuned substitution of the synonymous German words *Ursprung*, *Entstehung*, and *Herkunft*, all of which imply beginnings, sources, or provenances of some ilk.

THE GENEALOGY OF EFFECTIVE FORCE

As we saw in Heidegger's alternation of the first and third terms in the case of the "wherefore" of art, *Herkunft* is the genealogical expression, the signifier of effective force, because it implies an ongoing interspersal and reciprocal tracing back and advancing forward of the complex threads of force and action that impinge upon the "work." As Nietzsche's realized, history itself is such a "work" (*Werk*), but it only becomes "effective" (*wirklich*) when it becomes a "force" with impact (*Wirkung*). The aim of genealogy is to unravel from the weavings of historical "truth telling" the genuine forces that are forever and *marginally* as well as almost invisibly operating. Genealogy is distinguished from origin, according to Nietzsche. The quest for origins seeks to *site* the "truth" as the *why* of becoming itself. Such a situating of origins turns out to be a metaphysical sleight of hand, as implied in Aristotle's use of the word *aitia*, meaning "causal principle" or "explanation," that grounds our understanding of beginnings in a formal and conceptual manner of speaking. Whereas, Foucault proposes, "the origin makes possible a field of knowledge whose function is to recover it," engendering an *anachrony* that amounts to our own self-deceptions peering backward from our present vantage point, "it is a new cruelty of history" pursued by the genealogist that "compels a reversal of this relationship and the abandonment of 'adolescent' quests." For "the origin lies at a place of inevitable loss," a "site of a fleeting articulation that discourse has obscured and finally lost."[11] Thus "a genealogy of values, morality, asceticism, and knowledge will never confuse itself with a quest for their 'origin.'"[12]

But in its rejection of the idea that history has its own founding principles, its *aitia*, its own hidden, but unimpeded gateway to the *truth of history* from which we can learn and "apply" to where, what, and who we are now, genealogy also recognizes the *force of events*. Events, as philosophers from Nietzsche onward have grasped, are not general, but *singular*. The singularity of the event "within" history directs us toward the point at which historical particularities do not become intelligible in some comprehensive way but suddenly intrude as observable streamlets of becoming. These points are *event horizons*, virtual thresholds of the actual. It is the location of these event horizons that is the overriding task of genealogy. According to Foucault, the locution Nietzsche chooses for this singular and virtual vanishing point of all "explanation" is *Entstehung*. *Entstehung* refers to "emergence," which is "the entry of forces; it is their eruption, the leap from the wings to center stage."[13] The *Entstehung* or site of emergence "is not the unavoidable conclusion of a long preparation, but a scene where forces are risked in the chance of confrontations, where they emerge triumphant, where they can also be confiscated."[14] The theory of origins anchors history in a sense of identity, but genealogy "dissociates" all forms of identitatarian folly. Genealogy, in contrast, *insinuates* the artist, the political *force majeur*, the entrepreneur of the grand and "effective" notion into history. There is one use of genealogy, and that is to clear the ground for the yea-saying of the singular declaration, or deed, that manifests the will to power.

Nietzsche's exaltation of the artist, together with his insistence on genealogy over the "will to truth," contradicts the Platonic heritage, but it is not really at odds with the Aristotelian program, especially its *political* one. Aristotle is often misread by imputing the canons of "rationality" outlined in the *Topics, Physics, and Metaphysics* to the perfection of the *politeia,* as laid out in the *Nichomachean Ethics* and the *Politics,* which is a supplement to the former. In book 1 of the *Nichomachean Ethics,* Aristotle raises the framing question of how *logos* and *polis* can be properly coordinated with each other through a common *telos* resting on the pursuit of *eudaimonia,* conventionally translated as "happiness." Thus the Lockean formulation of the pursuit of happiness as the guiding teleology of liberal, "representative" democracy—immortalized in Jefferson's famous words from the American Declaration of Independence—is thoroughly Aristotelian to the core and informs all resultant discourse about the inseparability of an educated citizenry from the rightful exercise of their liberties. The liberal political ideal not only built on Aristotle's insistence that *eudaimonia* must be derived from intelligence and prudence (*phronesis*), but that the aims of the *politeia* itself are genetically intertwined with the pursuit of an informed kind of happiness, which is in essence the true happiness. Aristotle, unlike modern thought, which sees ethics as the "science" of individual decision making and action as somehow the baseline for political theory, reversed the relationship. "Political science," he says, is the "ruling science" because it "uses the other sciences concerned with action" that converge on the good of the *polis*. "Hence its end will include the end [*telos*] of other sciences, and so will be the human good . . . for though admittedly the good is the same for a city as for an individual, still the good of the city [*polis*] is apparently a greater and more complete good to acquire and preserve."[15]

Yet in his theory of poetics, or *mimesis*, Aristotle departs from Plato, who was famously suspicious of the relationship between art and politics, because the organization of the *politeia* must center on that form of *logos* that makes the truth evident. Plato banished the poet, the technician of *mimesis*, from the genuine *politeia*, because his "technology" seeks simply to reproduce, in inferior and degenerate guise, the shining *eidos*, the purest presence of the true.

THE FUNCTION OF MIMESIS

It was Plato who reduced the function of "representation"—the customary translation of the Greek *mimesis*—to a mere *eikon*, a cheap imitation of the supreme epistemic standard of both knowledge and value. But representation in Aristotle carries far more the connotation of imaginative performativity, where mimesis is more akin to the German *Darstellung*, or stylized enactment, than to the idealist *Vorstellung*, the sensuous idea or embryonic concept. If the philosopher must be king in the Platonic *politeia*, for Aristotle it is the dramatist or rhetorician who provides us with the models for emulation. The "objects of *mimesis*," Aristotle writes in the *Poetics*, are "men in action," who are of "a higher or a lower type," those who possess *arête* or a moral character who may be emulated.[16] The language of course anticipates Nietzsche. The chief role of *mimesis*, Aristotle adds in the *Rhetoric*, is "success in persuading audiences and speaking well on public affairs," which at the same time facilitates the kind of "authoritative decisions" necessary to the maintenance of the *polis*.[17] *Logos* as poetic persuasion and the true *techne* that we now refer to as the "science" of the political merge in the unitary Aristotelian depiction of *mimesis* that includes ethics, poetry, rhetoric, and, of course, the ordering of the *polis*.

The cipher, therefore, to any authentic theory for both constituting and administering the state lies in the realization that representation of political interests—that is, the proper mimetic performance that gives the *politeia* substance and significance as the fulfillment of informed human desires, that fashions "goods of the soul"—lies in the artistic idealization of what Nietzsche termed the "highest values." The Nazi exploitation for its own totalitarian purposes of Wagnerian grand opera, his *Gesamtkunstwerk* or "total art work," is a lesson in the hidden dangers of politics as imaginative performance. But it is neither an aberration of the "rationalist" or *logos* tradition in Western culture nor a cynical ploy at manipulating the masses. Contemporary "virtue ethics," descended from Aristotle and formulated to revision politics as a surrogate for the development of character, and Artaud's "theater of cruelty" where "high art" and street stagings with political ends in view blur into each other, are much closer cousins than we would like to admit.

But art to be "persuasive" and therefore politically effective must have force behind it. It must mobilize by elevating the phantasm of the self to an identification with imaginative action. This "creative" dimension of *mimesis*, as it perhaps applies to the representation of the political not as collective interest but as *collective performative act*, is strongly implied in Benjamin's essay "Doctrine of the Similar." In that short piece, composed in 1933, Benjamin emphasized the force of language itself. "Language is the highest application of the mimetic faculty: a medium into which the earlier perceptive capabilities for recognizing the similar had entered without residue, so that it is now language which represents the medium in which objects meet and enter into relationship with each other, no longer directly, as once in the mind of the augur or priest, but in their essences."[18] Benjamin calls attention to the manner in which the archaic genesis of written language was closely associated with the technique of conjuration and suggests that such a capability can be harnessed for the mobilization of social action. Having been influenced by Jewish Kabbalah, the surrealists, and the French symbolists, who experimented with what today we would call "altered states of consciousness," Benjamin generally implied that the "essences" that combine in the new imaginative politics of his era could become expressive of a will that linked the avant-garde "image spaces" of the present era to an eschatological kind of temporality.

It would not be going out on a limb to surmise that Derrida's democratic messianism evolved conceptually from such an analysis. The force of the imagination, which Romantic art had elevated to a kind of supernatural principle in its own right, and the force of the political could only combine effectively when such an eschatological temporality—in biblical language the power of the in-breaking *kairos*—came into play. The mimetic action, the reflective emulation of *arête* that guaranteed the integrity of the Aristotlean polis now could be transformed into the mobilizing vision of Marx's "universal class," shattering the self-contradictory industrial organization of production that characterized modern capitalism and would eventuate in a new, global order of *constitutive justice*.

But if messianic mimesis were to replace the reflective, representational system of signs established by the proper Aristotelian functioning of rational discourse and the ordering of the *politeia* in accordance with the principle of calculative choices made to secure happiness, it would be on account of a change in the fundamental understanding of the power of *logos* itself. The mimetic role of *logos* would no longer be to structure and hold together the natural communal dispositions of humanity, but rather to expand and alchemize the very "image spaces" in which human beings organically situated themselves, thereby fulfilling the tendency of language itself, as Benjamin noted in the "Doctrine of the Similar," to bind together the familiar sensuous object with what he termed its "alien" counterpart. This "alien" otherness identified in the force of the imagination as embodied in language *as* performance draws to itself the force of the political in a way the original notion of the *polis* never could.

As Richard Wolin stresses in his masterful study of Benjamin, "language [for the latter] is *rationalized mimesis*."[19] But the vector of this rationality points in the direction of what Benjamin terms the "disenchantment" (*Entzauberung*) of the mimetic correlation through the "logical" differentiation of the tokens of language, the elaboration of a propositional architecture for meaning, and the *predicative function*. The propositional edifice of discursive reasoning mirrors the rise of the hierarchical and bureaucratized state apparatus. It is, therefore, no accident that Hegel's identification of the "real" with the "rational" is congruent with his presumed incarnation of absolute Spirit as German *Recht*. The Socratic dialectic, first employed against the theocratic traditionalism of the original Athenian polis, now reaches its apotheosis in Prussian authoritarianism, the very incendiary condition for the "most terrible wars" of the twentieth century, which Nietzsche, the genealogist of the state, prophetically foresaw.

Implicitly, therefore, we can say that, for Benjamin, the downward spiral of decadence that has captured liberal democracy, inescapably dependent on a theory of representation that is at the same time intimately bound up with this very primal "fall" of discourse itself, can only be braked through "divine" intervention. Such an intervention is never predictable, as the messianic moment itself comes like lightning from the East. But this lightning is always that of the linguistic. The recapture of the prelapsarian "primal" force of language is only possible for the one who senses its imaginative energy as it suddenly erupts eventlike in the present—not the "general present" (*Gegenwart*) of the chronicler or the historian but the "flash" of inspirational presencing that seizes whomever glimpsing the "messiah," an instant that Benjamin (coining his own word) dubs the *Jetztzeit*, literally, the "immediacy-now."

We are naturally reminded here of Derrida's time that is "out of joint" when historical specters manifest and the messianic expectation of "undeconstructible" justice suddenly blazes across our temporal horizon. The "bearer" of the *Jetztzeit*, according to Benjamin, can never be any dialectical resolution of unfolding concepts, but a pure singularity, what he, in his very brief essay "On the Mimetic Faculty," terms the "semiotic element."[20] The singularity of the semiotic moment is not only messianic but "religious" in a profound sense. The *religious* is a word Benjamin himself uses, though, more tellingly, he also refers to the semiotic indicator as the unique, "redemptive" (*rettend*) force of language, which is the essential aim of literary criticism, the method he preferred to philosophy.

In his "Theses on the Philosophy of History" Benjamin offers a parable of the messianic force—and thus the true *genealogical force*—of language. Benjamin, whom Hannah Arendt called the "oddest of Marxists," wrote the theses perhaps as an answer to Marx's own declaratory "Theses on Feuerbach," as way of "Jewishly" thinking Marx in a way Marx himself could never have thought. Benjamin tells of a painting by Paul Klee showing "an angel looking as though he is about to move away from something he is fixedly contemplating. His eyes are staring, his mouth is open, his wings are spread. This is how one pictures the angel of history." The angel's "face is turned toward the past. Where we are perceiving a chain of events, he sees one single catastrophe which keeps piling wreckage upon wreckage and hurls it in front of his feet. The angel would like to stay, awaken the dead, and make whole what has been smashed. But a storm is blowing from Paradise . . . [it] irresistibly propels him into the future to which his back is turned, while the pile of debris before him grows skyward."[21] The angel of history cannot tarry, for the very force of history is constantly intensifying and impelling surge after surge of flotsam in its wake. But, strangely, this billowing wreckage is held together by another force that makes the litter of history appear as a coherent mass, the force of the symbolic, the force that constitutes a "symbolic economy" articulating what is meant truly by the "political."

Part 2

THE GENEALOGY OF CRISIS

5

Force and Economy

The abjection of our political situation is the only
true challenge today. Only facing up to this situation in all its desperation can help us get out of it.

—JEAN BAUDRILLARD

Hegel introduces the concept of force at the beginning of the *Phenomenology* because he must have designated a mechanism or process by
which the idea becomes conscious of itself. Without force there is no
dialectic. Without the dialectic, thought cannot disclose itself. At the
same time, without *history* there can be no dialectic either. Hegel's celebrated observation that the history of philosophy *is* the philosophy of
history, and vice versa, turns on this premise. History does not inject
force into the idea. Instead it materializes or concretizes the force of the
idea as it unfolds. History is the idea's progressive incarnation.

So far we only have a textbook summary of Hegel's "method," if it
can be called that at all. But it was Hegel's insight into the inextrica-
ble connection between force and idea that made him the triumphal
thinker that he was. When Marx sought rather rambunctiously to turn
Hegel "on his head," he was not really inverting Hegel's method. He
was only reasserting the deep affiliation between reason and "force"

in history that had been scuppered through the excesses of German idealism and was tacit in Hegel's own "speculative" take on rationality. The affiliation had already been noted by Kant himself in his essays on politics and history. The thoroughly idealistic or "right-wing" version of the dialectic has always been a straw man for Marxists and antimetaphysical critics of Hegel alike.

The Hegelian discovery of force, as we have already underscored in our survey of later innovations in philosophy and the arts, was the covert dynamo of postidealistic Continental philosophy from Nietzsche to Derrida and Deleuze. Not only Derrida's account of the deconstructive momentum of discursivity but also Deleuze's notion of signification as a "difference engine" rely on this discovery. But even though poststructuralist, or "postmodernist," differentialism commencing with Saussure has its genesis in the isolation of force within the Hegelian dialectic, its well-known antirepresentationalism does not consistently account for the production of representations themselves.

As Heidegger discerned in his own sort of archaeological "venture back" into the pre-Socratics in order to chart the circumstances of Western philosophy's "forgetfulness" of Being, Platonic representationalism arises within this epoch of amnesia. For Deleuze, the amnesia has to do principally with the the epochal failure of philosophy to register the differend at the heart of every repetition of the phenomenal present, a confusion of "re-presentation" with the perduring idea. Deleuze, with remarkably more epistemo-semiotic sophistication than Derrida and with a sly nod to the fundamental insights of structural linguistics, ended up hypostatizing the differentialism in all discourse with a fury that could only climax, as with in Nietzsche's declaration at the end of his life that "all is the will to power and nothing besides," in an acquiescence to a null metaphysics of "pure immanence."

Deleuze's pure immanence is merely the other side of the coin on which is inscribed Derrida's "impossibility." Thus the end of postmodernism as we know it leaves us as the same kind of impasse for which Heidegger faulted Nietzsche, who otherwise might have grandly succeeded in "overcoming metaphysics." The irony is that not even the most radical postmodernist project has decisively "reversed" Platonism, especially when it comes to a serious political venture. The reason is both obvious and not so obvious. The very possibility of a *politeia*—and not the kind of undeconstructible, *impossible* justice of which Derrida speaks—belongs to the sphere of the representation, not the unrepresentable. Even the divine monarchy of primitive Hebraic society required a positive articulation of an ethical and covenantal relationship that was inherently "representable" as Torah, or for Philo of Alexandria's divine *logos*. Thus in order to diagnose properly the crisis of representation we must pass from deconstruction to genealogy. And such a genealogy leads us to a different kind of "force field" than we find in Hegel's dialectic, the mirror image of the Deleuzean difference engine.

Nietzsche invented genealogy as a philosophical task by digging deeper into the generative process of representational thinking itself than even Hegel had done with the dialectic. Whereas Hegel posited the vague concept of force in order to designate a "driver" for the dialectic and to make both immanent and active the "power of the negative" innate within the predicative (i.e., Platonic) rationality peculiar to Western logic and language, Nietzsche isolated it as the dangerous secret of representation itself. The inspiration, however, had not been Hegel, but Schopenhauer with his metaphysics of the "will" as the cosmic source of all intelligible structures, or what Kant had called *Vorstellungen* ("representations"). A metaphysics of the will, of course, was the binding thread throughout all German philosophy in at least the first three-quarters of the nineteenth century. But, prior to Schopenhauer, *Wille* had always implied a sort of immanent teleology in all things that could be made philosophically meaningful, whether universal or simply subjective. Schopenhauer claimed, however, that *Wille* was a lawless, "blind striving." Moreover, it is not something that contends with our own indwelling capacity for reason, but masquerades as reason itself.

Schopenhauer himself had broken with the two-millenial tradition of a rational universe after reading a translated text of the Hindu Upanishads, which held out a similar perspective. Nietzsche was first infatuated with this non-Western view of things and saw a similarity with what he had uncovered through his own philological inquiry into the minds of the Homeric and pre-Socratic Greeks, a force he termed the "Dionysian." But his attraction to the heroic ideal of the ancient Greeks quickly left him with disgust at Schopenhauer's "pessimism," and he came eventually to work out instead a radically new way of reversing Platonism—his postulation of what he termed the "will to power" (*Wille zur Macht*).

The will to power was neither the rational, constitutive, representation-producing will of German idealism nor anything akin to Schopenhauer's blind will "in itself." Rather than representations, it produced "values" (*Werte*). Though Nietzsche never used such language, the will to power was in its essence the *force of valuation*, or a "will to value." What were values, for Nietzsche? They were representations that were indissolubly implicated with certain kinds of "moral" judgments—or propensities to make such judgments. When Nietzsche spoke disparagingly about the "Christian, moral view of the world," and when he dismissed Christianity as "Platonism for the mob," he was saying, in effect, that the seemingly objective, or what we would today call "value-neutral," philosophical as well as theoretical and "scientific" approach to things prized since the time of Socrates concealed a certain profound set of valuations. Nietzsche's call for a "transvaluation" (*Umwertung*) of these hidden values amount to the declaration that ideas are the consequences of the play of prerepresentational forces that are inherently vectored toward certain values and that the valuational quality of these forces must be exposed for what they are so that new vectors can be applied. "Power" (*Macht*) is the value-direction of these forces (*Kräfte*).

The Genealogy of Political Economy

The reduction of power to value was indeed the distinguishing mark of Nietzsche's genealogical approach. Nor should we try to imagine what a thoroughgoing transvaluation would have actually looked like. Nietzsche always saw his genealogy as a preparation for his more apocalyptic project of transvaluing all values—something that can only be inferred from the tragic philosophical opera script he titled *Thus Spoke Zarathustra* as well as numerous comments he made in his manuscripts from the period of his "insanity." However, since genealogy was also the powerful anecdote, for Nietzsche, against the "Western nihilism" he discerned as the rotten core of all ancient and modern thinking, most of his specifically "philosophical" writings are devoted to that purpose. We are still today embarked on the quest of genealogy, especially when it comes to addressing the crisis of representation. And the force of valuation is at once the very *force of the political*.

But the political also has an *economy* emerging from the play of force. Hence the older term for political theory itself—i.e., *political economy*. Whereas economic theory and political theory have gone their separate ways since the early twentieth century, there are intimations that a new trend toward rapproachment may be in the offing. The ever convulsing global economic crisis that struck full-blown in 2008 may be a significant factor in the emergence of this trend. The feckless mathematicization of economic theory (as if economic behavior and expectations could be realistically quantified) that began after World War II has proven itself wrong time and time again. Similarly, the campaign since the end of the cold war to promote "democratic politics" throughout the world as if it were an end in itself has had the ironic twist of spawning electorates in many countries, particularly Islamic ones, that have often been inclined to reject the very Western values on which the push was based in the first place. Secondarily, democratic majorities in many Western country have repeatedly voted their short-term interests as well as certain romantic fantasies that undermine their long-term collective good, as we see in the nations of the northern Mediterranean and to a lesser extent in the United States.[1]

A genealogy of the political in the present age of ongoing crisis requires a new synthesis—at least at the philosophical level—with the theory of economy. But the theory of economy has always been deeply political, a brute reality the "economic" profession has long ignored. A genealogy of the political, henceforth, requires a theory of value that understands the role and intriacies of what is denominated in a wider theoretical value as "economy" per se. It is for that very reason we must turn to the ideas and suggestions of the French language theorist Jean-Joseph Goux.

Goux, who was originally part of the Tel Quel group in Paris during the 1960s and 1970s that launched the careers of Deleuze and Derrida, has had little influence or recognition in contemporary postmodern philosophical thought. One of the key factors may be that Goux's important early writing were not translated early on and then later in various relatively obscure American university press contexts. In

addition, Goux has circulated through departments of French literature rather than philosophy in American universities, and in the last
two decades has only published occasional books. Finally, his inclination during the Tel Quel years to transpose classic thinkers such as
Freud and Marx into a new poststructuralist register involving anthropology and value theory did not have much appeal anymore in avante-
garde circles from the mid-1970s onward amid the global craze of
deconstructive theory and textual readings. Nonetheless, as we enter
the twilight of French postmodernism and edge into a brave, new era
of global *Angst* and uncertainty along with a new fascination with theories of political economy, Goux is suddenly quite timely and relevant.

Like Marx, and in contrast to Nietzsche's ontology of willing,
Goux's "genealogy" is erected upon a theory of exchange. According
to Goux, value can never be created. It is always what we might term
a *metaphenomenon* (as opposed to an *epiphenomenon,* which can be
simply derived from some primary, constitutive, and underlying process) that appears, like a magnetic field whenever current flows, as a
conjugate factor in the moment of exchange. Furthermore, values are
not necessarily economic values (contra Marx); they belong to the
very structure of exchange itself. "Metaphors, symptoms, signs, representations; it is always through replacement that values are created.
Replacing what is forbidden, what is lacking, what is hidden or lost,
what is damaged, in short, replacing something equivalent and what is
not in itself, in person, presentable."[2] Value theory, therefore, amounts
to a *semiotics of transactions.* "Now the notion of value, whether
for exchange, compensation, indemnification, purchasing, or repur-
chasing, is implied in every replacement. Whether this exchange
involves comparison, substitution—supplementation—or translation
and representation—value enters into it" (9).

But exchange generates more than values as sign substitutions, as in
algebra. It also gives rise to standards and measures that regulate these
substitutions. Ultimately, in every calculus of exchange, there has to be
a criterion for gauging all substitutions that Goux, following Aristotle
and later Marx, dubs the "general equivalent." The general equivalent
"finds a heretofore unsuspected significance that contributes to the
illumination of our cultural institutions as a whole," Goux writes. It
"pertains first of all to money: what is in the beginning simply one

commodity among many [that] is placed in an exclusive position, set apart to serve as the unique measure of the value of all other commodities" (3). Money, according to Goux, comprises the incubator for entire networks and systems of new cognitive associative mechanisms. Monetary economies are the infrastructure for a general *symbolic economy*. "Ths structural homology among the various registers of exchange could aptly guide an analysis of the historical correlations between particular symbolic institutions" (4). For example, with money in ancient Greece comes writing, philosophy, metaphysics, and the entire "logocentric" apparatus for simulating "presence" that Derrida has critiqued as our "white mythology." "Is there not a close congruence between Western reason, as conceived starting with the Greek philosophers, and this systematic institutionalized configuration of monovalent measure?" (5).

THE GENERAL EQUIVALENT

The "hegemony of the general equivalent" becomes the reign of representation and contributes to ascendancy in a hierarchial rather than a differential semiotics of the transcendental signified. Thus "the concept of the general equivalent is the concept of philosophy itself" (52). Gold, in the "numismatic" sense, computes out not only a semiotic equivalency for the Platonic "good" but also for the God of theology. It also functions at a second-order level as the ego/subject in psychology, the noun substantive in linguistics, the phallus in sexuality, the idol in religion, and, perhaps we might add, the *state* in political theory. Furthermore, the general equivalent becomes the general *representamen* in both political theology and political theory. *All economies are symbolic economies* insofar as, first, the mechanism of exchange engenders stable significations that serve to equilibrate the sign posits on either side of the transaction and, second, these significations are further correlated with a general equivalent whose "value" can always be assessed in terms of both previous and future transactions. There is no "floating rate"—i.e., a variable signification that fluctuates at the moment of exchange—for the general equivalent.

We might say that in Goux's value theory qua theory of general sign economies that the ever evolving Hegelian idea amounts to the supermonetary general equivalent. But that would be an oversim-plification. Goux's analysis, however, points up what can be consid-ered a basic weakness for political theory in Nietzsche's model of genealogy—and, by extension, Foucault's as well. For Nietzsche, value is what we might call the *crystallization of force*. Yet force is hardly a factor in Goux's theory of value as supplementarity. Force is intimately associated with what we might designate as the element of icono-clasm, the disclosure of the vacuity of representation, as in Nietzsche's philosophizing "with a hammer." In the theory of supplementarity the dynamics of exchange inevitablity lead to the hegemony of the general equivalent, a logic of domination. Such hegemony depends less on the suppression of force than on its realignment. Goux sees this hegemony as something built into the emergence through com-plex transactional economies that Marx originally identified as the "universal symbolic product." The universal symbolic product is the very teleology of the mediating process in exchange. "Instead of the relation, in which symbolicity is constituted; instead of exchange, through which subjects, in partially reversible fabric, can metabolize the signifiers that constitute them—the symbolic freezes into a rigid mediation that dominates them. If the symbolic relations introduces a *third entity*, a mediating element, by which the ceaseless floods of the imaginary are absorbed . . . a symbolic counteraction, operating like a forced currency, blocks the balancing process and dispossess sub-jects of their own activity, through the symbolic functions of the state, money, the concept" (163).

Here we have, of course, Foucault's spiderwebs of "power/knowledge." The symbolic exercises its own force on the system of signi-fication and exchange. It authorizes value and legitimates the represen-tations that operate as instrumentalities of domination. But exchange is a kind of *givenness* for the system overall. The relationship between exchange and domination was something that preoccupied Marx, both in his grasp of history and his anticipations of revolution. His theories of capital as surplus value together with the "fetishism" of commodi-ties arose from his endeavor to articulate this relationship. The "force" that ultimately undoes the relationship is the force behind the dialectic of history, the "relations of production," and class struggle. For Marx, in comparison with Goux, domination dissolves as a consequence of the "contradictions" that spring forth from the *dissymmetry* of value relations that ensue from distorted exchange relations. For Goux, in contrast, such a force remains "utopian." "What does *utopia* seek? To overthrow the tyranny of the symbolic?" (163). Utopia remains, as Lacan would say, the occasion of the "real." It is "desire itself, desire for the Face of God" (164).

It is difficult, if not impossible, to adduce a direct theory of political economy from Goux's postulate of the general equivalent. Our fallback is not, however, an otiose form of Marxist dialectical materialism. Goux compels us to rethink the political under the guise of "economics" as the manifestation of force that drives the semiotics of exchange functions. As to what that force might be, we cannot cite him straightaway. Goux's reliance on the "utopian" as a signifier that energizes the power of resistance against the symbolic seems a somewhat limp political gesture. If the utopian serves mainly as the trope that masks desire undiverted, free from the mediation of all symbologies, we in effect end up with an earlier, less sophisticated, version of Derrida's impossible demand for justice.

THE TWO PARADIGMS

A more recent and far-reaching foray into what we might describe as the genealogy of political economy is the third volume of Agamben's tripartite treatise on the question of sovereignty titled *The Kingdom and the Glory*. Agamben declares that, while taking Foucault as his point of departure, he is going where no "genealogist" has gone before. In short, Agamben frames his genealogy as a surprising study in historical theology. Agamben aims to show how the "form of an *oikonomia*" is always the configuration of human government in the West, largely as a consequence of the persistence of the *theological* norm of a triune divine nature. "Locating government in its theological locus . . . does not mean to explain it," however, "by means of a hierarchy of causes." Instead "the apparatus of the Trinitarian *oikonomia* may constitute a privileged laboratory for the observation of the working and articulation—both internal and external—of the governmental machine. For within this apparatus the elements—or the polarities—that articulate the machine appear . . . in their paradigmatic form."[3]

The genealogy of the political thus focuses on what Agamben names the "two paradigms" that derive from Western theology. He refers to these two paradigms respectively as "political theology," whch founds the transcendence of sovereign power on the single God, and "economic theology," which replaces this transcendence with the idea of an *oikonomia*, conceived as an immanent ordering . . . of both divine and human life." Modern political philosophy is inscribed within the first paradigm, and "modern biopolitics up to the current triumph of economy and government over every other aspect of social life" is within the second (1). Agamben credits Schmitt with clarifying the "concept of the political" as the exceptionalism of sovereignty. The political as sovereign power is what distinguishes it from other master formulations of the symbological. Paradigmatically and broadly conceived, we can perhaps read Nietzsche's *Wille zur Macht* as a kind of protorecipe for sovereignty as the nonrepresentational "first cause" of all chains of value. Heidegger's characterization of Nietzsche as the last of the metaphysicians may have something to do with this realization. But, contra Schmitt, the political is also about the "governmental," and it is at this stage that theories of sovereignty eminently falter. The governmental—or what we might term the "administration" of sovereign power—is founded on *oikonomia*, which "makes possible a reconciliation in which a transcendent God, who is both one and triune at the same time can—while remaining transcendent—take charge of the world and found an immanent praxis of government whose supermundane mystery coincides with the history of humanity" (50–51).

Modern liberal democracy, according to Agamben, is thus primarily a peculiar instantiation of the divine administrative apparatus identified by the church fathers. Hegel's infamous dictum that "the state is the march of God through the world" constitutes the kind of politico-theological fetishism of the symbol that Goux talks about. But it comes from the theory of state and government as divine administration. It is no accident that "Prussianism" and state welfare systems are historically and mutually implicated with each other. "The divine government of the world," Agamben says, "is so absolute and it penetrates creatures so deeply, that the divine will is annulled in the freedom of men (and the latter in the former)" (285). Liberal democratic *economicism* does not bespeak a "secularization" of earlier theological themes and rubrics serving to order the world symbolically. The "economic" paradigm is embedded in the Western mentality, and it persists whether God is dead, active, or senescent. "Theology can resolve itself into atheism, and providentialism into democracy, because *God has made the world just as if it were without God and governs it as though it governed itself*" (286), Agamben concludes.

Agamben's thesis, while provocative, seems to be more *etiological* than genealogical in Nietzsche's radical sense—or even Foucault's for that matter. We must conclude that any genealogy of this kind must explore the relations of force holding together the constellations of value, along with the structures of representation, that enter into the functioning of liberal political economy. Only those relations of force can somehow explain the crisis of such an economy. After all, Nietzsche's "death of God" proclamation was really *a genealogical summation in extremis* of the crisis of value and representation that he lumped together with the advent of Western nihilism. While giving much currency to Marx (something that should be seriously reconsidered these days, if we can ever have Marxist political economy *sans* ideological Marxists), Goux ultimately seeks refuge in a psychological theory of pure desire. Revolution and the smashing of symbological hegemony are dependent on the emancipation of the sex drive, a notion native to the kind of radical Freudianism that was current when Goux wrote in the 1970s. But today we know how "unrevolutionary" the sexual revolution turned out to be. The present crisis of liberal democracy as one of representation stems from a dysfunctionality of general economy itself, and it is in that light we must investigate the failure of the mechanism of semiotic value-production inherent in such economies that have led us to the current pass.

It is the modern democratic instinct in general—which Nietzsche prophetically foresaw in his own jaundiced fashion—to transmute the gold of the Christian sensibility concerning human history as the outworking of divine glory into the dross of ideological railing, electoral scapegoating, and blame gaming, what adds up in this day and age to an ever malignant and metastasizing *political economy of resentment*.[4] In this economy of resentment we crudely trivialize not only what is really at stake at the level of *deep politics*, but fail to discern the "invisible hand"—what early Christianity, according to Agamben, understood as a prevenient *donum gratiae*—at work within every worldly economy. For example, Augustine of Hippo in the fifth century, as the hungry barbarians wrecked the frail, fragmenting frames of what was once the "glory of Rome," envisioned the persistence and eschatological promise of the true *civitas Dei*, the "city of God," in which the collapse of empire served as a mere chrysallis for the emergence of a new hidden economy. Every age of global "shift" like the present one—indeed, the very term *postmodernity* signifies a transitional rather than an easily identifiable era—raises up prophets of such an invisible economy. We only have to consider Condorcet's formulation of the "idea of progress" as he pined in his jail cell before his execution at the height of the French Revolution. But how can we begin to ponder a similar prospect for a hidden *oikomonia*, perhaps in simply a thoughtful and less heroic manner, in this current age of global upheaval—less than a generation after the collapse of the vision of a worldwide, democratic, market-based, neoliberal future, as enunciated for example in Francis Fukayama's *The End of History and the Last Man* (1992), in light of the events of those fateful years 2001 and 2008?

Despite its limitations, Agamben's book *The Kingdom and the Glory* succeeds admirably in enunciating the notion of a hidden economy as an anticipation of the very world conditions from which Augustine in the fifth century did not avert his eyes. *The Kingdom and the Glory* completes a trilogy on the "genealogy" of Western political theory that includes Agamben's two very important earlier works—*Homo Sacer* (1995) and *State of Exception* (2003). Political theology, as Agamben is well aware, must of necessity center on the genealogical method, which Nietzsche invented. However, unlike Nietzsche, who saw both the theological and the political as metaphoric "masks" for the "reactive" force of *ressentiment* that has worked since the dawn of time to stifle the creative, *active* force of the "will to power," Agamben views the theological itself as the secret of the genealogical.

The theological is a cipher not for a hidden economy of *ressentiment*, or structural resentment, which for Nietzsche distinguishes the conjugate histories of Christianity and democracy, but for a different kind of "force" that works itself out in all secular "economies." We may characterize this force as the *eventful productivity of the Singular*. Agamben, in following the now fashionable line of reasoning introduced by Mark Lilla a number of years ago in his *The Stillborn God* (which traces the patterns of conceptual descent in current theories of democracy to early and medieval Christianity), sees the unmistakable footprint of Christianty in modern political theory.[5] This impression is most explicit for Agamben in modern and present-day models of political order, which distantly echo an "economic" doctrine of the Trinity. Economic paradigms in theology as well as political economy were introduced, according to Agamben, to provide a distinctively Christian counterweight to the absolutist doctrines of sovereignty, which were pervasive in the ancient world, enshrined in the Roman idea of *plenitudino potestatis* ("plenitude of power"), informing Caesarism and papal supremacy, as well as, *spiritually,* the Hebraic and Islamic theologies of unconditional monotheism.

The modern democratic ideal, starting with the Reformation, was essentially a revolution in religious thought that overthrew the reigning sovereignty paradigm for the economic-democatic one. The "economic" paradigm, as Agamben observes, is radically different from the state paradigm. The state paradigm, deriving from the notion of sovereignty, finds its ultimate expression in the National Socialist *Führer-Prinzip.* The economic paradigm, deriving from the division of labor and administrative responsibilities in a household, leads not only to the American constitutional principle of the separation of powers and formulations of "representative democracy" but even to the current global ideal of free markets and the neoliberal economic doctrine of "comparative advantage"—the international correlate to the domestic division of labor. Agamben's latest work is a treasure hoard of frequently arcane scholarly minutiae to buttress his highly persuasive genealogy of democracy itself.

But what Agamben is secretly longing for in such a tome is the recapture somehow in our *hypereconomic* new global order for the old ideal of "glory," which has historically been intimately connected with the doctrine of sovereignty. Agamben argues, albeit unfortunately not very convincingly, that the tradition of *gloria* previously associated with monarchial sovereignty is furnished today by mass media. We live in a vast, worldwide, *mediacracy* that encompasses both CNN and Twitter. However, even by Agamben's own reckoning, glory amounts to a charismatic focusing on the political singular (comparable in some ways to Walter Benjamin's notion of the "aura" in an original work of art), and it is questionable whether in a democracy we have no way of accomplishing that task other than in the obvious case of presidential pomp and ceremony. If we take Agamben seriously, we are caught in a kind of Derridean aporia involving a democracy without glory versus a sovereignty without economy.

ECONOMIES OF RESENTMENT

So much of the current new *global disorder* seems to reflect an entropic breakdown of world "economy" with the concomitant movement toward the reaffirmation of sovereignty (whether religious or political) in the rise of many, new authoritarianisms. As everyone familiar with the growing pathology of liberal democracy in the West in general, and America in particular, is aware, it rides increasingly on the promiscuous proliferation of special interests, factions, partisan hostilities, popular banalities, and all the "nihilistic" tendencies Nietzsche prophesied as the outcome of such an economy of resentment. It was this pathology that led Schmitt during the Weimar years of the 1920s to develop his own prototype of sovereignty, although we now know tragically what the alternative turned out to be.

Why does liberal democracy progressively degenerate into an economy of resentment, and what is the alternative, save a new authoritarianism or even a new totalitarianism? It was Kant, referring to epistemology, who famously said perceptions without conceptions are blind, and conceptions without perceptions are empty. We might adapt this precept to the questions of political theology and observe that sovereignty without economy is violent, whereas economy without sovereignty is "decadent" (Nietzsche's word). We can also say that when the "grace" of a divine economy is reduced, as in our ideological militantly secularist space, to nothing more than a flawed, "democratic" sense of personal political entitlement (which it is very much today) as well as rage against the lavishly refined sense of the "other," there can be no "glory begun," only resentment seeded. Can economy recover its own "glory," corresponding to divine glory, a glory without sovereignty? In short, can the "glory of god" radiate in a democracy?

It was Alexis de Tocqueville, perhaps the most perceptive "political theologian" of the modern epoch, who provides a clue. Tocqueville, the majority of whose family was guillotined during the French Revolution, was suspicious of the very principle of "sovereignty," be it monarchial or democratic. The danger of sovereignty, he argued in *Democracy in America,* is that its inherent principle of "exception" entails the assumption of *omnipotence.* Only God can be "sovereign" and thus "omnipotent without danger" because "His wisdom and justice are always equal to His power."[6] Since glory is necessarily attached to sovereignty, any pretension to the "sovereignty of the people" must be subordinate to the sovereignty of the Singularity that we identify as divine. The only true economy is God's economy. Democracy requires, according to Tocqueville, not only "virtue" to survive, but a virtue rooted in an acknowledgment of this *divine sovereignty and economy.* That is the only possible meaning of Derrida's "democracy to come."

One of the reason the very idea of a political theology, especially a "global" political theology, makes us uncomfortable is that we are virtually hypnotized these days, particularly in America, to think—*politically*—solely in terms of an economy of entitlement and resentment, which we mistakenly associated with some vague idea of "justice." Agamben has forced us decisively into rethinking our "economic" and "ecumenical" models of the new global political as ultimately the "God" question. *We are now all now political theologians,* mainly because all theology is political and all politics is theological.

Yet we still must ask: how does an economy of resentment supersede an economy of divine salvation, which liberal democracy originally saw itself as the "visible sign"? At this juncture, Agamben is of little assistance, and we must find our way back to Nietzsche, with some assistance from Peter Sloterdijk, who has carried Nietzsche's torch more faithfully than others into the public arena of discourse. We must further inquire: what precisely is an economy of resentment, how does it germinate, how does it manifest as a "decadent" supplement for divine economy in its protological and theological significations?

Nietzsche never crafted a theory of economy. But his development and elaboration of the concept of *ressentiment*, especially in his *Genealogy of Morals*, can be read with reference to such a theory. Nietzsche's theory of *ressentiment* was inspired by certain passages in the writings of the German political economist and social democratic agitator Karl Eugen Dühring, though the latter's militant anti-Semitism met with the former's stern contempt. Dühring regarded *ressentiment*, a French term used quite routinely after Nietzsche and without the technical philosophical nuances it has had in English, as the key to the feeling and formation of the concept of injustice.[7] In that sense he saw it as having a positive political implication. Scholarship surrounding Nietzsche has not focused seriously on the way in which his well-documented contempt for anti-Semitism, which he linked closely with social democracy, may have had as its source a disgust with everything Dühring himself advocated and stood for.

Dühring is generally regarded as having inaugurated the virulent type of "scientific" racism and anti-Semitism that culminated in the horrors of the Third Reich. Dühring's *Die Judenfrage als Frage des Racencharakters und seine Schädlichkeiten für Völkerexistenz, Sitte, und Kultur* (*The Jewish Question as a Question of Racial Character and Its Harmfulness for National Existence, Morals, and Culture*) purported to employ the "positivist" methodologies of Darwinism and the new empirical anthropologies both to warrant the policies of collective welfare and ameliorative justice advocated by the Social Democrats, and implemented in lesser measure by the German state, while villifying in an eerie, dispassionate way the ubiquitous and "contagious" decadence (*Verfall*) of Judaism, attributable to the "universalistic" perspective of Hebraism down through the ages.[8] It is not our aim in this context to dissect the pathology of antisemitism in the history of Europe or in Germany in the modern era for that matter. Nor is the issue of who were Nietzsche's own provocateurs interesting in itself. But we may surmise that Nietzsche, in fact, turned Dühring's scientific anti-Semitism on its head to reconstitute his own analysis of *ressentiment* as a noxious (*schädlich*) "affection" of the democratic masses with its roots in Christianity. Without attacking Dühring directly, but still referencing his work in a citation here and there, Nietzsche in the *Genealogy of Morals* depicts unnamed accounts of "the spirit of *ressentiment*" as a emanating from "this new shading of scientific shabbiness" (*diese neue Nuance von wissenschaftlicher Billigkeit*). Such shabby science, furthermore, "allow for accents of deadly enmity and bigotry."[9] Nietzsche is clearly alluding to Dühring.

The implication, of course, is that such a "scientific" economy, intended to cordon off Judaism as what Bataille would later dub an "accursed share" in the project of democratic socialism, is actually the bearer of the very *ressentiment* within which it seeks to frame "the Jewish question." In *Nietzsche and Philosophy* Deleuze captures a certain sense of what is going on with Nietzsche's own "transvaluing" of Dühring. "The man of ressentiment must turn misfortune into something mediocre, he must recriminate and distribute blame: look at his inclination to play down the value of causes, to make misfortune 'someone's fault.'"[10] An economy of resentment depends on the prevalence of the kind of sanctimonious "objectivity" that can no longer perceive its own internal psychological mechanisms of distortion. It conceals an entire nexus of warped valuations that pretend to be "value-neutral" when in fact they are mere value equivalencies for a seething, yet suppressed interplay of reactive forces where the will to power can no longer express itself in any affirmative creative fashion.

The mass cultural, communication, and opinion-making networks of modern democracy foment the thoroughgoing hedonism and economicism by which these systems of resentment are fueled and driven. They generate pseudosymbols of differentiation that are, in fact, repetitive signs of sameness, or *simulacra* in Baudrillard's terms, marketable but barely distinguishable objects for consumption and enjoyment, toward which Deleuze and Guattari's insatiable "desiring machines" are oriented. An excessively charged politics of *having* and *not-having*, a false dialectic that hides the imperiousness of political qua consumerist wish fulfillments themselves (forever limitless in their scope and intensity), is amplified by providers of commodified information customized according to one's own preferences and prejudices. Such a politics of vacuous slogans and symbolic "hot buttons" to arouse the passions of endlessly differentiated electoral factions and affinity groups is held together by a single common thread: the commodified representation of certain dangerous "others" along with their presumed noxious plots, policies, and habits of perpetrating alleged, sundry "injustices." *Ressentiment*, as Nietzsche most likely deduced, ironically, from Dühring's political influence and success, has morphed into the very metabolism of the economy of contemporary liberal democracy in the postmodern era—a pure economy of resentment.

But what is the "general equivalent" in such an economy of resentment? And can a genealogy of such an equivalent offer us insight into how to reverse such a path of "decadence"—not the path that Dühring envisioned because of Hebraism's peculiar history of a singular universalism, but something more akin to the trajectory Nietzsche discerned going forward from a democratic transmutation of the heroic and affirmative ethos of the ancient warrior classes into a mindless, resentful moralism of former "slaves," now emancipated from their mediocre lot by the retrogressive Christian form of transvaluation. As we have argued, Nietzsche's focus on valuation—both its intensity and direction, which Deleuze later stressed—as the source of this downward decadent spiral is necessary, but not sufficient, to a genealogy laying bare the evolution of the current crisis. Goux's recasting of the value question in terms of a semiotics of exchange seems to fill that particular gap, but it fails to deal with what forces, active or passive, are actually operative in this setting.

THE ECONOMICS OF HYPERREALITY

In order to comprehend the real task at hand, we must—surprisingly—revisit the thought of Baudrillard. In the last two decades, Baudrillard has become less fashionable—or at least less compelling—for a multitude of reasons, yet much of that neglect, perhaps, can be ascribed to a popular stereotype of his approach, which remains far removed from the sophisticated theoretical groundwork he laid earlier in his career for a new, many-pronged convergence of cultural theory, media theory, political economy, and philosophy. Initially Baudrillard did not make his mark as a pundit of popular media culture. But his groundbreaking *Symbolic Exchange and Death*, a tour de force in 1976 when it was first published, has never really been appreciated for its "prophetic" merits and its theoretical contributions, which are becoming suddenly relevant nowadays. Most aficionados of Baudrillard tend to skip over this densely theoretico-critical work and occupy themselves with his much later musings on America, consumer capitalism, and mass media. But such a work turns out to be even more timely after the global financial catastrophe of 2008 than it was in its own day.

Baudrillard's well-known break with Marxism was motivated by his realization that "value" was something that had become alien to the new mediocracy of the age of Marshall McLuhan. Marxism classically had defined value as something substantial, something irremediable and real that had nonetheless been sublimated and somehow stolen from those who produced it. Marx's theory of labor value as primary value had merely been lifted from classical political economy, which begins with Locke in the seventeenth century. The difference between the "value" assumed in its transit from the moment of material fabrication or production to market exchangeability—ground zero of the process of "commodification"—became, for Marx, the basis of its distension as *surplus value*, its expropriation in the form of capital or as alienated labor. It was this mechanism of distension that separated Marx decisively from classical political economists, effectively firing his vision of class conflict and "dialectical materialism." In Marxism, value remains a real attribute of production, use, and exchange, and the task of political economy is not only to secure and investigate the "crime scene" (the scene where the grand larceny that is the deployment of capital itself had taken place) but to devise a strategy of historical restitution through revolution.

For Baudrillard, however, the "law" of value in the era Fredric Jameson has described as "late capitalism," has become a "structural" law.[11] Baudrillard's use of the expression *structural* resonates with the semiotics of Saussure that weighed so heavily on so-called structuralism and poststructuralism in France from the late 1950s onward, and it is also reminiscent of the intricate study of cultural sign systems pioneered by Roland Barthes.

But structural also implies a kind of extremely thin ideality that turns out to be vaporous and virally self-replicating at the same time. In Marx's theory of commodities both human labor and the products of labor are increasingly exchangeable. But, from Baudillard's standpoint, nothing is really exchanged anymore, because nothing is "produced." Nothing is produced, because there is *nothing* to produce. "Now we have passed," Baudrillard writes, "from the commodity law of value to the structural law of value, and this coincides with the obliteration of the social form known as production."[12] The law of value predating its absorption into a pure semiotic "structuralism" was always based on the assignment of certain quantifiable and calculable use-values, a fundamental principle of political economy underwriting the so-called law of supply and demand. The allocation of such values, according to political economists up through Marx, rested on their variable determination within a system of exchange—in fine, their functioning as tradable commodities.

When Baudrillard writes that "nothing is *produced*," yet "everything is *deduced*" (9), he is somewhat hyperbolically stressing what Goux sees as the linchpin of the law of symbolic exchange: that all value fluctuates in accordance with its algebraic positioning within a system of sign equivalencies and standards of commensurability. But, for Baudrillard, such a fluctuation no longer signifies any sort of interaction between commodity production, exchange, and assigned values. Even the general equivalent—a totally irrelevant concept so far as he is concerned—becomes inconsequential. What are "produced" are simply signs and their endless proliferation as replicated sign functions. It is, furthermore, unnecessary to speak even metaphorically of some kind of agora for "symbolic" exchange, as there no longer exists an "economy" in this sense; therefore no "value" may be generated from so curious an *oikonomia*.

"A revolution has put an end," declares Baudrillard, "to this 'classical' economics of value, a revolution of value itself, which carries value beyond its commodity form into its radical form." This "revolution" amounts to a "dislocation of the two aspects of the law of value, which were thought to be coherent and eternally bound as if by a natural law. *Referential value is annihilated, giving the structural play of value the upper hand.* The structural dimension becomes autonomous by excluding the referential dimension and is instituted upon the death of reference. The systems of reference for production, signification, the affect, substance and history, all this equivalence to a 'real' content," is superseded somehow (6). Real value, derived from real transactions, is no longer "represented" by economic signs, but these values are merely *simulated* as signs. They are signs that "precede" anything they pretend to signify. In place of the production and constitution of value in its sign form through the determination of commodities, we have signs *as* signs producing signs "of" value, what Baudrillard dubs the "precession of simulacra."

Systems of representation, therefore, effervesce into clouds of sign ephemera—Baudrillard's celebrated "hyperreality." What we call "values" now have to be located amid these swarms. "All the great humanist criteria of value, the whole civilization of moral, aesthetic, and practical judgement are effaced in our system of images and signs. Everything becomes undecidable, the characteristic effect of the domination of the code." Finally, "this is the generalised brothel of capital, a brothel not for prostitution, but for substitution and commutation" (9).

Contra Goux, commutation does not engender signs functioning as valuations or even serve to conjure up a metaphysical phantasm of universal value proper to a general equivalency. Baudrillard's "brothel" for commutation implies the unrestrained promiscuity that sign-production, once separated in its entirety from commodity production, inevitably engages in. What we have is something that no longer resembles anything like a political economy, but rather one approximating an economy of political simulations. The dereliction of the present political order has everything to do with this transformation, which Baudrillard ruthlessly analyzes not simply as a metastasis of the representational order but as a complete *alchemy of substance into semblance*. Baudrillard wrote several decades before the advent of computer-based communications technology and social media. Such technologies, of course, have created their own global "brothel" of virtual transactions propagating and accelerating at a dizzying pace as well as runaway simulations of human interactivity, which have helped to define an epoch that is rarely referred to any longer as postmodern, but rather as *posthuman*.

Baudrillard is famous for his ironic statement that the "Gulf War didn't happen." But, following his logic, could we also say that the current world economic dysfunction "isn't happening," if only because *nothing* is really happening other than an ever quickening planetary buildup of sovereign debt by some nations matching obscene excesses of foreign reserves in others, the soaring and tumbling of stock and commodity "exchanges" at ever lightning speed, the "flight" across borders of capital that is no longer capital in the classical sense but unalloyed, generative simulacra of what Marx in his foolish "materialism" identified as cumulative surplus value. The precession of the simulacra, Baudrillard wryly notes, is immune to all Marxist, or would-be dialectical, "contradictions." There is a pure historical fatality in this endless precession, what he considers in a "hyperreal" sense of the term as the true *end of history.*

However, at a certain point one has to stop taking Baudrillard very seriously, even though he professes, like Nietzsche, Foucault, and others, to construct "the entire genealogy of the law of value and its simulacra in order to grasp the hegemony and the enchantment of the current system." Such a genealogy, he further contends, must encompass the "structural revolution of value" and must "cover political economy, where it will appear as a second-order simulacrum" (2). Yet a "second-order simulacrum" is exactly that. How can we have a genealogy of simulacra if we recognize, like someone who finally catches on to a very subtle joke, that the genealogy itself must be simulated? Is the joke, therefore, on us? Or does Baudrillard somehow offer, perhaps unwittingly, an opening to do the kind of genealogy that is truly urgent at this current stage of history, where history is not at its end so much as it has been *upended*?

The more trenchant implications of Baudrillard's work have probably been overlooked, because his readers, both before and after his death, have tended to read him more as a media or cultural theorist than as a philosopher, which he was. Baudrillard never developed his ideas through the interpretation of philosophical texts or by taking familiar philosophical issues straight on, but always through commentaries on cultural trends. But his well-illustrated notion of hyperreality as a strange ontology of the sign has stunning philosophical ramifications, many of which have not been carefully thought through, and it is here that we must begin to appreciate its genuine applications for both political philosophy and political theology. It is "economics," in the strict sense of a historical *hyperrealization* of traditional tokens of exchange, incentives, production, consumption, and value, where we must scramble for a new genealogy of liberal democracy. And that is where the "precession of simulacra" becomes far more suggestive.

No one doubts any longer that the financial collapse of 2008 was due overwhelmingly to the virtualization of the entire, emergent global economic system. So-called derivatives and special investment vehicles were traded, but they were barely understood, and once their "values" disintegrated, it became difficult, if not well-nigh impossible, to figure out how they had really been "sliced up," that is, how their worth could be appraised against any sort of referential corollaries for particular investors. Buying and selling, even on less esoteric equities and commodities markets, had turned into largely automated procedures driven by sophisticated algorithms basing calculations on different probability and "risk assessment" prescriptions, which in themselves remained instances of a pure computative ideality. Descartes's dream of a *mathesis universalis* had come true, not just in his charted method of science and philosophy, but in political economy as well, and with tremendous fallout.

After 2008, certain economic theorists, many who had previously been outliers in the profession, began to stand down against this juggernaut of mathematicization, which had historically justified itself as providing more reliable economic forecasts. As David Orrell, a mathematician, wrote two years after the debacle, the failure of mathematical explanations and predictions was not at all unprecedented. "Financial forecasts have an extremely poor track record of success, even when based on sophisticated mathematical models. This time though, not only did the models fail to predict the crash—they actually helped cause it."[13] Orrell's critique is, of course, a mathematical one—the kind of linear extrapolations about future market performance and investor behavior that have dominated the economics profession have shattered repeatedly against the obdurate complexity and *nonlinear* unpredictability of economic systems and agents, both individual and collective. The global economy amounts to what Deleuze termed a "chaosmos," a universe of both regular and aleatory processes as well as fleeting coherences that, viewed from one angle, seems purely anarchic and "chaotic," yet regarded from another has a certain, discernible *orderliness*, if not a transparent order per se. But, even as a mathematician, Orrell recognizes that this kind of robust formalism used by economists, increasingly sought and rewarded in the last half century, is not only inadequate, it leads to an official type of persistent conduct that Freud credited mostly to religion, what he termed a "universal obsessional neurosis."

Freud's diagnosis of religion in this light, and the growing recognition that economics also succumbs to the same symptomatology, rest on a historical/philosophical insight that we are not so much "under the bewitchment of our intelligence by means of language" (in Wittgenstein's renowned words) but remain still under the powerful spell of representation.[14] The "reversal of Platonism" may have happened in epistemology and language theory, but the reversal itself has been dramatically reversed when it comes to the codes and modes of symbolization that matter significantly in our personal lives. Political economy should have gone the way of structural linguistics, but instead it has reverted to Platonism of a very odd sort.

Such a reversal in political thought—atop which an entirely unanticipated *political theology* might float—can only be charted if we fully comprehend the ontological relationship between systems of exchange, especially symbolic ones, and the processes of virtualization and the *reidealization* that eventuates from the commodification of signs and tokens in the market setting (what Marx identified as "fetishism"). Baudrillard has clinically described and diagnosed these processes in his somewhat recondite discussions of the so-called hyperreal. The palpable reality of what comes to be exchanged in a market *oikonomia* vanishes in an occult alchemy where things reemerge as signs, and signs reappear as things—what Heidegger poses as the interplay between *Dichtung* and *Ding*.

If a political economy is to be authentically reinscribed as a political theology without resorting to the kind of dogmatic, "anticapitalist" moralizing that afflicts so much of Western political thinking nowadays, we must begin to grasp the dynamics of exchange and understand from whence any productive critique of these dynamics truly arises. It is as if the Western—and even the Westernized postcolonial theoretical imagination—has been captivated by the fantasy that human redemption requires the elimination of the exchange mechanism in its entirety. That legacy runs all the way back to Plato's *Republic* and the utopian spirit that has animated it. It is not accidental that Plato, unlike Aristotle, did not take consideration of the role of *oikonomia* in the specification of the *politeia*. It was, of course, Marx's merciless attacks on the idealistic mindset that distinguishes historical materialism from utopian socialism. The collapse of Marxism as a globally viable theory of revolutionary social transformation, which has only been exacerbated by the resurgence of what Walter Mignolo terms "decolonial" sentiment stressing geographical, cultural, and identitarian politics against all forms of Western universalism, has led us significantly to such an impasse.

GIFT AND DEBT ECONOMIES

Interestingly, in order to recover the meaning and importance of the exchange factor in political economy, we need to reappropriate Derrida's own project, to which we called considerable attention earlier. We inquired into the way in which Derrida "grounds" the transit of signs through the intricacies of textual elaboration—the self-displacing signifying movement we know as "deconstruction"—in the moment of force, an insight he derives from Hegel. In that respect Derrida may be considered a remote taxomon of the genus commonly referred to as radical Hegelians. Yet we have not considered the intimate connection between the moment of force and the principle of economy itself, something that Derrida does not address directly, but remains tacit within his full-flowered meditations on the signifying complexities of the Western philosophical tradition.

The opening to Derrida's thinking in this area principally occurs in his reflections during the early 1990s on the problem of the "gift," expressly in his well-recognized, but at times puzzling, ruminations on the tension between gift and economy. What we might dub Derrida's "thought experiment" along these lines comprised a portion of so many of his different "deconstructive" strategies of reflection throughout the 1990s of key aporias, undecidables, or paradoxes—e.g., messianism, forgiveness, friendship, hospitality. Derrida's thought experiments during this period were never intended as disengaged philosophical exploration. They were carefully crafted to work through the logic—or what might be better termed the *translogic*—of deconstruction as a whole in order to frame the larger, more compelling questions of the political, the religious, and the ethical.

The question of the gift, therefore, recapitulates in many important ways the more fundamental question of genealogy as the question of force in respect to the operation of all "economics." Is there a *force of economy*, as there is a force of *Recht*, that somehow traces itself to the true genealogical question of the force of valuation and the "founding" of an order of exchange, on which the "political" itself is founded? Can there be a genealogy of symbolic economies that have nothing to do with the presumed sui generis character of symbols and values, a genealogy of representation itself that recognizes the exchange process as a contingency and not a given, a contingency of history in something of the constellation or profile that Marx as well as the classical political economists seemed to be groping toward?

Like Heidegger, Derrida locates what he terms the "enigma" of the gift—and henceforth the fissuring of the operative symbolic order itself—in the impersonal donation within time of the indeterminate "other" of all origins, the *es* of the *es gibt* ("there is"). Furthermore, as we can say in English, the *there* of the *there is* indicates a specifiability that connotes no source of specification, a spatiality as well as temporality that is impossible to localize except in terms of its phenomenal manifestation. The *es* of the *es gibt* (in French the *ça* of the *ça donne*), "which is not a thing," *gives*, "and in this giving that gives without giving anything and without any giving anything—nothing but Being and time(which are nothing)."[15]

However, the enigma of the gift ultimately remains a conundrum for neither epistemology nor metaphysics. It is a problem of the "transcendental" disconnection between freedom and history, as it was for Kant. This disconnection is not something that admits, in any fashion, of a solution à la Kant through some kind of stipulation of the possibility of "pure practical reason," through a positing of a will to power (Nietzsche), or even some surpassing metaphysics altogether, through a declaration of a new, fundamental ontology (Heidegger). For Derrida, the enigma of the gift, like the "secret" of responsibility, can only be conceived philosophically in an aporetic context, and hence its solution is eminently "impossible." Yet it also suggests—like the question of responsibility—a horizon of signification beyond which all terms present themselves as decisively *undeconstructible*. Does the gift enjoy the same status in Derrida as justice? It does not exactly do so, because an undeconstructible justice constitutes the event horizon for all acts and gestures of ethical response toward the "other." As it was for Levinas, this horizon persists as a boundary for the interpersonal temporal as well as for the historical. It is eschatological, "messianic." But the gift does not condition the interplay of all possible ethical responses,

Kant's "kingdom of ends." As an incalculable condition of temporal occurences, it is constitutive—paradoxically—of both the exchangeable and the *calculable*. As "another name of the impossible," the gift is an "overrunning" of the circuit of exchanges and calculable signifiers. It is an "exteriority that sets the circle going," that "puts the economy in motion," that "*engages* in the circle and makes it turn" (30).

In the following sentence Derrida also refers to the gift as the "first mover of the circle." His language has a curious resonance with metaphysics. Yet that is not Derrida's purpose. Metaphysics is always, as it was for Aristotle, a matter of finding the proper "reason" (*aitia*) for any system of rationality. But the gift is "at once reason and unreason, because it also manifests that madness of the rational *logos* itself, that madness of the economic circle the calculation of which is constantly reconstituted, logically, rationally, annulling the excess that itself . . . entails the circle, makes it turn without end, gives it its movement, a movement that the circle and the ring can never comprehend or annul" (36–37). The "madness" of "economic circulation" amounts to an annulment of the gift, Derrida suggests, and can be regarded as "equivalence." Equivalence results from the "calculation of return" in the system of exchange and from the necessity of providing a unit of measure for such a calculus.

Similarly, although Derrida does not talk about it, the "general equivalent" is the broader measure for all calculations of return beyond the act of giving. "The most modest gift must pass beyond measure" (38). What we term "rationality" hinges irretrievably on the abolition of its very source or impetus. Rationality by its very nature winds up out of control, as in the fable of the sorcerer's apprentice. For Derrida, the *logos* is "mad," and it is mad precisely become of this aporia that implicates the essential connection between gift and exchange. If "politics" is always rational in this sense, it is at the same time insane, and its insanity springs not from the untenability of the requirement that any *polis* be administered justly or even efficiently, but that it is founded on the calculability of the economic—thus the very undecidability of any system of "political economy."

But if economy, both as the circulation of what is exchanged and the computative general measure of such a process, annuls the gift—and the gift in turn abrogates the principle of economy—does such an aporia then compel us to admit that "politics" per se is impossible? The answer itself—yes and no—remains paradoxical. Certainly Marx's intuitive recognition of this paradox, derived from his profound realization that the dialectic of history depends inexorably on the evolution of the relations of production and exchange, drove him to sacrifice all theories of the political to the "mad" fantasy of the dictatorship of the proletariat, for which the tragic consequences are well documented. The tragedy of Marxism, despite its perennial addictive allure for the Western intelligentsia, can be traced to Marx's own refusal to heed the aporia. In the end the Marxist vision yielded neither the kind of rational economy nor the political freedom it promised.

But now Marxism itself is history. And the pyrrhic victory of liberal democracy over communism during the brief beginning in 1989 can be taken for what it is—a purely utopian premise, a wistful flash in the pan. The steady unraveling of what we know as the "global economy," which today malignantly afflicts ever more of the peoples of the earth, calls our attention not so much to a crisis of democracy as a crisis of the very political economy on which the postcommunist rhetoric of democracy has been founded.

We are all familiar with the daily headlines. Governments throughout the democratic West teeter on the rim of financial insolvency—the so-called sovereign debt crisis, a phraseology that rarely found its way until relatively recently into the syntax of our everyday political discourse. Meanwhile, authoritarian regimes leverage their monopoly on political decision making along with their capacity to concentrate terrifying armaments used to suppress the protests of the population. The last two great challenges to liberal democracy during the era of world wars from 1914 to 1945, and to a lesser extent during the cold war that ended in 1991, came primarily from the force of arms. But now there is a dual threat that goes beyond the military might of democracy's adversaries and includes the specter of internal collapse, particularly the ability to raise the very arms that might at some point be necessary for these democracies to defend themselves.

The political crisis, however, is not so much one of policy failure as it is of a historical and "structural" crisis that only a genealogy can begin to elucidate. The notion of a structural crisis, of course, takes us back to Marx. But, whereas Marx understood crisis as a stage in the material dialectic where the momentum of history compels an "inexorable" transformation in the structures themselves, a genealogy can only envision the pathway along which the system unravels and slides into dysfunction, laying bear the deeper impetus or forces that both serve to precipitate the crisis and to reveal what was concealed within it all along.

Perhaps a clue to the way in which our genealogy can speak into the crisis and beyond it can be found in the second part of Derrida's curious little treatise on the gift, which he titles "Counterfeit Money." The title is drawn from a story by Charles Baudelaire of a gentleman who encounters a beggar with extended hand and gives him a counterfeit coin, for which the latter is exceedingly grateful. Derrida ponders the paradox of the gentleman's "generosity," which actually turns out to be a criminal deception that could either serve as a vehicle for the beggar multiplying his modest but spurious earnings or perhaps be "rewarded" by being jailed for passing bogus currency. The gentleman is not fazed by his own deliberate deception, which he justifies as a true gift because "there is no sweeter gift than to surprise a man by giving him more than he hopes for" (39). Such a surprise is a true gift, if only because it creates a pure event that defies every calculus of indebtedness and exchange. According to Derrida, "one can give only in the measure of the incalculable; therefore, only an hypothesis of counterfeit money would make the gift possible" (157).

Yet the gift itself, as Derrida maintains repeatedly, belongs to the realm of the impossible, not the possible. Derrida seems to be saying here that any "possibility" of the gift depends necessarily on a ruse that engenders the illusion of money as tokens of exchange, when in fact there is no real exchange, only the productivity of pure *signs of exchange*. In other words, a "gift economy" is impossible *de re*. Nonetheless, it is indeed possible *de dicto*, if simply because what *seems* to be the actual intension of the expression arises from a deceit—specifically, a deceit that could in its "criminal" guise destroy, at least theoretically, the credibility of the exchange system that it simulates.

Derrida uses Baudelaire's tale as an example of the very aporia that he sees encompassing the concept of the gift. Yet we know there are instances in real life, such as Ponzi schemes, where the consequences, especially for a functioning economy, can be profound as well as extensive. The notion of a Ponzi scheme, a prima facie criminal enterprise, is not equivalent to what might be termed the "white lie" of the donated counterfeit money, which the gentleman intended as a charitable gesture. Yet the principle remains the same. It is the "gift" of counterfeit money (or, for the victim of a Ponzi scheme, an investment that is "too good to be true") that activates the circuit of exchange, rendering it something that can be "credited" for future transactions, even if these bogus transactions ruin the *credibility* of the very circuit that the gesture enabled.

If the gentleman had simply offered praise, a blessing, or even a promise, the beggar would have most likely become angry or humiliated. Thus, as Derrida observes elsewhere, the *fiduciary* element in every interaction that drives an operative economy—the promise or guarantee of credit (literally, a "trustworthiness" or believability)—requires the assumption of a *noncalculative* intention, a certain generosity, that undermines the regime of economy. At the same time, it is this precise regime that marks the gesture as a gift, when in fact within such an economy the gesture serves no longer as a pure gift, but rather as a medium of exchange. The secret that the money is counterfeit must be preserved if the aporia of gift and exchange may remain fruitful for the system as a whole.

COUNTERFEIT MONEY

Derrida has also raised the question of the same aporia in reference to the religious, a question he derives from Levinas's paradoxical formulation of the "infinite" responsibility a finite being has toward the Other. The secret of this responsibility is the key to paradox itself in the act of faith, which Kierkegaard's elaboration of the story of Abraham and Isaac at Mount Moriah so emphatically illustrates.[16] Transposed into the context of *Given Time*, the Derridean paradox of fiduciary responsibility implicates as well the universal problem of a real economy that can only function as if it were, in a genuine sense, a system of acts of charity. The tokens of exchange inevitably must be perceived as "filthy lucre," although lucre is the key to life itself, unless one "titles" (Derrida's word) something different—as gift. We are strongly reminded of Max Weber's insight that capital as the promise of further gifts of "investment," giving life to the exchange apparatus, ultimately derives from an unwitting accumulation of nonconsumables that is a byproduct of the Protestant sense of fiduciary responsibility to God and his universal kingdom.

Marx naturally understood, without the benefit of having read Weber, that the calculus of the accumulation of nonconsumables had its obverse as well as *perverse* side—the expropriation of the value of the labor and of the laborer. But even the "capitalist" ideology in this sense cannot be separated from a certain axiology or theory of value. In Weber's model of the Protestant ethic, the labor value produced by the worker, which in turn is *appropriated* by the capitalist as capital, signifies a certain fiduciary "sacrifice"—i.e., a transmutation—of the real for the sake of God's eschatological purpose, the Christian form of the transvaluation of all values. "Perversely" speaking, we can say the "immiserated" laborer performs an act of "charity" in Derrida's sense. Capital is as much counterfeit money as anything that otherwise draws its value from the ruse of a "greater good," even if it be a strictly imaginary anticipation.

Marx's well-known denunciation of this sort of "mystification" naturally stemmed from a moral outrage that could not abide the subterfuge of systemic exploitation under any "providential" titling of God and the greater good. Adam Smith's "invisible hand" is a case in point. But we now know that even hard-nosed "materialist" allegiances, like those of Marxists, smack of the same metaphysical sort of arithmetic. Whether it be the now defunct gold standard, or the seemingly infinite possibility of American sovereign debt, the specter of an accelerating economy that is at the same time running off its track hovers over the *civitas terrena* nowadays like a darkening pall. While the giving of gifts as the secret of economies hinges on the proliferation of counterfeit (or "printed") money, therefore creating the illusion of an economy that is not really an economy at all, it is the general equivalent that is disclosed as genuinely *impossible*. The only general equivalent that can serve as such a balance wheel for any "economics" today is a sublimated symbolic one, an infinite one, the infinite impossibility that can only be named by not naming, a weird kind of political *via negativa*. The circuit of general economy has come *full circle*, from scarcity through generosity back to scarcity again, or what we now term "austerity," which

constitutes the abolition of such an economy. It is the circuit from God
to gold and back to God again.

The completion of the circuit can be reckoned in terms of a thoroughgoing dissociative tendency within the structure of economics as
a whole. Derrida has made a profound move in the direction of the
genealogy of all political economy, particularly a liberal democratic
one where the premise of the individual will pressures all other kinds
of considerations in the fashioning of a theory of sovereignty. The
familiar, modern paradigm of political dimorphism between the state
and the private citizen, as evinced primarily in the competing views
of Hobbes and Locke, largely presupposes a notion of sovereignty as
agency rather than embodiment, or instantiation, even though the latter was the prevailing norm from the Greeks through the entirety of
the sixteenth century. The language of political agency is, of course,
quite recognizable in these discussions, which continue from the time
of the English Civil War up to the present. It is no longer a question
of *cui bono* ("who benefits") but *qui decernit* ("who decides"). Such
an implied political disjunction between maintenance of the public
good and deference to the popular will has its origins, to be sure, in the
replacement during the seventeenth century of the organismic cosmology of Aristotle with the mechanico-materialism of the age of Newton.

However, especially in light of the duality of the distinctive Hobbsean and Lockean models, it can also be interpreted as an invocation
of long-standing theologies concerning the nature of human will to
put in perspective the outcome of England's almost half-century-long
"time of troubles" stretching from the outbreak of the Civil War to
the Glorious Revolution of 1689. In Hobbes the unbounded decrees
of Augustine's God, glorifying and damning whomever he so elects,
is reflected in the will of the absolute sovereign, in the *majestas* of the
state. In contrast, Lockean republicanism discloses itself as classical
Pelagianism that is now immanentized no longer as a kingdom of those
who have diligently earned their salvation but as a *civitas* made up of
those who have properly pursued their own happiness by transforming
nature into productive fruits of their labor. It is simply the collective
difference between worldly and otherworldly soul making.

What are the consequences of this shift to a model of agency, especially when it comes to the "economic" side of political economy? We

naturally arrived very quickly at the distinction, highlighted in every beginning textbook in the "dismal science," between "command" and "market" economies. This grade school distinction often, nevertheless, fosters the illusion that command economies are without real markets, and real markets are more like perpetual motion machines than merely semiautonomous mechanisms without any kind of command or control. The question of economy, as we have seen, in the end comes down to a question of force and the exertion of that force through the proper agency. Markets are exchange venues or operators, and the impetus to buy or sell, to offer something and demand a certain price for what the other has to offer, rests on how the agent responds, resists, or ignores the play of these forces. So-called free market theory—the inherent outgrowth of Lockean liberalism—was originally conceived to explain how both political and nonpolitical decisions are made in the emerging open exchange system that sprung up as feudal, or seigneurial, systems of social command withered away. It would have been impossible to develop any form of market model without the underlying presumptions of sovereign private agency that found their way into political economy after the seventeenth century.

Nonetheless, the ideal of the market economy is one of pure exchange rather than gift, even though "gifting" is an essential, if not critical, factor in all degrees of democratic governance. The ethical principle of the gift in social practice exceeds the bare rule in Derrida's analysis, which he based on the investigations of the classical French anthropologist Marcel Mauss, of gratuity and absence of reciprocity. A gift economy—or more specifically an economics of regular, *expected* contributions to the general welfare, which often morphs into the idea of social obligation, whether it be through *noblesse oblige* or progressive taxation—fits the general historical model of political economy, even if it appears to violate the putative automatism of the "free market." Gifting in some form is integral to the perpetuation of the *politeia,* whether it be through private charity or an institutionalized, tax-supported welfare state. If the gift amounts to that which initiates a transaction, even if it is itself *nontransactional*, the types of transactions that make political life possible are as often *dona gratiae* as market computations. Even the utilitarians grasped this fundamental truism.

Yet, in *exceeding* the calculative rationality of the market exchange mechanism, the gift itself generates a strange new form of *overcalculation* that turns out to be fiduciary, not merely volitional. In other words, the gift exacts from the calculus of commodities a *promise* that a future, yet undetermined calculation will restore its initial valuation. Derrida hints at this new calculus without actually naming it. It is a strange sort of faith calculus: *I give without expecting repayment, yet the recipient is indebted to me and will find a way to make recompense.* The gift is manifested within the calculus of exchange as "credit," which demands a certain *credulity* on the part of the creditor qua giver. *And if he doesn't repay, everyone will stop giving, because gifting is in reality a wager, a "dice throw," that at some point and by some odds the favor will be retured.* Increasingly, market economies run on credit as well as on credulity. They are gift economies that *genealogically* reveal themselves as *impossible political economies.*

The liberal democratic order today has become an impossible economy. Its impossibility is enabled by the unboundedness of desire for a pure gift economy—and a corresponding popular will that generates the political fantasies legitimating these desires, either through an ideology of resentment against the "haves" or the notion of endless "stimulus" of the market through debt instruments—that is mediated by the mathematicized mumbo jumbo of "public investment" inputs. Augustine's *civitas Dei* has finally come down to earth, not as an immanent presence in the form of a one-time "heavenly Jerusalem," a supramundane *politeia*, but as a virtualized complex of signifiers that offer the mere "promise" of a perfected *oikonomia*. This promise is realized by *Schuld*, the "gift" of both death and *debt*, the encumbering of future generations. The "law," as in Paul's cosmology, brings death, because as *nomos* it requires exchange, giving back, even if that giving back is not technically obligated. When gold as a general equivalent has been abolished, we must fabulate, perhaps politically, some variant of Heidegger's famous quip: *only a God can save us.*

6

Force of Exception

> As soon as any man says of the affairs of the State
> "What does it matter to me?" the State may be
> given up for lost.
> —JEAN-JACQUES ROUSSEAU

The current age may become the true Indian summer of the modern Western conviction of the genuine possibility of a global "civil society" founded on what Kant in the waning decades of the Enlightenment of the eighteenth century called a "universal commonwealth." The commonwealth is distinguished by a profound respect for individual freedom and carefully designed mechanisms in place for reciprocal and democratic accountability. As a creature of the German *Aufklärung*, Kant assumed that such a rational global order was inevitable—historically inevitable. But the inevitability of such a society could not be presaged, as far as Kant was concerned, from the intelligent capacities and good intentions of human beings in general or even canny, forceful autocrats and oligarchs who, at the time, were known to practice "enlightened despotism." The manifest destiny of such an order could be ascribed to a discovery—perhaps we should call it a "postulate" of the late Enlightenment—that, as in its more recondite guise today of "chaos theory," there is an implicit rationality in what seems obviously irrational.

This notion became something of a conceptual philosopher's stone for nineteenth-century Western thinking. It is also the key to the Hegelian, and by extension Marxist, confidence in the dialectical movement of history (what Hegel himself termed *die List der Vernunft*, the "cunning of reason"). The march of empire and the rise and fall of tyrannies, according to Hegel, brings not slavery, but liberty. Marx and Engels used the same argument to "raise consciousness" among, and mobilize, the uneducated and generally unmotivated proletariat in the pursuit of apocalyptic revolutionary goals. All collective ruthlessness and violence in the twentieth century has been justified through appeal to some version of this postulate.

Kant himself actually seems to have first applied this precept of what we might dub *larval mayhem* (i.e., the beastly and inhuman is not what it appears to be, and need not necessarily be morally condemned in an absolute sense, since it is really masks some kind of heuristic activity on the part of a hidden but beneficent agent.). As a lifelong apostle of reason promoting self-conscious and responsible moral action on the part of all citizens of the global cosmopolis, Kant's provocative adoption of the precept in his short essay "Idea for a Universal History from a Cosmopolitan Point of View" (1784) has not been appreciated for the way in which it suffuses so much internationalist thinking from World War I onward.

> The friction among men, the inevitable antagonism, which is a mark of even the largest societies and political bodies, is used by Nature as a means to establish a condition of quiet and security. Through war, through the taxing and never-ending accumulation of armament, through the want which any state, even in peacetime, must suffer internally, Nature forces them to make at first inadequate and tentative attempts; finally, after devastations, revolutions, and even complete exhaustion, she brings them to that which reason could have told them at the beginning and with far less sad experience, to wit, to step from the lawless condition of savages into a league of nations.[1]

But two grim cautions must be registered here. One of these cautions, ignored by Hegel and in lesser measure by Smith, Kant himself was cognizant of. Kant's recognition of how the notion might in the long run prove problematic can be traced to his own pietist religious heritage with its presumption, following Augustine and the sixteenth-century reformers, of ineradicable or "original" human sinfulness. Kant demythologized this theological dogma by renaming it "radical evil," a genetic defect not so much in human nature per se but in the human will—an insight he drew from Martin Luther. In opposition to the Enlightenment utopians who were about to unleash the horrors of the French Revolution, Kant insisted that the "will" was defective, not because it tended toward "disobedience," but toward capriciousness and "arbitrariness," i.e., *Willkür*. For Kant, *Willkür* was a kind of "parallel processor" in the computation of human decision making and ethical deliberation. Human will (*Wille*) is rational, but if denied the discipline of education (*Ausbildung*), and if it is not employed in more subtle strategies of moral reasoning, it can become refractory and unruly, even violent. In other words, there is a certain, built-in entropic tendency in "pure reason" whereby at some point the caprice of willfulness that is no longer "willpower" takes over. Goya's famous aphorism that "the dream of reason . . . produces monsters" is a poetic rendering of this sensibility. Kant hoped that such dreams, if the idea of reason were stretched to its limits, would prove to be just nightmares.

Kant did not live to experience the destruction of the Napoleonic wars. Throughout the long nineteenth century, during which German philosophy for the most part was dominated by neo-Kantianism, Kant's own anxieties gained traction. After the apocalyptic experience of the First World War, the prospects for a universal community grounded in common moral ideals seemed a pipedream. Wilson's Fourteen Points, which might be described loosely as Kantianism with a public face, were generally spurned and undermined by various interests, many of them by domestic opponents, from their very inception. Meanwhile, the dissolution of the Kantian liberal framework was gathering momentum in Germany, not simply in the chaotic parliamentary politics of the postwar Weimar Republic but within German political philosophy itself.

SCHMITT'S CONCEPT OF THE POLITICAL

The *enfant terrible* of this era, who has taken on a new, as well as a rather quizzical and perplexing, role in postmodern political thought was, of course, Schmitt. In his two precedent-breaking and highly controversial treatises, *The Concept of the Political* and *Political Theology,* Schmitt challenged the very foundations of internationalist idealism by advancing several crucial and untimely theses. The first thesis was that "politics" as a category belongs exclusively to the nation-state. It cannot be enlarged to compass some fantastic prospectus for a global polity. Schmitt thus, in one stroke, renders either inane or inconsequential the ancient Stoic ideal of the "cosmopolitan." Nor can it apply to such "imperial" models as the Roman *urbs et orbs*, the Germanic *Heiliges Römisches Reich*, the *dar al-Islam*, or the British "commonwealth." Schmitt's second thesis was that such a purely "national" politics, superseding the classical presumption of the *polis*, must of necessity be exclusionary.

In contrast to the Kantian longing for a global *Gemeinde* founded on the interests of pure reason and reciprocal respect for each person's humanity, Schmitt posited an irreducible binary. "The specific political distinction to which political action and motives can be reduced is that between friend and enemy," Schmitt wrote in offering his famously succinct yet unsettling definition.[2] Because politics is about "collectivities," any political undertaking must be understood strictly as an "existential" act of rebellion, or opposition, to those who form the countercollectivity, the *hostis*, the stranger in one's midst or on the borders, the one who cannot be assimilated. The political requires struggle against what is ontologically "hostile" to its self-constitution. The *polis* requires, by its own nature, a *polemios*, as Plato called such a person, a "public enemy." In many ways Schmitt in the 1920s was self-consciously laying the theoretical groundwork for what at least two generations later would become—perhaps unself-consciously—the principle of so-called identity politics. Identity by its very nature, contrary to Hegel, does not seek to subsume difference; *it demands difference*. Identity politics, furthermore, demands a sense of a differentiated *polis* driven by "hostility."

The third thesis of Schmitt is related to but not as obviously derived as the second is from the first. That thesis is, of course, Schmitt's most famous one—the thesis of *sovereignty*. Schmitt proposed this thesis in *Political Theology*, published originally in 1922 during the extraordinary troubles of the fledgling Weimar government: "Sovereign is he who decides on the state of exception."[3] The "state of exception" (*Ausnahmezustand*) is more than a political concept or perhaps even a "politico-theological one," as Schmitt envisioned it. Schmitt himself referred to it as a "borderline concept" (*Grenzbegriff*). Schmitt was employing the German term in a quite different sense from Kant, who in the *Critique of Pure Reason* characterized the *Grenzbegriff* as an idea that marks the limit of our understanding and of our rational faculties. "God" and "immortality" are well-known Kantian examples of *Grenzbegriffe*. For Kant in his political philosophy as well as his ethics all the various iterations of "borderline," "limiting," or what he elsewhere terms "heuristic" notions function exclusively to provide some logical justification for the use of terms and categories that cannot be captured within the net of empirical induction.

The Kantian *Grenzbegriff* was a vital prop for the development of the philosophical movement known as pragmatism. But Schmitt's deployment of the expression reaches ahead of its day, anticipating the postmodern. Such a "borderline concept," if we carefully unpack its syntactical positioning in Schmitt's politico-legal argument, is closer to the *khora* of Jacques Derrida—in other words, a space of critical undecidability that proves quite theoretically fruitful as a motivating force behind what, using fashionable parlance, we would dub the "deconstruction" of modern political theory, particularly the theory of international order and the nation-state. It is within this context that we must come to comprehend *der Ausnahmezustand* not so much as juridical construct but as an "event" intimately bound up with the decline of the nation-state and as the internal dynamism of global identity politics, which prioritizes the religious over the political.

THE SPACE OF EXCEPTION

In order to discern the character of this event, we must turn then to Agamben's analysis of the state of exception as formulated within his own sort of crypto-Hobbesean framework, which he developed in his earlier book *Homo Sacer*. In *Homo Sacer* Agamben starts from a fundamental aporia of Roman law, the "sacred" as a kind of violence that both "posits" and "sustains" law, a discovery he believes that Schmitt, in the 1920s, fatefully overlooked and that Benjamin, the Jew, during the same era, recognized as the real problem of the political in the twentieth century. The penumbra of the "sacral" in the heritage of Roman legal theory, on which the sense of secular human "rights" are at least provisionally founded, both rattles the seemingly ever fragile architecture of democracy and simultaneously illumines the apparently totalitarian anomalies of the twentieth century. These "anomalies" may turn out, Agamben implies, to be less anomalous than meets the eye. For increasingly contemporary law in its manic, programmatic, global expansiveness in driving to compass, protect, and regulate all persons, interests, and processes melts into pure force of law. Force of law is law in name only because it has lost its power to "signify" anything other than the numinous force behind the law. On the human side, the nakedness and absolute vulnerability of the permanently depoliticized subject before this kind of impersonal "sovereignty" is what Agamben dubs "bare life." It is the key not only to the *Ausnahmezustand* but also to Schmitt's radically revisionist identification of sovereignty with the declaration of the state of exception. "For life under a law that is in force without signifying resembles life in the state of exception, in which the most innocent gesture or the smallest forgetfulness can have the most extreme consequences."[4]

This *space of exception* (for it is not really a "state" at all in Agamben's analysis) is completely "deterritorialized" and depoliticized. It is a no-man's-land like the steppe, where a ruthless Attila or Genghis Khan can impose a brutal and arbitrary order that is truly "anarchy," *no-order*. As in Derrida's messianism without a messiah, the space of exception represents the hazy liminality of both Kantian and Enlightenment politics. In that space rear up nightmarish fantasies of theocratic and militaristic tyrannies.

But in the emerging global context, the "exception" is incrementally becoming the "rule." The assault on "democratic" politics comes from a plethora of different sources, but rarely any more is it the technocratic and intrusive state turned Frankenstein, the hypertrophy of some kind of *caesura* in the functionality of constitutional jurisprudence—for example, the military detentions at Guantanamo or the Patriot Act—

into full-blown Caesarism, a strange kind of postmodern absolutism. It is a force that in no way may be considered a "force of law." Rather, it is what we will call the force of *multitudinism,* the force of the *singular-multiple.* This language as a whole derives from an entire literature of very complex and technical discussions that have taken place in the past decade or so in what might be called the "third wave" of post-structuralist philosophy—particularly the writings of Jean-Luc Nancy as well as Michael Hardt and Antonio Negri. Hardt and Negri, in particular, characterize this concept as "the new science of the multitudes based on the common." The global commons is a key construction in Hardt and Negri's writings. It has little to do with any Kantian sense of a common and rational humanity, let alone any neo-Marxist fiction of some sort of "universal class." The "force" behind the development of the global commons is "the emergence of the common and the singular—the becoming common of singular forms of labor, the singularity of local human contexts in a common global anthropology."[5]

Similarly, Nancy understands this force as an ontological facticity, not necessarily as an artifact of political economy. It is the force of "freedom" in the sense of the assertion of bare identity. "It is a matter of responding to and from oneself as the existing of an existence," Nancy writes. "Nothing else." Any "commons" amounts to a simple "sharing of finitude."[6] As Nancy propounds in *The Creation of the World or Globalization,* this sharing is the very "law of the world." "The world does not have any other law, it is not submitted to any authority, it does not have any sovereign. . . . Its supreme law is in it as the multiple and mobile line of the sharing out that it is."[7]

The force of the singular-multiple as the "creation" of a global commons is not necessarily a world-shaping force. It is a force of what Deleuze terms "absolute de-territorialization," the reduction of *nomos* to nomadism, of generality to idiosyncrasy. Nancy is the latest prophet to declaim from the philosophical street corner about the "decline of the West," although, following his mentor Heidegger, he tends to regard this decline as destiny. "The civilization that has represented the universal and reason—also known as the West—cannot even encounter and recognize any longer the relativity of its norms and the doubt on its own certainty"[8] The crisis of the world, which has been gathering steam for almost a century is essentially the *crisis of postnationalism.*

And it is this crisis that is propelling the planet in its current fearful direction. The crisis itself generates an escalating momentum that cannot be attributed any longer to a "force of law" and an illimitable violence perpetrated in principle, if not in fact, by a totalistic state. The force of the singular-multiple works a violence that is diffuse yet equally exhausting, inscrutable, and seemingly unrepeatable. It is the violence of *centrifugal* rather than *centripetal* force. It is the violence of singulars grinding ever more clamorously against singulars in the name of infinite finite-multiples that claim in their own infinite ways a certain idiosyncratic, nonnegotiable, and infinite "authority." It is the violence of ever more "multiple" finite existential subject points that rattle around the planet, like so many metal beads in a jar rolling ever more rapidly downhill. It appears to be a cacophonous cry for "justice" but in reality is a cry for identity. But when the finite replaces the infinite in the name of a limitless multiplicity of possibilities for global existential freedom, the falcon can no longer hear the falconer, in the immortal words of the poet William Butler Yeats, and "the center cannot hold."

THE CRISIS OF POSTNATIONALISM

In order to acquire a sense, however, of the genesis of the crisis of postnationalism, we must turn our gaze briefly on the political and discursive formation we call the nation-state. In the vast sweep of world history, the nation-state, which from the Renaissance onward has served as the baseline for political—and international political—theorizing, is never the norm, but rather the curiosity. The utter contingency of the nation-state and its corresponding ideology—otherwise known as nationalism—has been dissected in careful detail by Benedict Anderson in his *Imagined Communities* (1983). Anderson ironically regards the nation-state not as some kind of political given, a departure point for more sophisticated inquiry into the foundation of "legal" rights, responsibilities, and their distributive ramifications, but as a simple "trope" for "two centuries of historical change." He contextualizes this argument in terms of what he dubs the "effort of Marxist and liberal theory" to "save the phenomena" of arguments about political economy, beginning with the assumption of the nation-state. He further argues that such an effort remains "Ptolemaic," and that a "re-orientation of perspective," that is, "a Copernican spirit is urgently needed." His own *point d'appui* is that "nationality or, as one might prefer to put it in view of that word's multiple significations, nation-ness, as well as nationalism, are cultural artifacts of a particular kind."[9]

Anderson traces the production of the nation trope to the subversion, decline, and *dispersion* of the monarchial and absolutist political figurations that arose in the seventeenth century, formations that in themselves were signifying instrumentalities that evolved to "imagine" both the formal and concrete relationships between new, slowly *secularizing*, hyperfeudal rulers and the masses of the ruled. The nation-state and the trope of the "sovereign" emerged from the wreckage of a never-quite-coherent, medieval, "holy" *imperium*, in itself a ghostly or "spiritual" knockoff of the distant memory of Rome. But the imagination of the nation-state per se only became possible when the authority of the dynastic and often God-enthroned "sovereign" itself became both administratively and philosophically questionable and when sovereignty passed over—not as much conceptually as practically—to the *populus*. The sovereignty of the *populus* could only be "imagined" itself if it had some kind of recognizable facticity, a collectivized *identity*. A common language, and the imagination of a historic, common culture based on that language, became the strategy of choice for nineteenth-century and early twentieth-century "nationalisms."

Ironically, however, it was not in Europe, with its crumbling multiethnic and multilinguistic empires, that the strategy of nationalism gained initial impetus, but in the New World, where ethnicity and linguistic priority—other than the argot of the landowner or slaveholder—were not so easily identifiable. The champions of early nationalism, in North America as well as South America, were the "creole" or mixed-blood and polyglot rising merchant classes, who clambered for "national unification" on cultural as much as political grounds, according to Anderson. In Europe, after the extreme difficulties of linguistic and cultural unification experienced in the late nineteenth century, the "imagined," pseudoscientific element of race became a temporary principle of cohesion, eventually with an apocalyptic outcome. That element, in turn, fueled colonialism and the colonial expansion of Europe and, to a somewhat lesser extent, America. In the "postcolonial" situation that developed after World

War II, the nativistic and revolutionary forms of nationalism throughout what used to be called the Third World, which functioned to disseminate the geography, and the provisional demography, of the present world order, mimed to a limited extent the modalities of European nationalism.

But, as Anderson points out, neither language nor race were anywhere nearly as prominent as a force of resistance to, and differentiation from, the structures of colonial occupation and regimentation itself. The current fragility of these new nationalisms, particularly in South Asia and Africa, can be explained, we might add, as the consequence of the natural dissipation of the countercolonial force of resistance, although it can also be accounted for by economic globalization, which has created, à la Hardt and Negri, a new kind of transnational "empire" of capital and capital flows in which the politics of the nation-state becomes progressively jejune and obsolete.

As that short-lived empire begins to unravel, which seems to be the case after the global financial meltdown of the autumn of 2008, we can only begin to speculate what "rough beast" might be "slouching toward" some global gravamen, ultimately to "be born." But the force of the singular-plural, as I have named it, continues with its own kind of uninterrupted logic. I will postulate, not so much with prophecy as with an archaeology of what can still be found after the worldwide collapse of the last intellectual "dynasty" in the three-century-old regime of the Kantian-European *Aufklärung* that we know as the theory of the state and its purification in the ideal of liberal democracy, that the crisis of postnationalism will resolve itself in a yet unchartered manner.

We need only make the observation that the "state of exception" has now passed from the state and become a space of multiple singularities that render the state not all-powerful but otiose. Identity politics has hastened the proliferation, through globalization, of this future exceptionality. Identity politics, given special currency by postcolonial theory, was always a brutal battering ram for delegitimating the Enlightenment universalism implied in Kant's democratic cosmopolis. Identity is a singularity. It is a "philosophical" construct, as Nancy argues, for the singular "existential" existent to be itself as itself. Identity politics is founded on an assertion of the singularness of what is existentially significant in a broad sense—gender, class, race, religious identification, nationality, sexual orientation, local peculiarity, etc. It is what Nancy names *freedom.* And freedom, he insists, is a "philosophical name for absoluteness." But freedom in Nancy's sense is merely the "absoluteness" of the secular and universal Enlightenment principle of voluntaristic politics. It does not name the singularity in certain identities. The singularity is the absoluteness of the *force of infinity upon the finite,* the force of the *religious.* But this force has nothing to do with the religious as marker of temporal identity, only as a *force of constraint and command,* not the "force of law," but the *force majeur* that expresses itself in the "majesty of the law," the sovereign ordained by God—the ultimate force of God himself. That is the force behind the "exception" in the postnational era.

RELIGIOUS MONOTHEISM

This force amounts to that of a religious monotheism, something Nancy himself is compelled to take more seriously than he had in his earlier work. In the case of Western "monotheism," with its Judeo-Christian coloration, Nancy does not necessarily recognize the religious as force so much as *precedent.* "A certain conception of 'human rights,'" he opines, "as well as a certain determination of the relationship between politics and religion, comes straight out of Christianity."[10] The idea that Christianity has seeded the political configurations of the current world is several generations old. It goes back to arguments quite fashionable in the 1960s, the decade of "God's death," that Christian monotheism is the genetic forbear of secularization. In the now vanishing moment of planetary neoliberalism, the numerous varieties of so-called liberal pundits still cling to a similar outlook, all the while substituting the term *globalization* for *secularization.*

That, of course, is what Nancy is really up to. Nancy purports to be a theorist of globalization, but such theory beyond the past decade since 9/11 has been impossible to carry forward without recognition of the religious, particularly religious monotheism, not as precursor but as *the real engine of globalization.* The pioneer theoretical contribution to this nascent genre is Olivier Roy's *Globalized Islam.* Fascinated with the spread of Islamist identity politics in Europe and its resurgence in the Muslim regions, Roy undertook a complicated empirical study that led him to elaborate a model of a transnational and a transnational

Muslim identity that has been forged out of the failure of Enlightenment secularism and the cultural-linguistic politics of ethnic "nationalism." Islamism, Roy asserts, "want[s] to bridge the gap between religion and a secularized society by exacerbating the religious dimensions, overstretching it to the extent that it cannot become a habitus by being embedded in a real culture."[11]

The broad model, as has been evident most recently, also applies to other forms of monotheism, including both Christianity and Judaism.[12] The religious is a force of "identity" that subsumes, and cancels out in many respects, the particularities of the components of modern nationalism. The "power of the universal" emanates, paradoxically, in the "singularity" of the monotheistic revealed truth that seeks to "deconstruct" all localities, nationalities, and empires. The monotheistic claim on the politically particular is the very "categorical imperative" of the infinite upon the finite, something Kant himself understood, when he correlated the "starry heavens" to the "moral law" within himself, but that he had to defer in terms of political theory to the Enlightenment goal of cosmopolitan rationality.

Such an insight lurks behind Badiou's starting contention that the "incarnational" monotheism of the infinitized finite found in Christianity is the real source—not the Enlightenment—of any moral or political universalism. "The conditions for the universal cannot be conceptual, either in origin, or in destination."[13] They originate in what Badiou calls an "event" of singularity—in the case of Christianity, the Cross and Resurrection. "There is singularity only so far as there is universality," and vice versa.[14] The singularity of the religious engenders a force, as we know, that is double-edged and double-valent. Especially in the monotheistic tradition, and frequently in its absolutist or "fundamentalist" manifestations, it claims a certain kind of *Recht* in the name of divine justice. The space of exception becomes the monotheistic conscience in its demand not simply to be exempt from Enlightenment standards, but to consecrate a whole new global politics. Religion challenges the perceived threat of violence of the state, often with its own threat of violence in the name of an absolute, transcendent, and stateless "justice." From diverse wars against the imagined "axis of evil" to apocalyptic struggles against the imagined "great and little Satans" the logic of postmodern global politics becomes increasingly "postpolitical" in the true sense of the word. It becomes *theopolitical,* though not necessarily "theocratic." *It becomes religious* in the sense of *the force of the singular,* a singularity that unleashes a certain kind of *Gewalt* that claims its own "redemption" (in Benjamin's sense) by eliminating the tentative economies and fragile equipoise that define the political in conformity with the liberal paradigm.

The future belongs, therefore, in this era of Deleuzean "absolute de-territorialization" wrought by globalization to those who harness the force of the singular. The inescapable yoking of the passion of today's singular minded to the classical monotheisms has been analyzed extensively by two of the current era's most important living philosophers—Sloterdijk and Badiou. Sloterdijk's method is what we might call *historic-hermeneutical,* Badiou's *logico-semiotic.* Yet the upshot is unmistakable. The singularity of the divine creative force—be it the unnameable Mosaic name, the *principium absurdum* of Christianity's crucified God, or the terrifying undifferentiability and "nonassociability" of Islam's absolute revelation as embodied in the rule of *tawhid* ("indivisibility") in these monotheisms—contains the secrets of the late modern and postmodern epochs. Any "philosophy of the future," as Nietzsche envisioned it, must take into account this force of singularity, this particular *force of God.* Such a force is not only *theogenic,* but "sovereignly" political in Schmitt's sense as the *force of exception.*

Badiou and Radical Politics

Badiou, in many ways an unreconstructed or undomesticated *provocateur,* grasps this force of exception, which he envisages as somehow proleptic to the radical politics of the late twentieth and twenty-first centuries. The universalism of such a radical politics is embryonic in what Badiou describes as Saint Paul's "antidialectic" of death and resurrection, as found in the latter's various epistles. It is *not* the case that somehow Badiou, like Derrida, underwent a "religious turn." As with all good "political theologians" of our contemporary era, Badiou understands that the political transformations of the modern era, and now of the postmodern age of upheaval, have their ultimate genesis in the curious Jew-Greek-Christian alchemy that first took place during the first three centuries. Secularism, as Nietzsche properly discerned, is nothing more than a form of what Gianni Vattimo has called a "weak Christianity."

But Badiou recognizes that the peculiar kind of "weakness" (*asthenes*) that Paul extols as the covert "power" of the crucified God is not the fulcrum of the dialectic as we find in Hegel. The divine weakness, as enunciated by Paul, is a *singular force* in Badiou that overcomes death, because death is no longer a pathway of salvation. More clearly than any updated version of the *theologia crucis*, Badiou's interpretation of Paul is an impressive rendering in the present-day discourse of sign and event of what Luther—contemptuously—called a *theologia gloriae*. Only Badiou these days can claim to be a postresurrection—and hence an eschatological—theologian of sorts. According to Badiou, "death sets up an immanentization of the spirit," which does not in any manner depend on a dialectical transformation, but solely on the "real as event."[15] Death belongs to the participation of God in the worldliness of the world, "becoming sin," as Pauline Christology would phrase it, even though it is at once the "configuration of the real through the subjective path of the flesh."[16] Universality has its provenance in the absolute singularity of this death-destroying *anastasic* moment at the impossible interface between time and eternity.

Furthermore, Paul's "universalism," Badiou insists, amounts to an "equality" that is neither egalitarian nor merely the zero-sum of all heterogeneities. Paul's universality defies every economy. It is a universality that is productive of a nonarithmetical "equality," a force of exception subtracting from all forms of difference as givenness. The thought of this force or "power" consists "in he who is a militant of the truth identifying himself, as well as everyone else, on the basis of the universal."[17] Militancy for Badiou, as for Žižek, is the marker of force, though Badiou is far more sophisticated in realizing (in a way at which Žižek himself fails) that the force is eminently *postdialectical*. It is the force behind the affirmation of what Schmitt understood as "sovereignty," although it is a sovereignty without a particular sovereign—the genuine meaning of the Kantian-Derridean slogan of "religion without religion." *Sovereign is the one who incarnates the force of exception.* Sovereign is the one who forces an exception to the iron rule of economies not in the name of the "individual" but of this "spirit of truth."

Badiou's analysis has the opposite outcome as Sloterdijk's, even while both thinkers nonetheless—remaining profoundly political in a much deeper sense—start from what we might term the *monotheistic imperative*. Badiou sees the monotheistic imperative as perpetually generating its own historical apparatus of signification to manifest the force of exception. Sloterdijk understands history as the cooling tank for this force. For Sloterdijk, monotheism amounts to what we might term a *sphere of negotiation* wherein we can begin to signify, and simulate, the reasons for the failure of our own epistemological economies. According to Sloterdijk, every monotheism is an attempt to reinscribe somehow "a monovalent primal language." They "want to make audible the monologue of things as they are, and reproduce the unconcealed facts, the first structures, the purest instructions of being, without having to address the intermediate world of languages, images and projections with its independent logic."[18]

At the same time, monotheism is not simply an epistemological fallback, as the familiar "God of the gaps" hypothesis renders it. Ninteenth-century theories of religion as human projection, on which the "God of the gaps" model rests, always assumed the sovereignty of a certain "rational" structure of knowledge. The nineteenth- and twentieth-century critiques of religion, of which today's popular atheism is merely a querulous bastard child at the tail end of a declining bloodline, were simply more sophisticated versions of the rage against transcendence characteristic of the entire *Aufklärung*. Sloterdijk, as a disciple of both Nietzsche and Heidegger, has always understood the limits of Enlightenment, even though Western philosophy has never been able to disown it.

GOD'S ZEAL

But this rage against transcendence was always misplaced and indicated more of a contempt for the alliance of religious with political authoritarianism than with a serious consideration of why religion is problematic in the first place. The historical source of any claim for religious revelation and doctrinal certitude has always, according to

Sloterdijk, been (as they are for Badiou) the impulse to universality. What defines the Enlightenment is not so much a suspicion or even a rejection of religion, but the assertion of a *counteruniversality* under the flag of a totalized regime of reason.

Sloterdijk's take on transcendence naturally reflects his positioning as a post-Enlightenment thinker. Post-Enlightenment philosophy from Kierkegaard onward has exposed the fractures, gaps, and indeterminacies in the regime of reason. But, as Sloterdijk himself stresses, the regime of reason had inevitably to crack and fissure, because it was simply one stage in the expansion of what he terms environing and comforting "spheres"—or as spherical microentities or subjectivities he terms "bubbles" that are constantly expanding into the endless space of the unknown and forcing an encounter with "monstrous" externalities, the transhuman or posthuman. Spheres are *autogenetic*, that is, they expand, like life itself, according to an internal "law" of self-formation. This process of expansion—a constant mutual attraction of fragile, film-sheathed, "airy" (that is, virtual) essences, which, as in fluid dynamics, aggregate and coagulate according to the level of surface tension, then, at the slightest disturbance or protrusion from without, separate or dissipate, only to reform at different magnitudes anew—is what is ultimately meant nowadays, according to Sloterdijk, by "globalization." "Since the start of the Modern Age, the human world has constantly—every century, every decade, every year, and every day—had to learn to accept and integrate new truths about an outside not related to humans."[19]

Yet, unlike contemporary French postmodern thinkers, who regarded these externalities mainly as an invasion into the distinctive "bubble" of Enlightenment rationality of factors that remain alien and irreconcilable with the structure of scientific inference and logical predication, or even postcolonial theorists such as Walter Mignolo, who view *Aufklärung* as the concurrent expansion of European spheres of language, territoriality, and racial classification that has now been pierced by the obdurate reality of the indigenous other, Sloterdijk regards the tension of globalization as something far more consequential than a clash of subjectivities. For Sloterdijk, the monotheistic *Sphäre* derives from a distension of the original bubble that was the all-embracing, metaphysically seamless unity of space and time the ancient Greeks named *cosmos*.

As with all spheres in their trajectory of expansion and reformation, there was something the sphere could not contain, something that provoked and destabilized it. The story of the first genuine monotheistic revelation—Moses on Mount Sinai—is instructive here, because in the account we discern a subtle, incommensurable element that intrudes on what at the time was the great cosmological bubble of Egyptian civilization ruled by and embodied in its pharaonic god-kings. The irritating externalities in this instance are the descendants of Abraham, the *habiru*, "outlaws" or outsiders. Moses as a secret *habiru* in royal dynastic disguise, who can no longer abide the enslavement and oppression of his people, slays an Egyptian and is forced into exile. While tending sheep in the land of Midian, he is confronted and addressed by a "presence" that outstrips all the boundaries and markers familiar to those who live within the sphere of sacred Egypt. This presence cannot be named. Indeed, when it discloses its name, it becomes a gargantuan surd, a nameless naming that expresses only its potency and might, in short, its pure *sovereignty*. After the exodus, new semiotic materials for the enclosure and preservation of this sovereignty are given once more on a mountain, the handing down of the tablets, the Torah. The Torah is the *Sphäre* for sojourning through history as God's chosen people; but it is a sphere in which the "law" is always a reminder of the dipolarity of the bubble itself—the I-am-that-I-am that constantly calls into question the subjectivity of the Jewish subject. It is the *voice that addresses,* whose "I-ness" constitutes the master subjectivity.

In all such instances, of course, what we are contending with is the manner in which the force of exception becomes, in Derrida's terminology, the "mystical foundation" of a new order. The same is true of the beginnings of Christianity. Christianity arose from the unique *antipolitical* identity of the Jewish people, living out their own exceptional and eminently irreconcilable relationship within the imperial *urbs et orbis*. The Romans wielded the penal form of torture we know as crucifixion to mark the incompatibility of any such exceptionalism, especially when it led to revolt, as often happened in the case of Judea. Crucifixion signified the violent consequences of the victim's claim of exception from the *imperium* through his or her extinction within the "civil" sphere. From the standpoint of the empire, anyone violating the rules of "civil society" did not deserve humane treatment. The notions *humanitas* and *Romanitas* remained indistinguishable. This form of "exceptionalism," however, became the instigation to a new and powerful force of universalization that continues to this day.

As Schmitt noted, every theology is political theology, and all politics is "theological." *Polis* and *cosmos* are heuristic signifiers for the envisioning of an immunized sphere of negotiation between the human and the transhuman, signifiers that are ever expanding their peripheries. Thus the force of universalization, which when restricted to the political sphere becomes *imperialism*, is driven both by a "transcendent" prompting of all *true believers* and the immanent reshaping of the *politeia* so that it becomes ever more inclusive. In Sloterdijk's words, "spheres are forms of destiny."[20]

In its early phases, liberal democracy had this universalizing force behind it. The push for inclusivity was tempered only by intractable racial animosities as well as resistance from indigenous cultures with their own self-perpetuating spheres of "local knowledge" and mythoethnic identification. The loss of any sense of a *divine imperative* or a sovereign mandate behind liberal democracy, manifested, of course, in the secular exclusion of religion from the public sphere, has had more to do with its crisis of legitimacy than many realize.

Where liberal democrats in the nineteenth century saw themselves as torchbearers for this theopolitical campaign of universalization (captured in such clichéd slogans as "the fatherhood of God and the brotherhood of man"), by the end of the twentieth century they had turned decisively consumerist and particularist. Liberal democracy was now a vast emporium for the exchange of dreams and desires as well as an apparatus for the policing of greed and excess. It also became a temple for money changers, as the millions of dollars poured into the financing of political contests in America testify. Where the money changers flourish, faith languishes, and democracy ultimately perishes.

But, as Derrida prophetically noted in the early 1990s, neoliberalism itself as a globalizing force has been troubled by the planetary "return of religion." Religion serves as a *counterdestiny* to the rampant technologization and economic absorption of the macrosphere that has now become the sole focus of globalization theory. Sloterdijk himself uses the immunological trope. The return of religion, particularly in the new, militantly charged political Islam, has been lamented by Western liberal pundits as an ignorant manifestation of counter-Enlightenment. But, from Sloterdijk's vantage point, it functions broadly as a strategy of reinvigorating the collapsed orb of a once proud Islamic suprema-cism, as a parallel form of "microspherology" in a completely decultur-ated and monetarized world system where all previous *Sphären* have been abolished.

If neoliberalism, however, has meant the obliteration of all previ-ous expansionary spheres with their encapsulated destinies, it has also deprived humanity of the profound immunological cover these spheres once provided. The immunizing role of spheres, so far as Sloterdijk is concerned, remains just as critical as their meaning-bestowing func-tion. Spheres often burgeon through the aggrandizing power of their dominant ideologies, their *virtual content*, which is tied directly to their universalizing impetus. "What is world history," Sloterdijk writes, "if not the war history of immune systems? And the early immune systems—were they not always militant geometries too?"[21]

BLACK SWANS

But these universalized ideologies serve as well to reweave and mend the tattered threads of previous, more parochial spheres of meaning where fundamental injustices are now perceived as fatal. They offer hope for the hopeless.[22] The universalistic impulse, which always seems to precipitate in a multidimensional spectrum of proselytism, moral militancy, and political as well as cultural imperialism, has proven an inexorable force of reunification in ages of social flux, cosmopolitan-ism, and conceptual relativism. Nietzsche's identification of liberal cos-mopolitanism with decadence and his call for a new set of "tablets" that would authorize the transvaluation of values along with the cre-ation of new ones reflect the dynamics of history more accurately than familiar cultural diffusion and global interactionist models. History is about the impact of what Nassim Taleb has termed "black swans," the sudden occurence of singular events that change the course of human civilization in unprecedented and unanticipated ways. We can trace the long-term causal nexuses spinning centrifugally from these singularities (e.g., the collapse of feudalism following the Black Death and the rise of robust, mercantile types of protocapitalism in Europe from the late fifteenth century onward), but the Black Death itself remains such a "swan" by a cognate color.

Broadly speaking, we use the analogy of the black swan anomaly and its subsequent effects to illustrate what we are terming the "force of exception." More often than not, the force of exception manifests itself as a world-transforming human enthusiasm that, over time, acquires the label of a *religious inspiration*, as a *revelation*. The historical topography of religion is always cultural, institutional, and *semiological* (in that sense that it can be identified and mapped by recognizable and comparative systems of human sign-functions). But its origins must remain obscure and ultimately inexplicable.

The historical irruption of the force of exception—the impulse to universality—can only be attributed to such singular eventualities, as Badiou clearly understands. If a team somehow could envision themselves—hypothetically—as "reporters" for a Jerusalem news outlet around 33 AD who were asked to cover another crucifixion of a Galilean "criminal" on Mount Calvary, could they imagine that within a century the legacy of such a ne'er-do-well would have begun transforming the entire Roman world and within three centuries it would have "triumphed" over all the imperial legions? If they had met an orphaned caravaneer named Mohammed in Mecca in the early seventh century, could they have imagined that within less than a century his reportedly "outlandish" preaching would have motivated Arab armies to conquer much of what had been the crumbling Roman imperium, and within another hundred years or so a vast new realm reaching as far as the Pyrenees in the West and Persia in the East? But these naked facticities are no longer the stuff of speculation. They consist in the very warp and woof of history and they can only be accounted for as world transmogrifications ensuing from the force of such exceptions or singularities.

Sloterdijk does not consider the force of exception as something that only inhabits the sphere of the religious. The tendency to universalistic "zealotry" is a kind of mysterious, coiled serpent lurking within the pluralistic—and ultimately entropic—play of cultural and historical particularities. If we may pose a brainteaser, the force of universality is the exception, not the rule within the scope of history. The course of human events naturally leads to the dissipation of the universalistic impulse, and a slow, meandering return to a more casual order of what is comfortable, familiar, and simply *parochial*. It is culture, not religion, that enforces repetition and ritualism. Even the most putatively antireligious trend of the last half millennium that we now term the Enlightenment followed the rule of the exception. The debilitating war of religions, starting in the early seventeenth century, had reduced the universalistic pretensions of the different sectarian camps within Christendom to bare, burned-out remnants of conviction that in the end seemed more like counterfeit coinage than precious species. As Sloterdijk points out, the Enlightenment did not break with the tradition of the "one God," but "produced a higher-level monotheism in which various universal articles of faith attained dogmatic validity. These include the a-priori unity of the species, the indispensability of the state under the rule of law, the destiny of humans to control nature, solidarity with the disadvantaged and the disability of natural selection for Homo sapiens." Sloterdijk adds: "'Enlightenment' is simply the popular name for the perpetual literary council in which these articles are discussed, fixed, and defended against heretics."[23]

Monotheism, therefore, can be considered the *strong force* of exception within the unified field of human significations that establishes the real intention of the concept we have in mind when we talk about human solidarity. The historic drive toward the formation of an ever more inclusive *politeia* amounts to a "secularized," or domesticated, rechanneling of the monotheistic impulse. That is why all militant ideologies of democracy, especially in their early Enlightenment phases (such as the French Revolution and the American-Jacksonian creed of the "common man") turn out to be *exceptionalist*. It is also why militant universalist ideologies in general are ultimately divisive rather than inclusive.

But the danger to the contemporary *politeia*—if that term may still be regarded as describing political life today—does not reside in the fanatical affections that disturb and threaten a sense of well-ordered and amply administered civic life. The fear of unrestrained spiritual enthusiasm, what in the eighteenth century was contemptuously named *Schwärmerei*, is the residual paranoid fixation of a fading *Aufklärung*. As Roy has provocatively postulated, one finds a more serious prospect of changing the world in religious "fundamentalism" than in any cultivated Western form of political progressivism. The reason is compelling, though not obvious. Fundamentalism is not the kind of paleoconservatism its enemies routinely make it out to be. Fundamentalism, especially in the contemporary era, constitutes an excess of irritability—what Derrida aptly describes as an "autoimmune" response—to a technologically overdetermined environment in which the passion for the singular, *all-truth* has been co-opted by the dicing up of great ideas into random sign tokens for the undiscerning conceptual consumer and by the trivialization of language and communication through the explosion of media. Where everything is permitted, nothing is any longer possible.

The fundamentalist, waving the battle flag of purified doctrine and holy text, critically and "prophetically" views himself, or herself, as a revitalized champion of the universal. Unlike the ancient founding prophets of the monotheistic proclamation on which such a contemporary "witness" slavishly relies, however, the fundamentalist has only the strange, historically effaced bare *scriptum*. There are no voices from on high, or instructions from angels standing at the door of a cave, to help forge the message. The force of exception that is the universal truth reconstituted in the fundamentalist's declarations remains strictly *literal* and emptied of all "spirit" save the bearer's own militant determination that the message is right and shall triumph.

Pace Derrida, we can genuinely say that in the *age of globalization*, as contrasted with former ages of universalizations, *il n'y a pas de hors-texte* ("there is nothing on the outside of the text"). Even if this oft-quoted phrase indicates nothing more than the unsurpassability of the context of a text, it still applies to the pathos of the fundamentalist. The fundamentalist somehow "knows" the power of what was once a universalized demand to challenge all secret and absurdly subtle trellis-works of relativized truthfulness—the general monotheistic assault on "paganism," the Islamic offense of a persisting *jahilyya* ("days of igno-rance") even when the teachings of the Qur'an dominate—and must therefore take up the sword of truth to do battle once again.

The revival of *jihad* today in its many religious guises is no aber-ration caused primarily, as cultural diffusionists sophomorically con-tend, by a failure of backward minds, peoples, and societies to adapt to the new "educated" civil society of an emerging global *saeculum*.

It is the imagined global *saeculum* that is indeed the aberration. Our aim here is not to launch or develop a comprehensive theory of what is really going on with the worldwide process we dub "globalization." But we can safely note that the pushback against globalization on a truly global scale in recent years—and not just among the clueless intelligentsia in the Western world—has had far less to do with grievances about inequalities of wealth than about incommensurabilities in value systems and worldviews. In fact, it comes down, as Mignolo forcefully argues, to inequalities in systems of rationality, in the emerging global *oikonomia* of signs and discursive actions.

In his trenchant, though garrulous, analysis of what is happening, titled *The Dark Side of Modernity*, Mignolo makes the implicit claim that the language of both secularism and Enlightenment is a holdover legacy of European colonial domination not just over peoples and economies but over the rules by the which the self-understanding and spiritual self-formation of once subjugated ethnicities are granted recognition. These languages of "enunciation" must be emancipated, according to Mignolo, from their protocolonial frameworks. Transposing Lacan's neo-Freudian version of the *talking cure* from individual clients to entire cultures that are currently "decolonizing," Mignolo views the emergence of these new discourses of enunciation, these novel grammars of subjectivity, as earning their rightful place in the global emporium of standardized epistemologies.

Mignolo focuses particularly on indigenous subjectivities. This preoccupation, in which he insists that the *geospatiality* of discourses (sources of "local knowledge") is somehow largely determinative, tends to obscure the more profound relevance of his investigation. Mignolo makes the mistake, which Roy so effectively diagnoses, of confusing the perdurance of the *remnants of cultural tradition* with tradition itself. The juggernaut of the global commercialized *saeculum* has "deculturated" most, if not all, religious traditions, according to Roy, insofar as cultural heritage requires a stable sociopolitical context, which was lost long ago with colonialism. For every refurbished form of indigeneity (which anthropologists far more than reformers have assisted in fostering), there arises on the global scene a corresponding site of *reactivity* on the part of deculturated natives who have only the curious descriptions preserved in historical reports and texts to rely upon. The confabulation of indigeneity (Anderson's "imagined community") does not bespeak any kind of delusion or dishonesty. It is the lot of all religious practice nowadays and has been the source of religious revival and reformation since time immemorial. One need think only of the Protestant Reformation with its conviction that it was restoring the primitive church.

Such a reactivity, as an immunological defense against the threat of all pluralist and sociological dogmas that relativize the subjective certitude of the believer or practitioner, results in a new kind of universalism that overcomes all the doubts of previous generations. After all, Allah—the one, true God—was originally nothing more than the generic god in the pluralistic flux of Byzantine Arabia. The same could be said for "Jesus the Christ" in a Romanized, de-Judaized, polyvalent culture of competing messiahs and messianic yearnings. If monotheistic universalism is not the norm, it is always the trend in any given epoch. And that trend itself emanates from a persistent force in all history, the force of forces we name, for want of a better term (and recognizing, of course, the "theological" questions it is *not* meant to provoke), *the force of God.*

Part 3

TOWARD A POLITICAL THEOLOGY IN THE TWILIGHT OF THE POLITICAL

7

Force of God

It is possible for a dictator to govern in a liberal way.
And it is also possible for a democracy to govern
with a total lack of liberalism.

—FRIEDRICH HAYEK

The crisis of liberal democracy today is a far different one from that
which beset Europe between the wars. We have moved on from
Hannah Arendt's analysis in *The Origins of Totalitarianism*, which saw
the earlier crisis as the outcome of liberalism's own self-deconstruc-
tion. Liberalism's historical preoccupation with formal liberty at the
expense of those traditional ties that foster a sense of communal identity (Tönnies's famous *Gesellschaft/Gemeinschaft* distinction), according to Arendt's narrative, ultimately led to a virulent metastasis of a violent and expansive simulated pseudopolis—what she termed a *totale
Herrschaft*. Such an expression better translates from the German as
"totalized sovereignty" in preference to the conventional "totalitarianism," which implies an ideological commitment on the part of certain
historical actors such as Hitler or Stalin rather than a golemlike bur-
geoning of certain propensities, as Arendt discerned, within the very
structures of modern representative democracy. The hollowing out of

representative democracy through the bourgeois obsession with negative freedoms and what Hegel and Marx together understood simply as
"abstract right," incarnated nowadays in the politics of what is known
as libertarianism, fostered the conditions for the rise of totalitarianism.

However, those conditions have abated, or at least morphed in the
wake of the collapse of global totalitarian movements, such as Marx-
ist-Leninism, along with their shrinkage into new oligarchic forms of
classical authoritarianism. Nor do older, cold war theories of totalitarianism account in any credible manner for such contemporary trends
as the new breed of mystico-anarchic tribalism and religious identity
politics manifested in today's Islamist jihadism.

The crisis of liberal democracy has less to do with violent assaults
on its internal makeup from either domestic or foreign agents than
with what has been identified, although in entirely different contexts
and sets of circumstances, by earlier political theorists as a "legitimation crisis." At the same time, such a legitimation crisis arises not
from the failure of liberal institutions to "represent" the generic will
or interests of their constituents but out of the impossibility of any
conceivable *politeia* emerging from the complete evanescence of
what we previously designated as the general equivalent for a global
political economy. Any economy, in fact, is impossible without a
general equivalent, whether it be gold or God. Therefore, the collapse of even the remotest surrogates for such a general equivalent
into the singularity that can only be named the Great Uncertainty,
around which swirl a planetary multitude of personal, social, and
ideological anxieties, leaves us with a thought of the impossibility
of politics altogether. If not only justice, as Derrida claimed, but
the political as well constitute "impossible" theoretical determinations, which remain at once "undecidable" and "undeconstructible,"
what then might be our options? The question, of course, is a foolish
one, because the apparition of the *singular indeterminable* takes us
beyond all considerations of politics and economy, stitched together
since Aristotle's time as implicitly conjugate variables in any thinking about human conduct and terms of mutual association. Yet the
question of the singular indeterminable is not irrelevant to economy,
as Agamben himself has demonstrated in his analysis of the "two
paradigms" of political thought that aboriginally have a religious, or

monotheistic, point of origin. Sovereignty entails the "just" distribution of political privileges and entitlements, and vice versa.

VIRTUAL ECONOMIES

But what exactly pregrounds the assertion of sovereignty along with the establishment of systems of exchange and the "just" distribution of myriad rights and rewards? Agamben brackets that particular question. If the "monarchy" that is tacit in monotheism must be necessarily complemented, as Agamben suggests, by the "republicanism" of the Trinitarian formulation necessary to make the "one God" truly God not only in heaven but in human affairs and in human history, then all expressions of sovereignty amount to the actualizing of certain purely "virtual" propensities for language and representation itself. If we follow Benjamin and Derrida, we realize that the "force" of this expression is eminently the *force of God. All political theory, therefore, is eminently political theology* as well, broadly speaking.

What does such a statement actually imply, especially as it collides with the master assumptions of most Western political thought since the late seventeenth century and would appear to undermine the fundamental secularist premises of most strands of Occidental avant-garde theory since at least Machiavelli? The intimacy of political theory with what presently we have begun to denominate as political theology does not by any stretch of the imagination boil down to some revival of ancient or medieval arguments for theocracy. The theocratic suspicion, which is cloyingly common these days and polemically deployed way too often whenever religious claims or "faith statements" find a voice in the debates of liberal democracy, derives from a fatal misunderstanding of the very *ontology* of liberal democracy itself. In recent years scholars such as Lilla, Critchley, and, more incisively, Agamben himself, have put to rest the tiresome false premise of those who routinely object to the insinuation of religious or quasi-theological discourse into political deliberations through their own genealogies of democracy. But the peculiar "theological" substructure of modern democratic theory, drawing not just on Christian but also Islamic sources,[1] is but merely the expansive historical evidence for the primal insight first articulated in a crude but penetrating manner by Benjamin himself that all foundational authority legitimating the *politeia* is in some sense both ahistorical and "mystical" at the core. The "force of law," on which all law depends, genealogically resolves into the force of God. This genealogical discovery—which at a certain level is also strictly "logical"— amounts to what Critchley himself terms the "transcendental solution" inherent in all political theory.[2]

Following Kant and contemporary social theorists since Thomas Luckmann, we must distinguish this unique type of "transcendental" anatomy from any "transcendent" or metapolitical justification of political values and structures in terms of religion, which underlies all theocracies. The transcendental argument rests on the realization that no politics is self-legitimating, as no cognition was self-authenticating for Kant. Kant's overleveraged formula of a "religion without religion," or a "religion within the limits of reason alone," bespeaks such an intuition. It is a phenomenon that can be intuited in both the starry skies above us and the demands of "conscience" within us. As Plato emphasized throughout the *Republic,* "justice," or *dikaiosyne,* is concomitantly a quality of external political organization and the inward "virtues" of the citizen.

But we must not make the Kantian mistake of confusing this distinctive "transcendental" gesture with some kind of immanent Platonic idea. Such unrepentant Platonism stalks even Critchley's brilliant reading of political theory from Plato through Rousseau in his *Faith of the Faithless.* Critchley elegantly dissects Rousseau's struggle to devise a theory of democratic sovereignty that innoculates the *politeia* against mob rule by enforcing collective virtue through the construct of the "general will." For Critchley, this same kind of transcendental solution, which he also finds in Badiou's political philosophy, is inevitably "Platonist" because political theory in essence is necessarily a transcendental exercise, as Socrates' famous pupil learned the hard way following the execution of his mentor. On the other hand, transcendentalism in political theory runs the terrible risk of legitimating dictatorship, as Karl Popper famously—or infamously—overanalyzed years ago.[3] It can, so far as Rousseau's impact is concerned, be taken as a primary justification for the reign of terror during the French Revolution.

Yet the wager is worth it, Critchley suggests, because the transcendental "political fiction" of popular sovereignty regarded as "association without representation" turns out, as Rousseau hinted, as "the only form of legitimate politics that can face and face down the fact of gross inequality and the state of war."[4] Like Hobbes, who he proposes was the chief influence on Rousseau, Critchley regards the "state of war" itself as a heuristic principle for the adjudication of any doctrine of sovereignty. Hobbsean anthropology thus is the only truly credible anthropology to undergird political theory, and such an anthropology always comes down to one of human depravity (Augustine, Calvin) or "fallenness" (Heidegger). Politics is irrelevant to the affairs of demigods. In Critchley's view, the roots of "representative" democracy intertwine extensively with the age-old Platonic distrust of the phenomenal order, a viewpoint later Christianized as the dogma of original sin. And it is this "transcendental" assumption of a reality more enduring than phenomenal disorder that enables any genuine "theory" of the political. Lacking the transcendental, politics immediately is unmasked as chaos.

It should be noted that Critchley is self-professedly leftish in his political persuasions, so his "Platonism" turns out to be more the utopian than the conservative kind. The convergence of conservative and revolutionary ideologies in their mutual adherence to a transcendental *idée fixe* was a central theme of Karl Mannheim in his efforts to construct a "sociology of knowledge" that might epistemically anchor modern political theory.[5] The risk of dictatorship, fanaticism, or even totalitarianism in the pursuit of such an *idée fixe* can be offset by what Critchley in later chapters characterizes as the "faith" factor. Critchley's own "catechism of the citizen" is inherently balanced out by the eventual political realization that the transcendental representation constituting the *volonté générale* is itself a heurism for the commitment of every would-be Rousseauean *citoyen* to a faith. "Faith is an enactment in relation to a calling."[6] And it is this transcendent calling that transmutes political theory into an unavoidable "political theology."

Critchley's exodus from Platonism would appear to occur in this sort of retro-philosophical fallback on existentialism. Critchley's affinity for Paul makes him a self-conscious bedfellow with Badiou, whom he regards as a Platonist without portfolio and therefore as a credentialed revolutionary thinker. Critchley is enamoured specifically with Badiou's theory of the "event," a peculiar Lacanian discrepancy in the order of being that establishes a nonpredicative ontology for politics that is tied exclusively to history. The "event" is the key to politics, because it is always unpredictable and unprecedented. As Kant would say, it is "acausal" and belongs to the realm of "freedom." Critchley considers the strength of the acausal event as the incentive for radical political commitment, insofar as its momentary effect upon the course of human affairs provides an unmatched transcendental incentive to exemplary action. Paul's "revelation" on the road to Damascus is naturally the paradigm case.

But existentialism and Badiou's novel political theory of the event does not provide us with any serious way out of the crisis of representation at the heart of the legitimation crisis of liberal democracy. The legitimation crisis, as we have seen, stems from a breakdown of the system of reflexive representation induced by the end of modernity and the dissolution of its colonial *episteme*, as Mignolo emphasizes, in which a classificatory system allegedly employed for scientific purposes resulted in the exclusion and suppression of the subjectivities and discourses of the colonized. This colonization was not simply external but internal as well.

DECOLONIALISM

Mignolo's project, which he describes as "decolonial," is sometimes criticized as identity politics in a much more sophisticated and philosophical disguise. Mignolo's tendency to privilege the indigenous *episteme*, as the ultimate outcome of decolonial "delinking" from the theoretical and disciplinary matrix of modern thought, is a theme that has recurred during the past half century or so, most notably in the writings of Vine Deloria. Mignolo's resort at times to a critique of "monocultural" and "monocentric" analysis heightens this suspicion.

Yet Mignolo, as it becomes evident as the book progresses, is not retailing identity but "difference"—what he calls the *decolonial difference*. The latter concept remains quite slippery, even while Mignolo rhetorically embellishes it with numerous contemporary illustrations. But, at the same time, he views the decolonial difference as an inexorable consequence of the breakup of the relatively short-lived, global hegemony of Western market capitalism that flourished in the immediate aftermath of the collapse of worldwide communism. The present

and ongoing economic trauma of both America and Europe is insepa-
rably intertwined, as Mignolo astutely observes, with the growing dysfunctionality of those international institutions and rhetorics that have
increasingly sought to expand Enlightenment "cosmopolitanism,"
first envisaged by Kant, through force of arms. What Mignolo dubs
"decolonial cosmopolitanism" derives from a recognition that the collapse of Western hegemony, beyond its own borders, all at once in the
political, economic, and cultural sphere means the emergence of new
postcolonial "subjects of enunciation" (a Lacanian term he generalizes
to peoples and epistemological formations). These new (collective)
subjects and subjectivities are the green grass and shrubs that inevitably start to grown amid the ashes of the burned-over forest. They are
not in any way susceptible to the Enlightenment coding system that
gave us the post-Westphalian international order of national sovereign-
ties, since there is a new semiosis of culture, practice, and communal
solidarity that replaces the ancient, Western model of the *politeia* of
free citizens.

One wonders, in carefully considering Mignolo's argument, however, if the very idea of the political is impossible within this framework. Curiously, Mignolo addresses this challenge by returning to
Schmitt's revisionism by injecting the friend/enemy distinction. In
Mignolo's view the distinction applies to the Western episteme versus
the plural communitarianisms of the decolonized. "Cosmopolitanism
in a decolonial vein," or what Mignolo otherwise dubs "cosmopolitan
localism," aims "at the *communal* not as a *universal model* but as a *universal connector* among different noncapitalist socioeconomic organi-
zations around the world. . . . Thus, communalism is not a model of
society, but a principle of organization. What comes after delinking
will depend on what has been at work in different local histories."[7]

The friend/enemy distinction, so far as Mignolo conceives it in
terms of indigenous communitarianism versus the current world economic system, is provocative, but misleading and somewhat disingenu-
ous however. Mignolo's assumption that neoliberal economic policy
is intimately intertwined with Enlightenment epistemic taxonomies
constitutes the weak link in his overall genealogical treatment of the
current global crisis. Moreover, his suggestion that any kind of anti-
Western pushback presages this new "decolonial cosmopolitanism"

ignores much of the actual histories and trajectories of different parts of the world. Even in Latin America specifically, Mignolo's recurring region of reference, there are major and telling differences between the politics of a Hugo Chavez in Venezuela, the Zapatistas in Mexico, or Evo Morales in Bolivia.

One elaborate example Mignolo gives of this new "decolonialized" variant on Schmitt's distinction is the writings of the Iranian activist and intellectual Ali Shari'ati, whom a contemporary scholar characterized as the "ideologue of the Iranian revolution."[8] Mignolo considers the theories of Shari'ati, who died in exile just before the Ayatollah Khomeini overthrew the shah of Iran, to be a shining example of "cosmopolitan localism." The events of 1978 to 1979 in Tehran illustrate, for Mignolo, the historical force of Shari'ati's view that "spiritual independence" precedes "economic independence."[9]

What ultimately left its stamp on Iran as Khomeini's "Islamic republic," an idea he took ironically not from the Qur'an but from Plato's *Republic*, was just such an assertion of this spiritual indigeneity that serves as the "universal connector" to all other streams and structures of "local knowledge" comprising the new decolonial cosmopolitanism. The Iranian regime's multidecade global campaign against Western values, including the enforcement of traditional female dress codes, supposedly, and by implication, activates within this new counter-Western *politeia* the same sort of awakening we find throughout the Andes.

Without trying to sound tongue-in-cheek, we may observe that the decolonial option itself is merely one important option among others when we examine how globalization has undermined and dissolved the utopian dream, if not the enduring paranoid fantasy of antiglobalists, of a true, *planetary politeia with its own state sovereignty*. In the case of present-day global monotheisms with their own distinctive, universalizing missions (e.g., Christianity's irrepressible evangelistic outreach, Islam's widening of the *dar al-Islam* through *jihad*), we find not so much a "decolonial" option as a *desecularizing* one. The force of exception is not a "mystical" force that founds secular orders, but one that subjects them to a singular and irreducible force, the *force of God*. All reductive analytics, which seek to account for any would-be political theology in terms of the historical configuration of certain computative factors and conditions, must shatter against the force that flows from the singularity behind the sign play of history and culture as a whole.

By employing the term *force of God,* we are not, in any way, making a theological claim, nor saying that all politics is *in nuce* religious. We are returning to Derrida's own argument, implicit throughout his political writings, which derives from Benjamin's critical distinction between *rechtsetzende* ("law-founding") and *rechterhaltende* ("law-preserving") force, the alternative translation of the German *Gewalt.* The force of God is determinative of all *Recht* in both the historical and mythic, or religious, sense. Even in the context of the ancient Greek *polis,* with its polytheistic backdrop, the relation between *nomos,* or "lawfulness," and *moira* (i.e., "fate," force of destiny), were closely intertwined.[10] Schmitt himself, whom Derrida routinely cites, understood the *Ausnahmezustand* as the effect of a declaration of sovereignty that was not merely arbitrary but grounded in the *theological* character of all politics, an insight Agamben has, of course, developed in elaborate detail. Schmitt's other key principle, the friend/enemy distinction, flows from this view of the political as the vicarious intervention of God in the person of the sovereign. The "enemies" of the *polis,* and those who therefore *homo politicus* seeks to exclude from the decision-making or *rechterhaltende* process, are those who, so to speak, are outside the realm—technically speaking—of divine authority and election, even if in a democracy they are functionally integrated as part of so-called majority rule. The "chosen" become the passionate partisans, explaining what we now experience powerfully as the "polarizing" inevitability of dual party politics in a country such as America. Political democracy becomes a clash of what Deleuze terms "active forces." But it is always *polemos,* rather than *nomos,* that authorizes *polis* and drives the future of even parliamentary democracy.

In the context of contemporary globalization, the power of *polemos* is its own inexorable engine for apportioning collective and private lots, the *moira* that turns out to be the strange new world order and disorder simultaneously—a genuine Deleuzean *chaosmos.* The benign Hegelian dialectic in which oppositions are resolved, or Smith's "invisible hand" where passion and perfidy work themselves providentially into a higher form of historical rationality, have to be radically reinterpreted perhaps with respect to Deleuze's "war machine." Decoloniality—if that is truly the master signifier for the movement of peoples, realignment of state power, and economic reapportionment currently underway—means more the visible result than the invisible causal complexity of what we are witnessing. Even if Mignolo is basically correct, what we are experiencing is something much more like the reassertion of the force of *ethnos* over *polis*, or *natio* (in the true etymological sense, not with the contemporary modernist connotation of the "state" as *statuary* authority) in preference to *civis*. It is a form of "statehood" that is primarily cultural and identitarian rather than political, more an epistemic formation than anything else. However, a real issue arises: is not politics itself quintessentially a matter of force, and is a purely identitarian "politics" merely an idealistic construct that down deep remains a Western rather than a non-Western self-deception?

The question arises as to what degree liberal democracy itself, as we understand it, is spun from such a deception. A superficial reading of Schmitt would seem to bear out such a conclusion. And the upshot becomes invariably the now tired debates of the postwar period concerning the apparent Hobson's choice between liberalism and totalitarianism. But what if democracy properly understood could be considered a distinctive instance of *rechtsetzende Gewalt*? What if this *Gewalt*, as Lilla has in effect propounded, were neither the tour de force of the heroic founder nor the "violence" that accomplishes the establishment of any given imperial regime? What if the violence were neither in the moment of founding nor in the process of sustaining, but in the *polemos* that arises when the force of God is finally dissipated, when it manifests instead as the *death of God*?

8

The End of the Political

The RIGHT OF NATURE, which Writers commonly call
Jus Naturale, is the Liberty each man hath, to use his own
power, as he will himself, for the preservation of his own
Nature; that is to say, of his own Life; and consequently,
of doing any thing, which in his own Judgement, and Reason, he shall conceive to be the aptest means thereunto.
—THOMAS HOBBES

In the collection of her unpublished papers collected under the title
Was ist Politik? (*What Is Politics?*), Hannah Arendt ponders whether
in the age of nuclear annihilation the very idea of the "political" has
any meaning, let alone a future. The question of the political, Arendt
writes, can no longer be easily approached in the way it has since the
time of the ancient Greeks because of the staggering and monumen-
tal violence wrought by twentieth-century wars as well as revolutions.
Not only does the twentieth century consist in a ghastly chronicle of
measureless and unimaginable destructive violence, it has been over-
shadowed since 1945 by the very real threat of global annihilation due
to the invention and proliferation of nuclear weaponry.

In assailing Schmitt without referencing him, Arendt argues that the
political requires neither the declaration of the exception on the part
of the sovereign nor the implementation of the friend/enemy distinction. Writing in the aftermath of the Nazi Holocaust and beneath the

disquieting, nimbus overcast of the cold war, Arendt is keenly aware of how Schmittian precepts can be responsible under critical circumstances for totalitarian outcomes. Arendt implies that the Schmittian formulation represents a kind of Frankensteinian modification of the historical meaning of the political rather than its purification or refinement. Politics, so far as it has been understood since the age of the *polis* itself, can never be reduced to the exception. Instead, it is intimately tied to the *Zwischenraum* ("space of the between") forged by social equals who both have the capacity for and assign the highest value to the power of discourse, to the determinations of *logos*.[1]

In this sense "parliamentary" politics, broadly conceived, is the only possible form of the political, even though, of course, it was the pathetic and otiose performance of constitutional democracy during the 1920s that led him to launch his manifesto against what amounted to the entire Western legacy of what we normally consider politics. Even Hobbes, with whom Schmitt is frequently associated, in a curious sense can be seen as maintaining this older tradition of *polis* as *embodied logos*. For Hobbes, the commonwealth cemented by the consent of its subjects to the sovereign in order to escape the *bellum omnium contra omnes* of the state of nature arises not from any assertion of incontrovertible authority but through the exercise of natural reason by those who wish to be governed. The commonwealth, therefore, functions much like the ancient Greek *polis*, insofar as it is constituted through the transformation of the motions of bodies and the agitations of brute desire as well as corporeal sense impressions into the type of structured discourse that renders the institution of monarchial sovereignty into something consensual, rational, and "constitutional" rather than a mere a tour de force. Essentially, that is the point of Hobbes's brief excursus on the origins of language in the seventh chapter of *Leviathan*.

POLITICS IN THE AGE OF TOTAL WAR

The *Zwischenraum* in which discourse both expresses and solidifies the political, including the core element of sovereignty, would seem to be something unsustainable, according to Arendt, in the epoch of total war and the means of total destruction that can be harnessed through the machinery of the totalistic state. The greater the threat of annihilation, the less room there is for the give-and-take of the kind of political discursity we conventionally connect to the conduct of democracy. Yet, paradoxically, Arendt writes, this *Zwischenraum* is, at the same time, the space of the market or agora, the space of the coliseum where games of athletic competition took place, the space finally of both the solemn assembly where *politeia* under the guise of "policy" debates are carried out and of the philosophical forum where truth is sought through the "double sentence" that is, the division of *logos* into its branching systems of oppositions (what is *dia-legein*, or "dialectic"). Moreover, the space of the divided *logos*, commensurate with the space of the *polis*, does not appear in time as some idyllic parenthesis in which we are allowed to set ourselves aside from what James Joyce termed the "nightmare" that is human history. The *Zwischenraum* that is also the *polis* can be construed as a kind of pacified space that presupposes an a priori struggle with the violence of the historical as a whole. The triumph of *logos* presupposes *polemos*. Democratic "revolutions" in the wake of which the dialectic can flourish are always violent.

Arendt points out that the heritage of the ancient Athenian *polis* was founded on the realization, memorialized in the Homeric epics, that an ancient enemy had been obliterated. The same could be said of the "civic pride" of the Roman republic in its rage to eradicate its enemies: *Carthago delenda est*. Benjamin of course had a point. A "critique of violence" ultimately is disclosed as a critique of politics itself. The agonistic spirit that underlies the culture of ancient Greece, and de facto the political in its essential determination, is not in tension with the meaning of either a healthy or a powerful *politeia*, as Nietzsche rightly understood. Only the "messianic" or the perpetual reign of peace can supersede this agonism, and even its historical threshhold must be marked by convulsive "birth pangs." The violence of revolutionary justice is a recurrent testament to this paradox.

Violence belongs to history, not, *sensu stricto,* to the political. But, ironically, the violence of history frequently, and perhaps inexorably, occurs for the sake of preserving the space of the political. As the Greeks—and Hegel later understood—understood, the political always centers on the realization of the possibility of freedom simply as "freedom from domination" (*Nicht-beherrscht-werden*).[2] And the preservation of freedom, as political liberals have reminded us time and time again, demands struggle against both external and internal antagonists.

The agonism of the political, therefore, is vital and necessary for its long-term sustainability. The proliferation of weapons of mass destruction in the modern world cannot be blamed, as many critics of the West are wont to do, on politics per se.[3] The violence of our times has more to do with a breakdown of the political than the political has to do with the proliferation of violence. "Violence is by nature instrumental; like all means, it always stands in need of guidance and justification through the end it pursues."[4] As Arendt stresses in her various writings, politics boils down to the pursuit of various aims and purposes, strengthened and animated by free deliberation through the play of *logos* in the public sphere over the methods, costs, and benefits of reaching those goals.

The much touted "critique of domination" dear to the hearts of Marxists thinkers masks a fatal, theoretical Hegelian *Aufhebung* in which the political in this sense is totally canceled out and transmuted into the shining idol of historical determinism or a righteous demand for an abstract, collective justice warranted by some absolute and non-negotiable moral imperative. Only when the praxis of politics becomes indistinguishable from the enforcement of pure ideology through the instrumentalities of terror and violence can we say that violence itself has gained ascendancy. Benjamin's notion of *rechtsetzende Gewalt*, on which much of Arendt's analysis of violence is based, therefore, would seem to inscribe the political within the realm of violence, a violence that guarantees the "right" of the state irrespective of the provisions of laws that may discursively constitute its authority. This interpretation, in fact, signals Derrida's own take on Benjamin's notion of *Gewalt* as the "force of law." There is no violence outside the law. Law in its foundational sense (*rechtsetzende*) is coextensive with law in its "preservative" (*rechterhaltende*) aspect.[5]

Thus Arendt's essential question whether politics can have any meaning at all in an age when the means of apocalyptic destruction are all too ready to hand would appear, contrary to her own insistence that violence and the political are separable operators within the historical equation, to yield a negative conclusion. Arendt would seem to have read Benjamin as the anarcho-syndicalist of 1921, who, following Sorel, believed that the wave of violence that washed away the foundations of the authoritarian state would eliminate the need for state violence entirely, and not the Benjamin of his later communist days when messianism and dialectical materialism were fused into a strange love-hate relationship with orthodox revolutionary Marxism. But the later Benjamin also embraced communism because he saw it as the only alternative to fascism. He recognized that the political had already been engulfed by the monstrous spectacle that was taking place during the 1930s in Germany and Italy.

Ironically, Arendt rescues Benjamin from his failure to grasp the implicit capacity for violence in this fusion of Marxism and messianism through her demand that we never strip away the political from any political theory, or from any political theology for that matter. Any political theory cum theology that serves to abolish the necessary historical functioning of the idea of the *politeia* in its original Greek implications, as the form of community life embodying the agonism of freedom, irreversibly leads to totalitarianism and the illimitable violence associated with it. Even though her unpublished *Nachlass* demonstrates her preoccupation with the means of preserving the political in the epoch of the total state, the sketchy and fragmentary character of these texts offer no coherent solution to the very dilemma she sets forth.

Arendt died in 1975, a decade and a half before the specter of totalitarianism and of inevitable nuclear Armageddon suddenly seemed to go up in smoke with the collapse of militant global communism. She would not live to witness the autodeconstitution of so many familiar, modern totalitarian, or quasi-totalitarian, ideologies under the impact of a newly empowered critical theory among the Western intelligentsia that asserted the priority of personal, cultural, and historical identity over the sort of abstract universalism of the various libertarian and "humanistic" dogmas prevalent throughout modernity. However, in the new situation that has prevailed since the demise of militant communism more than two decades ago, the issue of the political remains just as potent, but for somewhat different reasons.

THE CRISIS OF CIVIL SOCIETY

The quandary of the political, and by extension the difficulty of the task of any political theory or theology, no longer rests on what Arendt diagnosed as the principal cause for the rising of the rough beast of totalitarianism during the twentieth century—the systemic failure to forge any semblance after 1918 of the traditional order with its assigned ranks, hereditary rights, and social responsibilities.[6] It was the abolition of the political, not its hypertrophy, as Arendt correctly saw, that made the totalitarian menace unavoidable. The total absorption of civil society by the state in the totalitarian equation arose from the complete emptying of what had passed for political currency or authority in the defeat by the Western democracies of the central powers as the consequence of World War I and, after World War II, in the denuding of any semblance of political legitimacy among previously sovereign nations, especially in Eastern Europe and East Asia, on the part of the brutal fascist occupying forces.

But this atrophy of civil society with its vital sinews of social recognition and regard for political authority—the phenomenon that Richard John Neuhaus metaphorically and with specific reference to religious concerns once dubbed the "naked public square"—today proceeds apace, yet not at all because of the totalitarian project, which for the most part has been relegated to the historical discard pile.[7] It is the direct outcome of very historical processes that led ultimately to the rapid extinction of the totalitarian species. One can cite the famous testament of the anonymous resident of the Deutsche Demokratische Republik (DDR) who told a media interviewer in November 1989 that he was willing to join with the mob battering down the infamous Berlin Wall because he had secretly been watching West German television for years and wanted desperately to visit its shopping malls.

It was not so much political freedom as economic freedom—consumer choice, in effect—that he coveted and connected in his propagandized, parochial mind with what "democracy" was really all about. It was about his "right" to enjoy what his free brethren on the other side of the wall took for granted. Was this admission simply a somewhat laughable, simple-minded anecdote symptomatic of the complete inability of the communist overlords to deliver the "worker's paradise" that had long been promised as the trade-off for the absence of "bourgeois" political liberties in the DDR? Or was something deeper betrayed in such an apparently naive confession?

Some insights into what this possibly ingenuous incident tells us about the problem of the political can be derived from the work of Claude Lefort, whose notion of the political as the symbolic self-constitution of society has tremendous relevance here. Lefort is one of those giants of French political thought who is not easily placed among the partisans of the left, whose flirtations with totalitarianism he has routinely castigated, or with the neoliberals, whom he also has subtly criticized for ignoring the symbolic and legitimating purpose of politics. Lefort's assaults on the modern social sciences for their reductive methodologies along with their inclination to, at best, regard the religious à la Durkheim as a prosthesis of the social and thus incidental to the political and, at best, dismiss its relevance entirely are familiar to us. But what remains even more compelling is Lefort's contention that the disappearance of the religious from the "theory" of the political in the post-Enlightenment milieu undermines the very possibility of theorizing any form of *politeia* in general and in fact may have reached a certain stage of crisis—a crisis far more epochal than Lefort himself realizes—because of the disappearance in contemporary democracies dominated by purely market-based consumer economies of any prospect for politics itself other than its mere semblance or "precession" of simulacra.

First, we need to consider how Lefort's analysis of the disappearance of the political through the excision of the religious works out in terms of his actual argument. Lefort sketches his general theory of the relationship between the religious, the symbolic, and the political in his essay "The Permanence of the Theologico-Political?" first published in the 1980s. For Lefort, the symbolic operation of the political consists in a set of signifying instrumentalities for self-conscious subjects "that determine *their manner of being in* society—and that guarantee that this regime or mode of society has a permanence in time, regardless of the various events that may affect it."[8] Lefort chastises the formalism of modernist critiques of ideology—the varieties of the so-called hermeneutics of suspicion, in particular, Marxism—that construes the political as something other than it really is, as a mere "superstructure" beneath which is concealed various configurations of productive, power, or ethnofamilial relations. "The criterion of what is *political* is supplied by the criterion of what is *nonpolitical,* by the criterion of what is economic, social, juridical, aesthetic, or religious. This operation is not innocent."[9] It is such reductionism that has made the political conceptually impotent in the contemporary situation and has, as a consequence, delegitimated it. The political always has a concrete placeholder in society. Through most of early modern history it was the "body of the king," whose symbolic function (his "glory" in Agamben's terms) coincided with his corporeal occupation of the public sphere we recognize as the state. Politics is what Lefort dubs the "generative" dynamism of what we otherwise identify as a system of social relationships. It is what makes that social configuration cohere and sustain itself; it is what indeed gives it real "life." "If we fail to grasp this primordial reference to the mode of the institution of the social, to generative principles, or to an overall schema governing both the temporal and the spatial configuration of society, we lapse into a positivist fiction."[10] That fiction in many ways is responsible for the failure of the political itself in the modern world, requiring not simply a new political theory but an entire political theology.

In a sense, as Lefort suggests, modern forms of polity are ultimately traceable to Christianity—a datum that many have exhaustively concluded, but for quite different reasons—because they are based on the principle of the corporealization of sovereignty, in short, the visible manifestation of the symbolic presence of the divine rendered incarnate. But modern secular democracy has witnessed a steady *disincorporation* of political symbolization. It is no longer driven by a "politics" of the Word made flesh but rather one of the empty tomb. And this "empty place" that now stands for the political has fateful consequences. According to Lefort, it is

> this peculiarity of modern democracy . . . [that] of all the regimes of which we know, it is the only one to have represented power in such a way as to show that power is an *empty place* and to have thereby maintained a gap between the symbolic and the real. It does so by virtue of a discourse which reveals that power belongs to no one; that those who exercise power do not possess it; that they do not, indeed, embody it; that the exercise of power requires a periodic and repeated contest; that the authority of those vested with power is created and re-created as a result of the manifestation of the will of the people.[11]

What is the long-term outcome of such a transformation, which in some ways parallels the kinds of processes of secularization Charles Taylor describes but with a different spin as well as emphasis?[12] The outcome is a stripping away of the signifying interagencies and symbolic performatives of a society that makes political reality appear as something far more substantial and impinging than a simple heuristic construct. The fabric of the political withers away. "When an empty place emerges, there can be no possible conjunction between power, law, and knowledge, and their foundations cannot possibly be enunciated. The being of the social vanishes or, more accurately, presents itself in the shape of an endless series of ... And so the symbolic dimension of the social passes unnoticed, precisely because it is no longer masked beneath a representation of the difference between the visible world and the invisible world."[13]

Straightforwardly stated, it is the political that guarantees the continuance of the social as a productive unity and the social that, as we have indicated, forms the conjugate dimension of the political as a whole. Although Lefort does not reference the ancient Greeks the way Arendt does, we should observe that the historic notion of the *polis* assumes this essential interchangeability of the political and the social. After all, the Greeks did not really have a name for the latter. The word *social* derives from the Latin *socius*, meaning a kind of voluntary affiliation or comradeship. Since, by the time of the Stoics, the Romans had largely replaced the *polis* with the fictive *cosmopolis,* which was in truth the "free society of equals" for a tiny elite of citizens from the former republic. By the days of the empire, *society* meant something entirely different from what it had connoted in Aristotle's generation.

Thus the persistence of politics today—Arendt's concern—has never really depended on the ability somehow to keep alive something that had long ago become extinct. The maintenance of a more than an arbitrary semiotic linkage between "politics" and "society," as Lefort rightly discerns, depends today on the capacity to regulate in an effective symbolic and ceremonial fashion, even if it be merely the metonymic residue of the ancient "body of the king" invested, for example, in the republican office of the presidency. In her perhaps hasty identification of the possibility of the political with the survival of at least the bare form of the *polis*, Arendt finds common ground with Lefort in her insistence that the a priori of politics, what transpires in a *Zwischenraum*, is, at the same time, the condition of *Zusammenleben*, the unthematized givenness of "life together."

Yet any historical procedure or institution that ensures a political thematization cannot succeed without the symbolic, legitimating agency that the religious provides. It is for this reason that politics as practiced inevitably comes down to some implementation of an implicit political theology. If Lefort is correct, it is not merely an oddity of American culture that its electorate always seems to demand of its officials some palpable expression of customary, and never in any way countercultural, religiosity. With his doubt concerning the utility of the ancestral gods, Socrates, like Jesus, was as much a political as an intellectual rebel for ostensible reasons.

THE EMPTY SPACE OF DEMOCRACY

But the weakening, if not the outright ideological suspicion, of this religious, or quasi-religious, symbolically authorizing factor common to modern secular democracies has very genuine perils. Minus its procedures of symbolic authorization, the empty space of democracy, the political "public square," becomes a place for pit fighting. The result is "that the delineation of a specifically political activity has the effect of erecting a *stage* on which conflict is acted out for all to see (once citizenship is no longer reserved for a small number) and is represented as being necessary, irreducible, and legitimate." The much maligned, but completely intelligible, "polarization" of politics today satisfies Lefort's grim prophecy.

The new "politics," bereft of any symbolic codes that might incorporate, directly or in surrogate guise, the imagined social consolidation of a functioning *polis*, is no longer merely agonistic, but *gladiatorial*. It becomes a "fight to the death" at the social level, because all sense of *as-sociative* obligation has dissipated. Only the quest for power now matters. This new terrain of democracy, which Lefort famously, and perhaps hyperbolically, suggests through the guillotining of Louis XVI and the final disappearance of the "king's body" as politics incarnate, is also a vacant throne as well as a naked public square. The thump of the guillotine and the rolling of heads in the marketplace represent something more than a historic figuration. They are emblematic of what might be termed the *crucifixion*—my metaphor, not Lefort's—of the body politic. But for the body of a crucified democracy there is no Easter morning. Political theory now comes down to a "science" of the *agony*, not the dramaturgy, that precedes the formation of the *polis*, but without the "generative" force of the political as a whole. This brave new world of political thought "allows us to identify a field specific to politics: the field of competition between the protagonists whose modes of action and programs explicitly designate them as laying claim to the exercise of political authority."[14]

In early modern societies, especially from the seventeenth century on, the agonism of the political, however, was not yet either explicit or apparent. In an essay that first appeared in France in 1981, Lefort focuses on human rights, which become the new "generative" element in democratic polity. The assertion of inherent human rights, which turn out to be substantially and qualitatively different from the classic notion of inherited rights, preserves the symbolic legacy of the political sphere. What Lefort designates as the *état de droit*, a political configuration that emerges with the rebellion against absolute monarchy that occurred in England in 1688, in France in 1789, and in Germany in 1848, signals the reinvesture of the symbology of the "body" within the space once occupied by *le corps du roi*, the body of a king who had already begun the process of *disinvestititure* by identifying his personal sovereignty with the abstraction of the state ("L'état, c'est moi," as Louis XIV infamously declared).

This symbology nevertheless remains "generative," only because it somehow embodies the idea of the "people," the baseline signifying pole of the modern duality that encompasses in Lefort's other writings the state, on the one hand, and what, on the other hand, discloses *la place de la politique* as an empty place. The people's "rights" are never fixed, but constantly come to be redefined, morally enshrined, as well as animating the very passion for democracy. In democratic society overall "the symbolic dimension of right is manifested both in the irreducibility of the awareness of right to all legal objectification, which would signify its petrification in a corpus of laws, and in the establishment of a public register in which the writing of the laws—like any writing without an author—has no other guide than the continuous imperative of a deciphering of society by itself."[15]

At the same time, Lefort would seem to ignore the way in which democratic "rights" often become operationally indistinguishable from desires or interests. Lefort's critique of Marx, as scanting the symbolism of rights in his dismissal of the prerogatives of civil society as a "bourgeois" subterfuge, misses a critical point here. Even if the symbolism of rights retains its own autonomy in the crystallization of the democratic *polis* and serves thereby to *materialize* the concept of the people in a historically more credible fashion than the Marxist construct of "class consciousness" ever did, there persists an attenuation of the very symbolism itself by virtue of the fact that what I believe is "entitled" to me as a provision of ever mutable human rights can increasingly become a simple material need. Franklin Delano Roosevelt's redescription of "freedoms" in materialist terms is one indicator of how this evolution can naturally take place.

One of the major shortcomings of Lefort's sweeping, but intuitively compelling, analysis of the vanishing of the political under the conditions of modernity is that it sidesteps the general issue of economy. Lefort's disdain for the hypocrisy of socialist systems in claiming to manifest the true value of human relationships as social productivity emancipated from the dictatorship of capital, while fostering a ruthless and privileged political elite that was always supposed to be inconceivable and indefensible in a "communist" context, perhaps prevented him from employing such a category. The majority of Lefort's most significant writings came out when world communism was nearing its final breakdown and when the "contradictions" and fraudulent representations in Marxists' long-cherished ideology of economic determinism were unraveling before everybody's eyes.

In his preoccupation with the fraud perpetrated by modern Marxism, Lefort misses the historical rationale for the reasons why the kinds of "economism," raised almost to the lofty station of unassailable religious dogma, came to dominate political economy in the nineteenth century and why they remain attractive even decades after the collapse of the communist systems. It is not our role to venture into a labored analysis of how the "economic turn" among political economists, starting with Adam Smith, secured such a powerful foothold in the first place. But we would have good cause to observe that the crumbling of the various *ancien régimes,* along with revolutionary waves that first struck Europe around that time, had the unintended effect of raising serious doubts about the cogency of the entire heritage of political thought harking back to Plato.

THE SUSPICION OF THE POLITICAL

We find a suspicion of this heritage of what might be termed the "speculative" tendency in political thought in the work of Adam Smith. As has been noted by different commentators in different ways, Smith did not intend to write treatises on "economics," but mainly on *moral philosophy* with an eye to affirming what he considered, as did many late nineteenth-century thinkers, the natural "sociability" of human beings. Smith was not only highly critical of mercantilists but also of the *philosophes* of the Age of Reason who underwrote the policies of "enlightened despotism." In a well-known passage from *The Theory of the Moral Sentiments*, Smith seems to have this particular early variant on the *la trahaison des clercs* in mind. He attacks the so-called man of system who "is apt to be very wise in his own conceit . . . and is often so enamoured with the supposed beauty of his own ideal plan of government, that he cannot suffer the smallest deviation from any part of it." Smith adds that such a man "goes on to establish it completely and in all its parts, without any regard either to the great interests, or to the strong prejudices which may oppose it. He seems to imagine that he can arrange the different members of a great society with as much ease as the hand arranges the different pieces upon a chessboard."[16]

The reduction of politics to economics originally was a response to the imperatives of democracy in the settling twilight of eighteenth-century autocracy. As Strauss and Cropsey in their class survey of the history of political thought underscore, Smith's fascination with *homo economicus*—and to a certain extent that of Marx—can be attributed to his grim realization that the entire effort to "reform" or legitimate society in accordance with certain guiding transcendental ideals, as political theory had done all along, did not take into account the way in which society as a whole naturally is composed. "Democracy is the regime that minimizes the distinction between rulers and ruled, the fundamental political phenomenon; and in that sense it can be said that democracy or liberal democracy tends to replace political life by sociality (private lives lived in contiguity) at the same time it diffuses political authority most widely." Furthermore, "the abstraction of morality from the demands of political life proper is in a way impossible; political life has to be lived, and support for it must be provided in the form of economic organization."[17] Hence, Lefort's protest that economism has abandoned the social sources of political life, the transfiguration of the bare *Zussammenleben* into the life of the "citizen," is countermanded by Smith's own implicit method. An understanding of the political as simply the symbolic interactivity that warrants a more purposeful and self-conscious strategy of "living together" is not in itself sufficient. Moreover, when these mechanisms of solidarity are themselves vitiated by economic forces—something Smith well understood as likely, especially as "natural" tendencies are manipulated and corrupted by the intervention of the state—the political itself becomes increasingly problematic. At that point, political economy itself breaks down and what James Joyce termed the "terror of history" rears its monstrous head. Statecraft seems to substitute for the political, but in the vacuum of the latter an even darker specter is gestating. It is the specter of the militant, the specter of revolution.

9

God, the State, and Revolution

Rebellion to tyranny is obedience to God.
—THOMAS JEFFERSON

Wherever revelation does not awake faith, it
must awaken rebellion.
—CARL SCHMITT

Everyone is familliar with Mao Tse-Tung's famous dictum, first formulated during the Long March in the 1930s, that "all power flows from
the barrel of a gun." The saying often has gushily romantic overtones
for even the most weapons-abhorring political progressive while setting off paroxysms of indignation perhaps among American conser-
vatives solely because of the source, even though it is the latter who,
in their fanatical defense of the Second Amendment, probably have
more in common with Mao than they care to admit. But few would
be inclined to view the precept as a fundamental formulation of modern political theology, let alone take it as a cipher for decoding somehow the current debate and growing political nastiness in the United
States over gun control. Furthermore, few would dare to ponder the
"gun" itself as the master signifier for political thought in the context of
globalization as a whole today—not the benign, neoliberal "world is flat"
version of globalization, but the darker sort of implosive, "decolonial,"

post-Eurocentric vision we find, whether implicitly or explicitly, in such writers as Mignolo, Žižek, or Badiou.

It is Badiou's analysis in particular on which I want to zero in eventually. But first we need to offer a few warnings and disclaimers in these concluding remarks. First, what we are about to say will probably shock and enrage many conventional readers, conditioned as we all are to viewing guns and weaponry, particularly when mobilized for "military" purposes, as instrumentalities of political reaction or unrestrained violence. Second, the automatic assumption within most contemporary politico-theological discourse of a certain *summum bonum* that might be best described as a "Christian liberal state pacificism" needs to be assertively challenged—not because it is false as a normative teleology of human societies, or that it must be zealously sought, but because it fatefully misreads history and human nature. The ongoing controversy over the Second Amendment is often misplaced, because it usually comes down to rather trivial questions of whether individual citizens should be armed, whether and to what degree there are constitutionally sanctioned limits on the type and quantity of weapons individuals can possess, and so forth. Moreover, regardless of what the Second Amendment actually means, or was "intended" to mean, the polemics nowadays tend to be framed—at least from the side of gun control advocates—in terms congenial to the advocates of "soft" (in Foucault's terms we should say "softly repressive") power—the "prevention" of violence, which conjecturally flows from the profusion of deadly weapons throughout society.

As a fallback, partisans in both camps have their own competing preferred, albeit dogmatic, theories about the explanation for armed mayhem. Whether indeed it is truly "guns" or "people" that cause violence, the acrimony turns out to be rather superfluous, because the obvious answer is *both*. Empirical comparisons between societies, or demographic groups, or historical eras to prove particular points are trotted out endlessly, all of which miss the essential point, namely, that the issue is really *the role of the state* and whether the state should—*normatively speaking*—play a critical role in the shaping the life of *homo politicus*.

The Second Amendment, which is unique in many ways for modern constitutional republics, was of course inserted at the instigation mainly of Jefferson into the Bill of Rights to complement the First

Amendment. Both amendments can be understood not merely in light of Jefferson's concern and determination in preserving for the future of the new democracy "the spirit of 1776" that recognized both the right and the obligation of the colonists to revolt against state tyranny. Revolution without arms is like a motorcyle without wheels, and it is the "revolutionary" principle—which implies the utter contingency and frail legitimacy of state power—that Jefferson feared would disappear once the Constitution was established as the sacred font of future legislation and the people became comfortable, if not complacent, with the blessings of their New World experiment in democracy. Jefferson's antistatist sympathies—sometimes bordering on what today we would regard as "anarchical"—are well-documented. Jefferson's principle of "permanent revolution" is in truth not that much different from Trotsky's, although the Marxist/materialist matrix of the latter's theorizing departs substantively from the Jeffersonian Enlightenment-based (almost Rousseauean) belief in the moral "virtues" of the people.

Jefferson was convinced in principle that the more powerful and far-reaching the state, the better armed should be the people. Call it the "ammunitional" rendering of Montesquieu's separation of powers. "What country can preserve its liberties if their rulers are not warned from time to time that their people preserve the spirit of resistance. Let them take arms," Jefferson wrote in his letter to James Madison on December 20, 1787. The current political context, where it is impossible to look at the issue apart from reflexive political prejudices that blind us to the context in which Second Amendment rights were originally formulated, needs to be set aside, and what we need to consider seriously is the way in which guns as a signifier of political power compel us to examine the fundamental question behind all modern political economy, the very question the age of revolution starting in the seventeenth century first brought to the fore.

The Danger of the State

That question amounts, as we have seen, to the authority and legitimacy of the state overall. The familiar nineteenth-century insistence on "limited government" was not originally a defense of laissez-faire economics, but a cautionary tale against the expansion of despotic prerogatives with the resulting arbitrary exercise of state power that had been historically witnessed by absolute monarchies since the seventeenth century. It was the co-optation of the limited-government principle by the infamous "robber barons," especially in America, in the second half of the nineteenth century to create a de facto political aristocracy based on predatory accumulation of wealth that changed the equation. The creation of corporate empires as ministates, operating as corrupt political hegemons, within the legitimate but feckless democratic *res publica* of that day and age that transformed the general social valuation of the state apparatus in general from oppressor to savior.

But this valuation has been gradually eroding since the end of World War II, largely because of what is perceived as the increasingly ineffective role of the state in mobilizing the productive interests of the general population against predatory economic power. Instead the state is seen as allied with that predatory power, as may be seen in the populist disgust with the alliance between Wall Street and Washington following the worldwide financial collapse of 2008. In the developing world, it has taken the form of indigenous socialist and grassroots collectivist movements that have won democratic elections, such as we see in South America, which resist ideologically the neoliberal fantasy of an economically integrated global superstate pursuing broader secular goals (e.g., the charter of the International Monetary Fund). The Arab Spring, with its antiauthoritarian passions and insurrections, has been the manifestation within the Islamic world of the same tendencies. The gun, therefore, has become the token of both resistance and insurgency against the neoliberal state in all its cultural and regional guises. The familiar adage about firearms as the "great equalizer" reflects the original Jeffersonian insight that democracy to be sustainable must somehow be permanently weaponized.

But let us get to Badiou, who has "axiomatized" as a political thought operation (Badiou's own phrasing is "truth procedure") the intuitions of a Jefferson. In his *Metapolitics,* first published in French in 1998 and translated into English less than a decade later, Badiou builds out the theoretical—and by extension the nascently *theological*—latticework for the assertion of the quintessentially *political* in opposition to the claims of the state.[1] Every state—even a putatively "democratic" one—is inimical to the political. The political, which Badiou identifies with the concept of "democracy," arises from a "fidelity" to an "eventual singularity" made known epochally in the resistance to state power. But it is only in this resistance that the state discloses itself for what it is, i.e, *antihuman* and *antipolitical*. The notion of a benevolent state is just as hypocritical and contradictory as the oxymoron of "enlightened despotism."

"Whenever there is a genuinely political event, the State reveals itself. It reveals its excess of power, its repressive dimension." Consequently, we have, according to Badiou, in the *"political prescription* the posteventual establishment of a fixed measure for the power of the state."[2] Although Badiou does not say it outright, the fixing of the "measure" is of course the equilibration of the previously unequal power between the state and the people through the "barrel of a gun." As an unrepentant Maoist, Badiou clearly has something like this analysis in mind. Without the "equalizer" of weaponry, the state's power is unlimited, crushing the political virtues of its citizenry that Jefferson so prized. "It is not the simple power of the state of the situation that prohibits egalitarian politics. It is the obscurity and measureless in which this power is enveloped."[3]

The division of armaments apportions this erstwhile "measureless" in such a way that what Nietzsche's Zarathustra termed the "pale monster," namely, the state, is slain, butchered, divided up, and consumed as the nutrient power of the politically awakened *demos*. As we have already suggested, therefore, the gun becomes the projective symbol of the empowered *demos* rather than of an antidemocratic lawlessness or of some sort of vicious reactionary, nativist, *anticosmopolitan* cabal. The debate over gun rights, which has taken on its own strange, idiosyncratic overtones in the current American context, needs to be further contextualized in terms of its meaning for the democratic revolutions that continue to percolate everywhere on the planet. It is not insignificant that when Secretary of State John Kerry met with the leaders of the Syrian rebels in Italy in early 2013, offering them humanitarian aid, he was angrily rebuked. Kerry was told, in effect, by the leadership that all gestures of assistance were meaningless without proffering the weapons material for democratic empowerment that would allow the rebels to level the playing field against the ruthless Assad regime, which initially triggered the uprising by mowing down unarmed demonstrators with tanks and machine guns.

If one is against arming the democratic citizenry under any circumstances, one must have the justifiable conviction that the state that preserves the imbalance of firepower cannot be presumed to run the risk of ever becoming "tyrannical." History itself continually gives the lie to that presumption. Yet we must ask ourselves: if guns are the cipher for revolutionary resistance to the state, or at least the power of the authentic *politeia* in opposition to the inevitable encroachments of power on the part of the state, on what is that resistance founded? And is it not only the Jeffersonian resistance to an *imbalance of power*, deeply feared by the Enlightenment theorists of civic virtue, that constitutes the "force of God," countervailing the "force of law" expressed through both the founding and regulating violence Benjamin identifies as the very metaphysical substance of the state itself? Jefferson himself certainly thought so. The vast majority of revolutionary thinkers from the English revolutionaries in the seventeenth century forward certainly grasped these dynamics.

But Jefferson was not a revolutionary like Mao in the modern sense. Jeffersonian democracy was the ultimate praxis of the Lockean argument, outlined extensively in Locke's *Two Treatises on Civil Government*, that the state has limited rights when it comes to the creative power of the individual, especially expressed through the transformation of nature by the force of labor. As is well understood in political theory, it was Locke, not Marx, who invented the labor theory of value. Marx only "socialized" the theory of value and radically construed it anew as a historical phenomenon, as part of the dialectical redirection of the transformative process through class consciousness and ultimately via class conflict. We discern, therefore, in the genealogical link between Locke and Marx the key to the difference between the Enlightenment and the modern view of the "force" that sets itself against the power of the state. It is inconceivable to think of modern revolution without some variant on the Maoist dictum about the provenance of power. The dictum rests, explicit in most of Marx's writings, on the tacit view that the repressive state is the inexorable outcome of a culture of "possessive individualism."

Whether this repression is through the highly "enlightened," nuanced, discursive, and putatively benign therapeutic apparatuses Foucault documents, or whether it comes from the paranoid reactivity

of monopoly capital and its political extensions, which was the revolutionary experience in Europe from the early nineteenth century
up through the late 1960s, are in a large sense irrelevant. The issue of
state repression is as ancient as Greek democracy itself. *Political theory
begins as a response to tyranny.* The state and the *polis*—therefore, the
state and "politics" per se—signifies the rudimentary antinomies of
political theology overall. The dilemma of whether to render to God
or Caesar is eminently one of deciding between, in Tönnies's phraseology, *Gemeinschaft* and *Gesellschaft*. The repressive mechanisms of
the former come into play only when one who has, either by birth or
voluntary association, assented to its strictures opts to reject them for
whatever reason. In the former instance repression follows from a challenge to the "artificial" legitimacy of the state—an idea introduced by
Hobbes that has become unshakable in the modern venue—that frequently arises as the command of "conscience" or, as is more often than
not the case, from God.

THE REVOLUTION OF THE SAINTS

In short, the state exists, as Hobbes himself well understood, in order
to preserve individuals from the intrinsic consequences of their
fallen condition, from their unsociability in the state of nature. But,
as Michael Walzer in his famous study of the origins of revolutionary thought notes tellingly, this uniquely Hobbesian insight, which
in many respects may be considered the *primum mobile* of all modern political thought, has profound implications that necessitate the
very revolutionary theory that challenges the state itself. The concept
of a so-called state of nature reflects in actuality the complete breakdown of a sense of prevailing "natural orders" and its attendant anxi-
ety that characterized the transition from the medieval to the modern
worlds. It is in the midst of this breakdown that the notion of revolution, according to Walzer, is born from the experience of a divine
calling among a select company of "saints" to combat the chaos. The
first revolutionary "saints," of course, were Calvinists—specifically,
the Puritans of the seventeenth century. "These men," Walzer writes
in his classic from the 1960s, "are marked off from their fellows by an
extraordinary self-assurance and daring. The saints not only repudiate

the routine procedures and customary beliefs of the old order, but they also cut themselves off from the various kinds of 'freedom' . . . experienced amidst the decay of tradition. The band of the chosen seeks and wins certainty and self-confidence by rigidly disciplining its members and teaching them to discipline themselves. The saints interpret their ability to endure this discipline as a sign of their virtue and their virtue as a sign of God's grace."[4]

Revolutionary politics arises as a reaction against the "fall," against the chaos, in the name of an imminent—and *immanent*—republic of godly community and mobilized virtue. The "grace" need not be heavenly; it can also be historical, as Marxist materialism recognizes. The discipline is the same. The saints fight against tyranny—and they always fight with arms—in the name of a God-ordained community with God-anointed leaders that will replace the mere restraining mechanisms of the state per se as the harsh, but unavoidable remedy to the disorder of the state of nature.

But what if the state itself no longer functions as the means of "restraining" sin? In Walzer's analysis the eighteenth century rejection of the Calvinist conscience in favor of the liberal laissez-faire—what we would now term *libertarian*—view of the minimalist state as the protector of property and industry was only possible because the Calvinist revolution had succeeded by and large in its objectives. Locke, the architect of modern liberalism, was a second-generation Puritan. Calvinism had employed the tools of civil repression and community discipline in pursuit of a godly commonwealth. "Liberalism also required such voluntary subjection and self-control, but in sharp contrast to Puritanism, its politics was shaped by an extraordinary confidence in the possibility of both, a firm sense of human reasonableness and of the relative ease with which order might be attained. Liberal confidence made repression and the endless struggle against sin unnecessary. . . . The Lockean state was not a disciplinary institution as was the Calvinist holy commonwealth, but rather rested on the assumed political virtue of its citizens."[5]

Liberalism's assumption of such virtue ironically created the conditions for its eventual demise. If there is one point on which Calvin and Marx agree, it is that an affirmation of private virtue without the discipline of the community, or, regarded in the classic context, without the oversight of the *politeia*, readily degenerates into acquisitive excess. Acquisitive excess has, in fact, been the destiny of liberal democracy, even if this excess has been fostered by the credit of the state, as we have witnessed since the advent of Keynesian economics, with its mission of "rescuing" capitalism. The mounting critique of ideology throughout the nineteenth century unmasked liberal virtue as a smokescreen for this very excess. "Law, morality, religion are . . . so many bourgeois prejudices, behind which lurk in ambush just as many bourgeois interests," Marx and Engels wrote in *The German Ideology*.[6]

It is no coincidence that *liberalism* in the past century, or at least since it became synonymous with *progressive,* continues to retain the same kind of *hypocrisy,* in the etymological sense of a lack of penetrating critical judgment that Marx first brought to our attention. The hypocrisy now extends to the pretense that it is advancing the interests of the downtrodden, when in fact it is simply keeping the downtrodden marginally secure—a strategy first adopted during the rise of the second German Reich under the "Iron Chancellor" Bismarck—while building a vast, bureaucratic army of civil servants and better-paid administrative professionals. Max Weber himself foresaw this development in the nineteenth century with his observation that social idealism, an inalienable property of progressivism in all its historical countenances, inevitably generates an "iron cage" (*stahlhartes Gehäuses*) of rigidified, impersonal, and collectivist bureaucratic behavior because of the need to concretize—or as we should say "enforce"—our moralistic sentiments.[7] The crisis of this new bohemian bourgeois "socially responsible" state corporatism, with its feigned "collective conscience," consists in the current global debt disaster, just as in Marx's time the crisis amounted to one of overaccumulation and the immiseration of the productive classes. The working classes of today have been abandoned by the new capitalists just as they were in the early nineteenth century.

Jefferson envisioned a virtuous citizenry as a sort of Archimedean balancing point against which the hegemony of the state must be held in abeyance and the metrics of power judiciously weighed. But he did not anticipate modern social bureaucracy, designed to administer the intricacies of the new, rationalized, "capitalist" order, in the way that Weber, as a German state employee, did for the first time. Marx, who competed indirectly with Weber to be the most "scientific" observer of the social trend lines of his day, did not anticipate it either. He understood the private "captains of industry," but not the faceless functionaries of what nowadays we refer to euphemistically on a global scale as the benevolent toiling angels of "civil society." Neither, of course, anticipated the rise to virtually unmastered power of the *bureaucratic, bohemian bourgeoisie.* The bohemian bourgeoisie is horrified at an armed citizenry, let alone a *revolutionary* armed citizenry, and seeks to disarm it by whatever measures it can muster and justify. It is also horrified at religious enthusiasms of all sorts of deeply feared "fundamentalists" who might somehow upset the equipoise of its brave new world of well-ordered, pluralistic, infinitely subtle and all-permeating Foucauldian networks of virtualized "disciplinary power." Foucault's revision of the Baconian formula to make power absolutely identical with and indistinguishable from "knowledge" (i.e, in the form of "power/knowledge") adumbrates the crisis of representation, therefore, in modern liberal democracy because no longer is there a "balance of power" between the principle of sovereignty and any kind of "material" interests. *All interests are now immaterial*; they are coded as the rarefied "social good" for which the engineers of the new virtue, like Plato's guardians in his utopian scenario, assume rigorous and unrelenting oversight.

The crisis of representation in modern liberal democracy thus emerges from a historical process whereby the "substance" previously signified in modern political economies, be it real property, labor, or capital equipment, relentlessly and systematically deliquesces into purely "symbolic economies." The underlying values of these economies are no longer genuinely exchangeable other than as promissory notes. In addition, material goods now are transmuted into "social goods," meaning that the promise no longer turns on the eventual exchange of one tangible item (or even a useful service) for another, as in the theoretical redemption of banknotes for gold or silver, but instead on the alleviation of certain abstract wrongs and the acquisition of indefinite symbolic credits toward ill-defined "extramundane" rewards. But the fiduciary compulsion of these virtualized tokens is only as good as the vanishing material economy that undergirds them. In his prophecy of an inevitable crisis of capitalism Marx did not foresee the political substitution of these symbolic tokens engineered by the ingenious social marketing mechanisms we now regard as democratic politics. The crisis Marx predicted finally appeared full-blown in the 1930s, but it was Keynes who, in a curious way, launched the process, which he believed would "save" capitalism, whereas, in fact, he only postponed it.

THE TASK OF POLITICAL THEOLOGY

But our job is one of geneaological discernment, not alarm mongering and doomsaying. As the crisis of liberal democracy approaches—and it is indeed very near—it does not avail itself of any straightforward political and economic solutions. The *solution,* if we are to employ the term appropriately in this setting, is ultimately not one of politics but of political theology. What are we really setting forth by such a contention?

In order to arrive at some sense of how to navigate our way through such thinking about what we can imagine as a political theology of the future, a future darkened and thoroughly rent by constant economic crisis and attendant political confusion, we need to turn back, as many Christian philosophers do at such junctures, to Augustine's *Civitas Dei.* However, we are not seriously concerned, as many political theologians in the past have been, with the possibility of either a Christian state, as the Roman Empire was nominally in Augustine's era, or the destiny of the "church" in an age of social and political collapse. All theologies of the "two kingdoms," first crafted by Augustine, have exhausted their implications.

The last twitchings of the expiring corpse of an intellectual heritage we might term *Christian Augustinian Romanism*, which yokes the salvation of the world to a beneficient—or at least a theologically authorized—state form can be found, of course, in the radical orthodoxy movement of today: John Milbank's call at the end of *Theology and Social Theory*, the book that launched the movement in the early 1990s, where he characterizes Christian life and praxis as a "counter-ethic" and "counter-ontology," securing in terms of *chronos* as well as *kairos* an activist and ethically integral community that struggles against secularity because it discloses itself as "different from all other cultural systems, which it exposes as threatened by incipient nihilism."[8] Theology must become "ecclesiology," according to Milbank, because politics itself must become a theologically suffused "social theory," or at minimum a strategy of installing virtue within the *polis*, of preserving the "commonwealth" against the constant encroachments of the *nihil*. All species of modern "cultural conservatism" conform to this model in some fashion. And, even though it is possible to read *Theology and Social Theory* as a curious sort of mongrelized, Reformed-Anglican manifesto calling for the church to take a less passive and perhaps even a strengthened "militant" role in resisting the moral and political deterioration of society nowadays, familiarity with Milbank's style and rhetoric persuades us that he is outlining a typically British Romantico-Gothic (ironically, one dubbed *postmodern* by the radical orthodox movement) vision of a neo-Constantinian world order.

Whereas there are certain similarities between the Christian militancy of a Calvin, the "saints" in radical orthodoxy are never revolutionaries. The latter model assumes the persistence of an identifiable and, in certain respects, "sovereign" entity that becomes the torchbearer for an enduring "cultural system," especially one that is eternally "alternative" to the prevailing *saeculum*. There is neither a need nor a compulsion toward revolution, because it is the state—and the state alone—that can provide the historical apparatus for the shaping of the Christian "citizen" of the "city of God." It is no accident that Milbank, coyly in this context, cites Hegel as the touchstone for what an ecclesiology qua theology qua social theory would actually look like. The new theology "refuses to treat reason and morality as ahistorical universals, but instead asks, like Hegel, how has Christianity affected human reason and human practice? Veering back to the "Church Fathers," and mainly Augustine, such a social theory turns for its paradigm of the *politeia* to the very sacramental *mythos* of community found in "the incarnation and Pentecost." It "seeks to define a Christian *Sittlichkeit*, a moral practice embedded in the historical emergence of a new, and unique community." The complex Hegelian "task," therefore, is "situated in the re-narration of Christian emergence, a story which only constitutes itself as a story by re-narrating previous stories, both of past and history, and of the relation of creation to Godhead."[9] To be sure, as Hegel himself made clear, this task is nothing else but the job of the state. "The march of God in the world, that is what the state is."[10]

In radical orthodoxy we have intimations once again of a spectral Christian statism, which, like its liberal counterpart today, understands its distinctive moral and spiritual role in combating the "barbarism" that, for the former, consists in the retreat of the religious from public life. In the latter instance, even without the pretension to any kind of religious morality, we have the perceived horror on the part of new and entrenched secular, educated elites of an increasingly armed but atomized social constituency, a horror arising from their purely rationalistic and "casuistic" type of ethical conscience dedicated to the expansion of ever new frontiers of "social justice" enforced by the enlightened despotism of their own knowledge aristocracy. But both models are not only statist; they are decidedly Roman. Augustine in his own odd way—in a way airbrushed to its extremities by radical orthodoxy—was the last true apostle of triumphal *Romanitas*.

The consecration of the state form goes all the way back to book 19 of the *Civitas Dei*. Ironically, it is here we find the implicit assertion of the divine legitimacy of the Christian state. Contrary to all the attempts over the generations to make Augustine into a "political theorist," the label cannot be properly attributed to him, if only because he was not concerned with arriving at a cogent construct of the *politeia* per se, only at trying to understand how the Roman ideal of the *res publica*, or commonwealth, had fatefully and most brutally degenerated into empire, which, as he wrote, was on its last legs. Rome pretended to be a *polis* when it was not one at all. Even the Stoic dream of an aristocratic, self-controlled "cosmopolitan" *polis*, or a *cosmopolis*, had long lost its traction as well as its *attraction*. Thus, in response to rampant accusations among the populace that the sack of Rome by the Goths in 410 was a kind of divine judgment on the empire's somewhat recent rejection of the pagan gods in favor of the new monotheistic *Christos pantokrator*, at one time Constantine's "conquering sun," Augustine sought not so much to offer an "apology" for the new Christian imperium as to demonstrate why all previous forms of the *polis* were not what they appeared to be.

Modern readers are usually baffled, and largely bored, by the seemingly overweening attention Augustine gives, up until the very last sections, to what might be termed a thoroughgoing narrative deconstruction of the Roman gods and the historic pillars of what were once considered "republican" piety. The entire *Civitas Dei* is a sustained critique, therefore, of the idols—the *politico-moral representational syntactics*—of what today we know as liberal democracy. The "liberal" or republican state, as Schmitt profoundly and prophetically realized, is not really a state at all, because it is a product of a play of natural and self-seeking interests, interests linked to forces that the Enlightenment was convinced, as an act of faith, were instruments of the providential hand of God. The moral quality of these forces was merely assumed to be beneficent. But over time these forces are exposed for what they really are—expressions of what Augustine termed *cupiditas,* or "avarice," the basis of all "base" desires that lead to moral depravity, greed, ruthless ambition, exploitation, and unceasing social violence. *Radix malorum est cupiditas.* For Schmitt, as well as for contemporary historical thinkers like Lilla, it was the separation of the theological from the moral within the computative scheme of the political that undermines the current crisis. Schmitt's solution, of course, was even more draconian than Augustine's. For Schmitt, it would require the force of exception in the agency of the sovereign, who literally performs the divine but political act of *creatio ex nihilo.* Thus the political can only be resuscitated in the present "dark age" of social and moral breakdown by the embodied theological. In a sense, the body of the king returns. The king is dead. Long live the king.

Augustine seems to have little interest in the question of sovereignty, even as it might have been couched conceptually in his own era. His project is to redescribe the *res publica* through a Christian semantics, a reformulation that was only thinkable within the century after Constantine's conversion. Constantine's vision of the Chi-Rho at the Milvian Bridge, the cross subtly and symptomatically transmuted into an imperial signet, has had far greater consequences for Western political thinking than can be imagined; it became the linchpin for the struggle between popes and emperors throughout medieval Europe.

On the other hand, Augustine—in contrast to Eusebius, or later Hegel, for that matter—did not see the imperial regime as necessarily the march of God on earth. The coming of a "Christian" state was both a blessing and a challenge. It was a challenge because, as Christian reformers have lamented over the centuries, it made conversion and the discipline of personal as well as communal sanctification seem much too easy. It was a blessing because now what might be considered the lost "virtues" of the *res publica* could be freely developed and elaborated without the fear of persecution. But, for these virtues to be realized, a different sort of *res publica* was critical, one more akin to what Calvin later called the "holy commonwealth"—though not with his militant overtones—than even the most pastoral ideal of the ancient *ekklesia* with its hierarchial and professional cadres for the curing of souls had indicated. To lay the foundational argument for a true Christian *res publica*, Augustine had not only to dismantle the authority of Roman's great "civil theologian" Varro, which he spends so much of the book doing, but to show how civil theology itself was always an impostor theology. Only a *political theology* would rescue the *res publica*.

THE NEW "CITY OF GOD"

In section 21 of book 19, referring to earlier meditations by Roman authors on the demise of the Roman republic, Augustine poses the *metapolitical* question of what a *polis*, or *res publica*, is truly seated upon. In book 2 he had cited Scipio's critique of Cicero that the Roman *res publica*, or commonweal, never really existed because there was not "justice" (*iustitia*) in it. A "republic," Augustine argues in book 19, is defined as the "weal," or well-being, of the people (*res populus*), the *populus* itself understood as "a multitude 'united in association by a common sense of right and a community of interest'" (*coetum multitudinis iuris consensu et utilitatis communione sociatum*).[11] And thus without *iustitia* there can be no *ius*, or "right," that binds together the *polis*, or *res publica*. For the *res publica* to function as a "state," that is, to have operative power and authority, it must have both *iustitia* and *ius*. However, in the Roman republic this failure to establish justice can be blamed on the false gods themselves. These false gods, who were in reality "demons," were exposed for what they were in the sack of Rome, "for the gods would not drive off those who assailed the walls of Rome from outside unless they themselves first drove out all morality from within the city."[12]

Elsewhere in book 14 of *Civitas Dei* Augustine, as most readers are already familiar, defines the question of the "city," the *politeia*, in terms not so much of its historic precedents or organizational makeup but of its general "character." This character is a reflection of what we might term its "conative" structure (from the Latin *conatus*), its composite of expressive desires. "We see then that the two cities were created by two kinds of love (*amores*): the earthly city was created by self-love (*amor sui*) reaching the point of contempt for God (*contemptum sui*), the Heavenly City by the love of God (*amor Dei*) carried as far as contempt of self (*contemptum sui*)."[13] These two loves constitute the historical destiny of each type, a type that is forged through the very nature of its own mode of devotion, its *religio*. Secular liberal democracy, that is, a non-Jeffersonian democracy where desire rather than virtue is all that matters, would in Augustine's typology obviously fit into the destiny of the *civitas terrena*, the destiny of the damned. In this "earthy city its wise men who live by men's standards [*secundum hominem*] have pursued the goods of the body or of their own mind, or both," which lapsed into a dominion of pride (*superbia*) and a genuflection to the whims of the leaders of the "general public" (*duces populorum*). The state, therefore, as a functionary and intermediary for these desires, has no gravity or authority. Its only claim to rule is to rule by tyranny, which is not rule but violence, and in Augustine's reimagined geneal-ogy of Rome the history of the putative *res publica* is precisely that, the tyranny of collective *amor sui* masquerading as both *Romanitas* and *humanitas* simultaneously.

The state can have no virtue, or even a "moral authority," in the *saeculum*, according to Augustine, because it is the ensemble of wills that readily manifests as mundane vanity, thus effectively as tyranny. But within the state, within the *saeculum* as a whole, the contours of the city of God can be discerned. That is why Augustine regarded the church, the *ekklesia*, as a sort of *predestined* antidote to the vitiation of the state within the secular habitat. The church is not a *polis*, but its politico-theological instrumentality leavens the state, bereft of its "political" authority, which is ultimately a moral authority. It is a *cer-tain agency that has the force of God behind it.*

Augustine seemed to grasp that the state was in crisis, because the republic as the fantasized, moral bulwark of the Roman *imperium*, supposedly restored by Constantine, had never really been present to history. He foresaw the inevitable collapse of the state form for this very reason, yet he was ever hopeful because he knew that God was "with" his true people, his half-heavenly, half-earthly *civitas Dei*, who would persist beyond the historical verdict on the state itself. We have our same "Romanist" fantasies today about the endurance of the democratic state, the *res publica* of American secular interests. We assign a "virtue," particularly in the debate over guns, to the state that is not there and has never been there perhaps. Or we enjoy Milbank's Romantic fantasy of a medieval church *redivivus*, which always requires the temporal sword to back it up; a church aligned with a Christian "state" can keep its finger in the dike against the onslaught of "nihilism."

Augustine was always more modest than that. His aim was immediate. He wanted to dispossess us of our fantasy of the omnicompetent Roman state, which everyone had taken as a given, now emboldened by the arrival of the presumed "Christian" iteration until the sack of Rome. He wanted to scotch that fantasy because he knew that something inconceivable was in the works, something that would not happen right away, and in his own lifetime would remain unfulfilled, especially when the Vandals later sacked Carthage, and he died a martyr's death. The state is never genuinely competent, only God. We cannot expect the "church," contra Milbank in any political guise, to make history from the divine point of view. Only the saints, the *communio sanctorum*, have historical authority. And what, or who, are these saints—today?

We live at a time when the baton of political theology passes to the saints, the revolutionary saints, the Christian insurgents, the visible signs of the operative and indefensible *force of God*. We are not talking, despite the inevitable nattering complaints of "exclusivism" and "hegemony," contra Milbank or any of his congeners of Christian "triumphalism" in any meaningful sense of the word. The lengthy "parenthesis," as the dispensationalist say of Christendom, is over. The church has played well its historic supporting part. It is now the age of militancy, not of the virtuous state. The state cannot be virtuous any more than a dung beatle can be free of excrement. The virtue of the saints is the new knowledge that emerges from the event of the absolute Christ encounter—the force of God!

Strangely, Augustine himself anticipated this at the end of his *Civitas Dei*, a historical compendium, a *Heilsgeschichte*, that continues to require decoding even today. Augustine talked about "the power of knowledge" that "will be very great in the saints."[14] Furthermore, we live in an age "consecrated" by the resurrection, the ultimate sign of the force of God. This event, let alone this force, we do not yet understand. Christian theology has no advantage when it comes to such saintly "knowledge."

Today we find ourselves truly as "militants" who cannot resist and are the historical embodiment of this force. Perhaps that is what is meant by the "church militant" (*ecclesia militans*), the spiritually, socially, and political engaged "community of saints" propelled by both contemporaneous and eschatologically framed *insurrectionary* power. The militant is the execution of what Badiou in his *Metapolitics* dubs the "infinite of the situation," the "evental" manifestation of the immeasurable force that finds its measurable dimensions in the moment of insurrection.[15] But this insurrection also brings to presence eventally, if we may indeed speak "theologically," the God force driving history that Augustine remotely sensed, the force for which the material sign is *resurrection*.

Both insurrection and resurrection derive from the same Latin root through which we obtain the word *surge*. It is the power of resurrection that eventually decides the minute of insurrection. According to Badiou, the truth of all politics expands into a "destination" that "reactivates a subject in another logic of its appearing-in-truth, resurrection." Such a resurrection "presupposes a new world, which generates the context for a new event, a new trace, a new body."[16] A genealogy of the political yields the truth of this resurrection power, by which the militant, the visible agent of the *communio sanctorum*, is eminently sustained. It also reveals the insurrectionary moment. That is the task of political theology today amid the enveloping crisis of liberal democracy.

Notes

PREFACE

1. Jeffrey W. Robbins, *Radical Democracy and Political Theology* (New York: Columbia University Press, 2011), 190.

1. LIBERAL DEMOCRACY AND THE CRISIS OF REPRESENTATION

1. For a general overview how this revolution has unfolded, particularly in the realm of religious thought, see my own *Postmodernism and the Revolution in Religious Theory: Toward a Semiotics of the Event* (Charlottesville: University of Virginia Press, 2012).
2. C. B. MacPherson, *The Political Theory of Possessive Individualism: Hobbes to Locke* (Oxford: Oxford University Press, 1962), 1.
3. Ibid., 3.
4. This argument, bolstering the critical importance of Schmitt today, is laid out rather forcefully by Heinrich Meier. According to Meier, Schmitt is a dominating presence for today's political theology—like Nietzsche for poststructuralism—because he liberated the term from its "old negative valence" and helped gain the term gain worldwide prominence, set across "all political and theological fronts as well as across disciplinary and national boundaries." Heinrich Meier, *The Lesson of Carl Schmitt:*

Four Chapters on the Distinction Between Political Theology and Political Philosophy, trans. Michael Brainard (Chicago: University of Chicago Press), xvi. For other important scholarship on Schmitt, see also William Scheuerman, *Carl Schmitt: The End of Law* (Lanham, MD: Rowman and Littlefield, 1999); Michael Salter, *Carl Schmitt: Law as Politics, Ideology, and Strategic Myth* (New York: Routledge, 2012); Kam Shapiro, *Carl Schmitt and the Intensification of Politics* (Lanham, MD: Rowman and Littlefield, 2008); David Dyzenhaus, *Law as Politics: Carl Schmitt's Critique of Liberalism* (Durham, NC: Duke University Press, 1998).

5.   Christopher Lasch, *The Culture of Narcissism: American Life in an Age of Diminishing Expectations* (New York: Norton, 1979).

6.   Friedrich Nietzsche, *The Will to Power,* trans. Walter Kaufmann and R. I. Hollingdale (New York: Random House, 1967), 9.

7.   "Therefore nothing but the idea [*Vorstellung*] of the law in itself, which admittedly is present only in a rational being . . . can constitute the preeminent good which we call moral, a good which is already present in the person acting on the idea." Immanuel Kant, *The Moral Law: Groundwork of the Metaphysic of Morals*, trans. H. J. Paton (London: Routledge, 2005), 45.

8.   Friedrich Nietzsche, *Untimely Meditations,* ed. Daniel Brazeale (Cambridge: Cambridge University Press, 1997), 67.

9.   Ibid., 62.

10.   Gilles Deleuze, *Nietzsche and Philosophy*, trans. Hugh Tomlinson (New York: Columbia University Press), 75.

11.   Michel Foucault, *Language, Countermemory, Practice: Selected Essays and Interviews* (Ithaca, NY: Cornell University Press, 1980), 148.

12.   Friedrich Nietzsche, *Beyond Good and Evil*, trans. Walter Kaufmann (New York: Random House, 1966), 50.

13.   For example, see Leo Strauss: "[*Politeia*] is the order, the form, which gives society its character." Leo Strauss, *What Is Political Philosophy and Other Studies* (Chicago: University of Chicago Press, 1957), 34. See also Mary Nichols, *Citizens and Statesmen: A Study of Aristotle's Politics* (Lanham, MD: Rowman and Littlefield, 1992); as well as William Bluhm, *Theories of the Political System: Modern Political Analysis* (Englewood Cliffs, NJ: Prentice-Hall, 1978).

14.   Alan D. Schrift, *Nietzsche's French Legacy: A Genealogy of Poststructuralism* (New York: Routledge, 1995), 45. See also David Owen, *Maturity*

and Modernity: Nietzsche, Weber, Foucault, and the Ambivalence of Reason (New York: Routledge, 1994); Yvonne Sherratt, *Continental Philosophy of Social Science: Hermeneutics, Genealogy, and Critical Theory from Greece to the Twenty-First Century* (Cambridge: Cambridge University Press, 2005); C. G. Prado, *Starting with Foucault: An Introduction to Genealogy* (Boulder: Westview, 1995).

15. Plato, *Republic,* 330d. *The Collected Dialogues of Plato, Including the Letters,* ed. Edith Hamilton and Huntington Cairns (Princeton: Princeton University Press, 1961, 579.

16. See Jacques Derrida, *Acts of Religion,* edited by Gil Anidjar (New York: Routledge, 2002), 228–98.

17. Raschke, *Postmodernism and the Revolution in Religious Theory,* 109ff.

2. FORCE OF THOUGHT

1. Alexandre Kojève, *Introduction to the Reading of Hegel: Lectures on Phenomenology of Spirit,* ed. Allan Bloom (Ithaca: Cornell University Press, 1980).

2. The motif of deconstruction amounts to the continual exertion of a force on inert structures of meaning by dint of the fact that these structures are the sediment of writing, which is dynamic. Derrida makes this point (forcefully) about force in his book *Limited Inc.* He argues that "a written sign, in the current meaning of this word, is a mark that subsists, one which does not exhaust itself in the moment of its inscription and which can give rise to an iteration in the absence and beyond the presence of the empirically determined subject." Furthermore, "a written sign carries with a force that breaks with its context, that is, with the collectivity of presences organizing the moment of its inscription." Derrida terms this force a "breaking force" (*force de rupture*), which is the key to deconstruction. The breaking force "is not an accident predicate but the very structure of the written text." Jacques Derrida, *Limited Inc.,* trans. Samuel Weber (Evanston, IL: Northwestern University Press, 1988), 9. Even the notorious "undecidability" of readings, according to Derrida, can be ascribed to conflicts of force. Derrida insists that the reason that he prefers the phrase *undecidability* to *indeterminability* is because the former constitutes and is based upon "relations of forces" and "differences of force," which permit, "precisely, determinations in given situations to

be stabilized through a decision of writing." Ibid., 148. See also David Wood and Robert Bernasconi, eds., *Derrida and Différance* (Evanston, IL: Northwestern University Press, 1988).

3. A similar presentation and discussion along these lines can be found in John Russon, "Reading: Hegel in Derrida's Understanding," *Research in Phenomenology* 36 (2006): 181–200. See also Kathleen Dow Magnus, *Hegel and the Symbolic Mediation of Spirit* (Albany NY: State University of New York Press, 2001); Stewart Barnett, ed., *Hegel After Derrida* (New York: Routledge, 1998); Catherine Kellogg, *Law's Trace: From Hegel to Derrida* (New York: Routledge, 2010).

4. Jacques Derrida, "Preface," to Catherine Malabou, *The Future of Hegel: Plasticity, Temporality, and Dialectic* (New York: Routledge, 2004), viii. See also Catherine Malabou, "Is Confession the Accomplishment of Recognition?" in Slavoy Žižek, Clayton Crockett, and Creston Davis, eds., *Hegel and the Infinite: Religion, Politics, and the Dialectic* (New York: Columbia University Press, 2011), 19–30.

5. Derrida, "Preface," ix.

6. Ibid., xvii.

7. Gilles Deleuze and Félix Guattari, *What Is Philosophy?* trans. Hugh Tomlinson and Graham Burchell (New York: Columbia University Press, 1994), 101.

8. Malabou, *The Future of Hegel*, 13.

9. Gilles Deleuze, *The Logic of Sense,* trans. Mark Lester with Charles Stivale (New York: Columbia University Press, 1990), 100.

10. Malabou, *The Future of Hegel*, 172.

11. Jacques Derrida, *Writing and Difference*, trans. Alan Bass (Chicago: University of Chicago Press, 1978), 11.

12. Ibid., 12.

13. Ibid., 26–27.

14. Ibid., 27, emphasis mine.

15. G. W. F. Hegel, *Phenomenology of Spirit*, trans. A. V. Miller (New York: Oxford University Press, 1977), 81.

16. Jacques Derrida, "The Pit and the Pyramid: Introduction to Hegel's Semiology," in *Margins of Philosophy*, trans. Alan Bass (Chicago: University of Chicago Press, 1982), 69–108.

17. G. W. F. Hegel, *Enzyklopädie der philosophischen Wissenschaften im Grundrisse* (Hamburg: Felix Meiner, 1991 [1830]), 372. Von Humboldt's

importance for understanding Hegel, as well as later Hegelian scholarship when it comes to the problem of language, has been stressed by Jere O. Surber. See his introduction to Jere O. Surber, ed., *Hegel and Language* (Albany: SUNY University Press, 2006), 3. An overview of Hegel's treatment of language more from a conventional Anglo-American than a Continental perspective is John McCumber, *The Company of Words: Hegel, Language, and Systematic Philosophy* (Evanston, IL: Northwestern University Press, 1993. See also Jere Paul Surber, ed., *Hegel and Language* (Albany: State University of New York Press, 2007); Quentin Lauer, S.J., *A Reading of Hegel's Phenomenology of Spirit* (New York: Fordham University Press, 1993).

18. Hegel, *Enzyklopädie*, 373.

19. "Diese Kraft is in der Tat die Intelligenz selbst, das mit sich identische Ich, welches durch seine Erinnerung ihnen unmittelbar Allgemeinheit gibt, und die einzelne Anschauung unter das bereits innerlich gemachte Bild *subsumiert*." Hegel, *Enzyklopädie,* 367.

20. Friedrich Nietzsche, *The Gay Science*, trans. Walter Kaufman (New York: Vintage, 1974), 182.

21. Hegel, *Enzyklopädie,* 367.

22. Ibid., 370.

23. Jacques Derrida, *Of Spirit: Heidegger and the Question*, trans. Geoffrey Bennington (Chicago: University of Chicago Press, 1991), 5.

24. Ibid., 5.

25. Jacques Derrida, "Force of Law: The 'Mystical Foundation of Authority,'" in *Acts of Religion*, ed. Gil Anidjar (New York: Routledge, 2013), 228–98.

26. Ibid., 9.

27. According to Simon Critchley, the Derridean *Kehre* is predicated on Heidegger's own recognition that "all questioning requires the prior pledge, or *Zusage* of that which is put in question. Thus, for the later Heidegger, the primary datum of language is das *Hören der Zusage*, listening to the grant or pledge. Derrida picks up, according to Critchley, on the close correlation in the German of Heidegger's philosophy between *zusagen* and *versprechen* ("to promise"). Simon Critchley, "The Question of the Question: An Ethico-Political Response to a Note in *Derrida's De l'Esprit*," in David C. Wood, ed., *Of Derrida, Heidegger, and Spirit* (Evanston, IL: Northwestern University Press, 1993), 96.

28. Derrida, *Writing and Difference*, 68.

29. Ibid., 76.

30. As Derrida's biographer Jason Powell quips, "writing is the original Valley of the Other within Being, and it is from the Other that writing comes." Jason Powell, *Jacques Derrida: A Biography* (New York: Continuum International, 2006), 54.

31. Derrida, *Writing and Difference*, 77.

32. Ibid., 153.

33. Ibid., 145.

34. Jacques Derrida, *The Gift of Death*, trans. David Wills (Chicago: University of Chicago Press, 1995), 80.

35. Ibid., 50.

36. Ibid., 109.

37. Jacques Derrida, *On the Name*, trans. David Wood (Stanford: Stanford University Press), 25.

38. Ibid., 17.

3. FORCE OF ART

1. Friedrich Nietzsche, *Thus Spoke Zarathustra*, trans. Walter Kaufmann (New York: Modern Library, 1995), 51.

2. Ibid., 141.

3. Ibid., 87.

4. Friedrich Nietzsche, *The Will to Power,* trans. Walter Kaufmann and R. I. Hollingdale (New York: Random House, 1967), 333 (my emphasis). Kaufman's translation of the phrase "inner event" seems to be something of a waffle based on doubts concerning what exact German word Nietzsche in his handwritten literary remains actually employed. According to Marie-Luise Haase, Nietzsche's original editor, Peter Gast, who put together the various aphorisms from the *Nachlass* in collaboration with the former's sister Elizabeth, apparently deciphered the expression "an inner event" as *ein inner Wille* ("an inner will"). Yet other scholars have claimed that the phrase should be *eine innere Welt* ("an inner world"). See Marie-Luise Haase, "Nietzsche und . . . ", in Volker Gerhardt, Renate Reschke, and Jørgen Kjaer, *Ästhetik und Ethik nach Nietzsche* (Berlin: Akademie, 2003), 27. Given the context in which the aphorism appears, Gast's original rendering is probably closer to what Nietzsche intended,

although Kaufman's translation also most likely captures a good deal of whatever meaning was originally projected.

5. Gilles Deleuze, *Nietzsche and Philosophy*, trans. Hugh Tomlinson (New York: Columbia University Press, 1983), 49.

6. Ibid., 50.

7. Nietzsche, *The Will to Power*, 550.

8. "Because Nietsche's fundamental metaphysical position is the end of metaphysics . . . it performs the grandest and most profound gathering . . . of all the essential fundamental positions in Western philosophy since Plato and in the light of Platonism." Martin Heidegger, *Nietzsche,* trans. David F. Krell, 2 vols. (San Francisco: HarperSanFrancisco, 1991), 1:205.

9. Nietzsche, *The Will to Power*, 550.

10. Friedrich Nietzsche, *Thus Spoke Zarathustra*, trans. Adrian del Caro (Cambridge: Cambridge University Press, 2006), 17.

11. Michel Henry, *Seeing the Invisible: On Kandinsky*, trans. Scott Davidson (New York: Continuum, 2009), 13.

12. Ibid., 16.

13. Wassily Kandinsky, *Concerning the Spiritual in Art*, trans. Michel T. H. Sadler (Boston: MFA, 2006), 96.

14. According to Hans Belting, Kandinsky in no way simply wanted to "paint music." He was "inspired" instead by Arnold Schoenberg's invention of atonal music, which "opened up new spaces of freedom" for the painter. Kandinsky strove to show in atonality a "dissonance" that "would become the 'consonance' of tomorrow," in other words, the "new harmony." Such a harmony was tantamount to a "field of force" that served as the fundamental condition of "an absolute color painting." Hans Belting, *Das Unsichtbare Meisterwerk: Die Modernen Mythen der Kunst* (Munich: C. H. Beck, 2001), 337. See also Igor Aronov, *Kandinsky's Quest: A Study in the Artist's Personal Symbolism, 1866–1907* (New York: Peter Lang, 2006); Christopher Short, *The Art Theory of Wassily Kandinsky, 1909–1928* (Bern: Peter Lang, 2010); Klaus von Beyme, *Das Zeitalter der Avantgarden: Kunst und Gesellschaft, 1905–1955* (Munich: C. H. Beck, 2005).

15. Kandinsky, *Concerning the Spiritual in Art*, 97.

16. Henry, *Seeing the Invisible*, 66.

17. Ibid., 122.

18. Ibid., 123 (my emphasis).

19. As art historian Arthur Jerome Eddy noted in 1914 at a time contemporaneous with the pre–World War I incarnation of *Der Blaue Reiter*, citing
one of Kandinsky's essays in the "almanac," which his friends published
with the same name as the actual group established during the 1920s,
Kandinsky's argument is that "our inner forces . . . mature and the result
is a longing to create something, and we try to find a material form—
manifestation—for the new value that exists in us in spiritual or intellectual form." This new value that is art is immanent in both the material
world and the spiritual insight of the painter. "Matter is but the store
house out of which the spirit selects the necessary elements to secure the
objective result." Arthur Jerome Eddy, *Cubists and Post-Impressionism*
(Chicago: McClurg, 1914), 131. See also Peg Weiss, *Kandinsky and Old
Russia: The Artist as Ethnographer and Shaman* (New Haven: Yale University Press, 1995); Frank Dersch, *Über das Geistige im Expressionismus:
Der Blaue Reiter und der Glaube* (Norderstedt: GRIN, 2005).

20. There are always "tensions," Kandinsky asserts, within the materials, and
these "tensions, for their part, permit the inner nature of the element to be
expressed." Such elements vary from lines, to colors, to "number." Composition feeds on such tensions. Composition is "nothing other than an
exact law-abiding organization of the vital forces which, in the form of
tensions, are shut up within the elements." Wassily Kandinsky, *Point and
Line to Plane*, ed. Hilda Rebay (New York: Courier Dover, 1979), 117.

21. Charles Harrison and Paul Wood, *Art in Theory, 1900–2000: An Anthol-
ogy of Changing Ideas* (London: Wiley-Blackwell, 2003), 251.

22. For example, consider Kurt Pinthus's "Speech for the Future" in 1918:
"die Wirklichkeit ist nicht außer uns, sondern in uns." Kurt Pinthus,
"Rede für die Zukunft," in *Die Erhebung. Jahrbuch für neue Dichtung und
Wirkung*, ed. Alfred Wolfenstein (Berlin, 1919), 1:412.

23. "What is great in man is that he is a bridge and not an end: what can be
loved in man is that he is an overture and a going under. I love those who
do not know how to live, except by going under, for they are those who
cross over." Nietzsche, *Thus Spoke Zarathustra*, 15.

24. Ibid., 4. Kaufmann's translation here seems to miss much of the subtle
implications of Nietzsche's rhetoric. *Genügsamkeit* implies more the
self-satisfaction of the conventional, "bourgeois" thinking of the "last
man," a thinking that the "lightning" (*Blitz*) of the "overman" dispels.

Furthermore, *Geiz* suggests less simple mean-spiritedness than the kind of invidious, rationalistic, and pragmatic kinds of calculation that hold back philosophy and culture.

25. Deleuze, *Nietzsche and Philosophy*, 77.
26. "We will never find the sense of something... if we do not know the force which appropriates the things, which exploits it, which takes possession of it or is *expressed* in it." It is the manifestation of the force that articulates the sentence, or proposition, as semiosis rather than as predication. "A phenomenon is not an appearance or even an apparition but a sign, a symptom which finds its meaning in an existing force. The whole of philosophy is a symptomatology, and a semiology." In effect, "Nietzsche substitutes the correlation of sense and phenomenon for the metaphysical duality of appearance and essence and for the scientific relation of cause and effect. Deleuze, *Nietzsche and Philosophy*, 3 (my emphasis).
27. Deleuze, *Nietzsche and Philosophy*, 2.

4. FORCE OF THE POLITICAL

1. See Victor Farías, *Heidegger and Nazism* (Philadelphia: Temple University Press, 1991).
2. Richard Wolin, "French Heidegger Wars," in Richard Wolin, ed., *The Heidegger Controversy: A Critical Reader* (Cambridge: MIT University Press, 1993), 274. See also Philippe Lacoue-Labarthe, *Heidegger, Art, and Politics*, trans. Chris Turner (Oxford: Basil Blackwell, 1990); Tom Rockmore, *Heidegger and French Philosophy: Humanism, Antihumanism, and Being* (New York: Routledge, 1995); as well as Tom Rockmore and Joseph Margolis, eds., *The Heidegger Case on Philosophy and Politics* (Philadelphia: Temple University Press, 1992); more recently, Mahon O'Brien, "Re-assessing the 'Affair': The Heidegger Controversy Revisited," *Social Science Journal* 47 (2010): 1–10; Jeff Collins, *Heidegger and the Nazis* (London: Icon, 1996).
3. Philipp Lacoue-Labarthe, *Heidegger and the Politics of Poetry*, trans. Jeff Fort (Chicago: University of Chicago Press, 2007), 104.
4. F. W. J. Schelling, *Critical and Historical Introduction to the Philosophy of Mythology*, ed. and trans. Mason Richey, Markus Zisselsberger, and Jason M. Wirth (Albany: State University of New York Press, 2007), 23.
5. Ibid., 10.

6. Joseph Lawrence, "Philosophical Religion and the Quest for Authenticity," in Jason M. Wirth, ed., *Schelling Now: Contemporary Readings* (Bloomington: Indiana University Press, 2005), 14.

7. A comparison can also be drawn here between Schelling, Benjamin, and Schmitt, who understood sovereignty as akin to *creatio ex nihilo*. For a general overview of the question, see Jens Bartelson, *A Genealogy of Sovereignty* (Cambridge: Cambridge University Press, 1995).

8. See Karl Popper, *The Open Society and Its Enemies* (New York: Routledge and Kegan Paul, 1945).

9. Michael Gagarin, for example, has shown that the ancient Greek ambivalence about the relationship between *eris* and *logos*, not to mention their mutual conditioning necessity, is not merely a Platonic, or post-Platonic, concern. It can be found in Hesiod himself. In Hesiod and subsequent thinkers "a unity divides into opposites, which then recombine into a new unity, resulting in a complex tension among the unity and its parts." Michael Gagarin, "The Truth of Antiphon's Truth, in Anthony Preus, ed., *Essays in Ancient Greek Philosophy VI* (Albany: State University of New York Press, 2001), 173. Thus because Hesiod's "ambivalent truth" runs throughout Greek thought, it is perhaps only an irenic misreading of the origins of the Western ontological tradition that we tend to associate *logos* with pacification. Indeed, Gagarin suggests, *eris* (discordant or disruptive strife) and *agon* (integrative or competitive conflict) are intimately bound up with what today we call reason. All the major "idealist" thinkers, particularly Kant, Schelling, and Heidegger, have engaged with varying ventures of this kind of genealogy into the interplay of myth and reason. The temptation to "totalitarianism," of course, can be found in the Hegelian dialectic, where the eristic component becomes the all-sufficient and all-comprehending comprehension (*Begriff*) of *logos* as pure, mediated opposition. The real hence becomes totally rational, and the rational totally real—the formula of totalization. By "sublating" myth into reason, as critics such as Lacoue-Labarthe perhaps would prefer, and many detractors from the use of myth in philosophy would prefer, the kind of political totalitarianism attributed to Heideggerianism is far more inviting.

10. F. W. J. Schelling, *The Ages of the World*, trans. Jason Wirth (Albany: State University of New York Press, 2000), 107.

11. Michel Foucault, *Language, Countermemory, Practice: Selected Essays and Interviews* (Ithaca, NY: Cornell University Press, 1980), 143.

12. Ibid., 144.

13. Ibid., 149–50.

14. Ibid., 159.

15. Aristotle, *Nichomachean Ethics*, 1094a–b, trans. Terence Irwin (Indianapolis: Hackett, 1985), 2–3.

16. Aristotle, *Poetics* 1448a, in *Poetics and Rhetoric* (New York: Barnes and Noble, 2005), 5.

17. Aristotle, *Rhetoric*, 1365b, ibid., 167–69.

18. Walter Benjamin. "Doctrine of the Similar," trans. Knut Tarnowski, *New German Critique*, no. 17, special Walter Benjamin issue (Spring 1979): 68. Taken from Walter Benjamin, *Gesammelte Schriften*, ed. Rolf Tiedemann and Hermann Schweppenhauser, vol. 2, 1 (Frankfurt: Suhrkamp, 1977), 204–10.

19. Richard Wolin, *Walter Benjamin: An Aesthetic of Redemption* (Berkeley: University of California Press, 1994), 243. See also Lutz Peter Koepnick, *Walter Benjamin and the Aesthetics of Power* (Lincoln: University of Nebraska Press, 1999), 213ff.; Jan Mieszkowski, "Art Forms," in David S. Ferris, ed., *The Cambridge Companion to Walter* Benjamin (Cambridge: Blackwell, 2004), 35–53. See also Andrew Benjamin, *Art, Mimesis, and the Avant-Garde* (New York: Routledge, 1991); Michael Taussig, *Mimesis and Alterity: A Particular History of the Senses* (New York: Routledge, 1993).

20. See Walter Benjamin, *Reflections: Essays, Aphorisms, Autobiographical Writings*, trans. Edmund Jephcott (New York: Harcourt Brace Jovanovich, 1978), 335.

21. Walter Benjamin, *Illuminations: Essays and Reflections,* ed. Hannah Arendt, trans. Harry Zohn (New York: Harcourt, Brace, and Jovanovich, 1968), 257–58.

5. FORCE AND ECONOMY

1. According to Richard Posner, the paralysis of competing demands and desires in our fractious democracy has become unsustainable. "Every sensible path to a long-run solution to the nation's long-run fiscal problems seem blocked by special interests and political demagoguery." See

Richard Posner, *The Crisis of Capitalist Democracy* (Cambridge: Harvard University Press, 2010), 241. See also Nolan McCarty, Keith T. Poole, and Howard Rosenthal, *Political Bubbles: Financial Crises and the Failure of American Democracy* (Princeton: Princeton University Press, 2013).

2.   Jean-Joseph Goux, *Symbolic Economies: After Marx and Freud*, trans. Jennifer Curtiss Gage (Ithaca, NY: Cornell University Press, 1990), 9. For a careful analysis of Goux's project, see Martha Woodmansee and Mark Osteen, eds., *The New Economic Criticism: Studies at the Intersection of Literature and Economics* (New York: Routledge, 1999), 13ff.; also Robert Markley, "Boundaries: Mathematics, Alienation, and the Metaphysics of Cyberspace," in Robert Markley, ed., *Virtual Realities and Their Discontents* (Baltimore: Johns Hopkins University Press, 1996), 70.

3.   Giorgio Agamben, *The Kingdom and the Glory: For a Theological Genealogy of Economy and Government* , trans. Lorenzo Chiesa and Matteo Mandamini (Stanford: Stanford University Press, 2011), preface, lov. 207 of 6397.

4.   I am using the more common English word *resentment* here in place of Nietzsche's *ressentiment,* which is normally employed for the kind of technical purposes this analysis pursues. My motive is less a deference to common usage than a preference for a certain stylistic smoothness with a secondary importation of Nietzsche's French usage, which sounds more natural in German than in English. Furthermore, the specific subject of "economy" here requires instead the contemporary construal of resentment as a political phenomenon, which Nietzsche's psychological and exclusively "genealogical" method unfortunately forecloses. For a consideration of this issue from a variety of viewpoints, including different takes on the role of resentment in the formation of political theory, see Richard Schacht, ed., *Nietzsche, Genealogy, Morality: Essays on Nietzsche's Genealogy of Morals* (Berkeley: University of California Press, 1995). See also Peter Poellner, *Nietzsche and Metaphysics* (New York: Oxford University Press, 1995), 130; Jeffrey Metzger, "How Deep Are the Roots of Nihilism? Nietzsche on the Creative Power of Nature and Morality," in Jeffrey Metzger, ed., *Nietzsche, Nihilism, and the Philosophy of the Future* (New York: Continuum, 2009), 135ff.

5. See Mark Lilla, *The Stillborn God: Religion, Politics, and the Modern West* (New York: Knopf, 2007).

6. Alexis de Tocqueville, *Democracy in America* (New York: Penguin, 2004), 290.

7. See Robin Small (1997), "Ressentiment, Revenge, and Punishment: Origins of the Nietzschean Critique," *Utilitas* 9:39–58. Dühring's ideas are mostly expounded in his *Der Werth des Leben: Eine Philosophische Betrachtung* (Breslau: Eduard Trewendt, 1865). "Tracing the concept of justice traced back to *ressentiment* or revenge is no frivolous effort, but has for years been considered a [genuine] insight" (ibid., 70, translation mine).

8. See Karl Eugen Dühring, *Die Judenfrage als als Frage des Racencharakters und seine Schädlichkeiten für Völkerexistenz, Sitte, und Kultur* (Berlin: Personalist Verlag von Ulrich Dühring, 1901).

9. Friedrich Nietzsche, *Zur Genealogie der Moral,* Projekt Gutenberg. 56.

10. Gilles Deleuze, *Nietzsche and Philosophy*, trans. Hugh Tomlinson (New York: Columbia University Press), 110.

11. Frederic Jameson, *Postmodernism, or The Cultural Logic of Late Capitalism* (Durham, NC: Duke University Press, 1991).

12. Jean Baudrillard, *Symbolic Exchange and Death*, trans. Iain Hamilton Grant (London: Sage, 1993), 10.

13. David Orrell, *Economyths: Ten Ways Economics Gets It Wrong* (Mississaugo: Wiley, 2010), 1. Other recent books that take the same line of approach include John Cassidy, *How Markets Fail: The Logic of Economic Calamities* (New York: Farrar, Straus, and Giroux, 2009); Franklin Allen and Douglas Gale, *Understanding Financial Crises* (New York: Oxford University Press, 2009); Justin Fox, *The Myth of the Rational Market: A History of Risk, Reward, and Delusion on Wall Street* (New York: HarperBusiness, 2011); Carmen M. Reinhart and Kenneth Rogoff, *This Time Is Different: Eight Centuries of Financial Folly* (Princeton: Princeton University Press, 2009).

14. See Ludwig Wittgenstein, *Philosophical Investigations* (Hoboken, NJ: Wiley, 1999), § 109.

15. Jacques Derrida, *Given Time I: Counterfeit Money*, trans. Peggy Kamuf (Chicago: University of Chicago Press, 1992), 20.

16. See Jacques Derrida, *The Gift of Death* (Chicago: University of Chicago Press, 1995).

6. FORCE OF EXCEPTION

1. Immanuel Kant, "Idea for a Universal History from a Cosmopolitan Point of View," quoted from the full online text of the essay that originally appeared in "Idea for a Universal History from a Cosmopolitan Point of View," in Immanuel Kant, *On History*, trans. Lewis White Beck (Indianapolis: Bobbs-Merrill, 1963). The online version can be found at http://www.marxists.org/reference/subject/ethics/kant/universal-history.htm#n1.

2. Carl Schmitt, *The Concept of the Political*, trans. George Schwab (Chicago: University of Chicago Press, 1996), 26.

3. Carl Schmitt, *Political Theology*, trans. George Schwab (Chicago: University of Chicago Press, 1985), 5.

4. Giorgio Agamben, *Homo Sacer: Sovereign Power and Bare Life*, trans. Daniel Heller-Roazen (Stanford: Stanford University Press, 1998), 52.

5. Michael Hardt and Antonio Negri, *Multitude: War and Democracy in the Age of Empire* (New York: Penguin, 2004), 211

6. Jean-Luc Nancy, *A Finite Thinking* (Stanford: Stanford University Press), 13.

7. Jean-Luc Nancy, *The Creation of the World or Globalization,* trans. Francius Raffoul and David Pettigrew (Albany: State University of New York Press), 109.

8. Ibid., 34.

9. Benedict Anderson, *Imagined Communities: Reflections on the Origin and Spread of Nationalism*, rev. ed. (New York: Verso, 2006), 4. See also Partha Chatterjee, "Whose Imagined Community?" *Millennium: Journal of International Studies* 20 (March 1991): 521–25; Roland Robertson, "Global Connectivity and Global Consciousness," *American Behavioral Scientist* 50 (October 2011): 1336–45.

10. Jean-Luc Nancy, *Dis-Enclosure: The Deconstruction of Christianity*, trans. Bettina Bergo, Gabriel Malefant, and Michael B. Smith (New York: Fordham University Press, 200), 33. The same point has recently been argued exhaustively and effectively by political theorist Mark Lilla in *The Stillborn God* (New York: Knopf, 2007).

11. Olivier Roy, *Globalized Islam: The Search for a New Ummah* (New York: Columbia University Press, 2004), 40. For related research, see Johan Meuleman, ed., *Islam in the Era of Globalization* (London: Routledge-

Curzon, 2002); Ali Mohammadi, ed., *Islam Encountering Globalization* (London: RoutledgeCurzon, 2002); Stephen Vertigans and Philip W. Sutton, "Globalisation Theory and Islamic Praxis," *Global Society* 16 (2002): 31–46.

12. Roy's argument is tacit, if not explicit, in the latest work of historian Philip Jenkins. See Philip Jenkins, *The Next Christendom: The Coming of Global Christianity* (New York: Oxford University Press, 2002). This analysis is also deployed in a slightly different manner in my own book *GloboChrist* (Grand Rapids: Baker Academic, 2008). See Caryn Aviv and David Shneer, *New Jews: The End of the Jewish Diaspora* (New York: New York University Press, 2005).

13. Alain Badiou, *Saint Paul: The Foundations of Universalism*, trans. Ray Brassier (Stanford: Stanford University Press, 2003), 109. For a good collection of essays on this trajectory of argument, stemming from a conference at Syracuse University, see John D. Caputo and Linda Martin Alcoff, eds., *St. Paul Among the Philosophers* (Bloomington: Indiana University Press, 2009). See also Simon Critchley, "On Alain Badiou," in Heidrun Friese, ed., *The Moment: Time and Rupture in Modern Thought* (Liverpool: Liverpool University Press, 2001), 91–112.

14. Badiou, *Saint Paul*, 97.

15. Ibid., 69.

16. Ibid., 68.

17. Ibid., 109.

18. Peter Sloterdijk, *God's Zeal: The Battle of the Three Monotheisms*, trans. Wieland Hoban (Cambridge: Polity, 2010), 96–97.

19. Peter Sloterdijk, *Bubbles: Spheres I*, trans. Wieland Hoban (Los Angeles: Semiotex(e), 2011), 21. See also Willem Schinkel, "The Global Sphere: Peter Sloterdijk's Theory of Globalization," *Cultural Politics* 3 (2007): 393–98; my own "Peter Sloterdijk as First Philosopher of Globalization," *Journal for Cultural and Religion Theory* 12 (Spring 2013): 1–18.

20. Sloterdijk, *Bubbles,* 61.

21. Ibid., 65–66.

22. As Jonathan Berkey notes in his probing and nuanced analysis of the rise of Islam, the entire millennium beginning with Alexander of Macedon's lightning conquests of most of the known world in the fourth century bc can be seen as a time when localism—which within a context of political consolidation implies pluralism—became increasingly difficult, if not

impossible. Empire and religious universalism go hand in hand. On that score, Berkey intimates that Constantinianism, spawning both growth of both the Roman church and Byzantine caesaro-papism, was therefore historically inevitable. The "union of Roman state and Christian religion . . . built upon a connection between religious truth and political power." When the Roman state in the West collapsed in the fifth century, "the rise and success of Islam followed rather than digressed from older patterns." Jonathan P. Berkey, *The Formation of Islam: Religion and Society in the Near East, 600–1800* (Cambridge: Cambridge University Press, 2003), 7.

23.   Sloterdijk, *God's Zeal*, 135–36.

7. FORCE OF GOD

1.   For a substantial discussion of the origins of democratic theory in the major religious traditions, see not only Mark Lilla, *The Stillborn God: Religion, Politics, and the Modern West* (New York: Vintage, 2008), but also Abdulaziz Sachedina, *The Islamic Roots of Democratic Pluralism* (New York: Oxford University Press, 2001). For a discussion of Sachedina's argument, see M. A. Muqtedar Khan, "The Politics, Theory, and Philosophy of Islamic Democracy," in M. A. Muqtedar Khan, ed., *Islamic Democratic Discourse: Theory, Debates, and Philosophical Perspectives* (Lanham, MD: Rowman and Littlefield, 2006), 158ff. See also Minaz C. Chenai, *Recueil de textes du professuer Abdulaziz Sachedina* (Paris: Publibook, 2008), 126.

2.   See, for this particular line of argument, Simon Critchley's opening chapter, "The Catechism of the Citizen," in *The Faith of the Faithless: Experiments in Political Theology* (London: Verso, 2012).

3.   See especially Karl Popper, *The Open Society and Its Enemies: The Spell of Plato*, vol. 1 rev. ed. (Princeton: Princeton University Press, 1971).

4.   Critchley, "The Catechism of the Citizen," 89.

5.   See Karl Mannheim, *Ideology and Utopia: An Introduction to the Sociology of Knowledge* (Whitefish, MT: Kessinger, 2008).

6.   Critchley, *The Faith of the Faithless,* 161.

7.   Walter Mignolo, *The Darker Side of Western Modernity: Global Futures, Decolonial Options* (Durham, NC: Duke University Press, 2011), 275. See

also Walter Mignolo, "The Geopolitics of Knowledge and the Colonial Difference," in Mabel Moraña, Enrique D. Dussel, and Carlos A. Jáuregui, eds., *Coloniality at Large: Latin America and the Postcolonial Debate* (Durham, NC: Duke University Press, 2011), 225–58; Walter Mignolo, "The Communal and the Decolonial," *Pavilion* 14 (2010): 146–55.

8. See Ervand Abrahamian, "Ali Shariati: Ideologue of the Iranian Revolution," in Edmund Burke and Ira Lapidus, eds., *Islam, Politics, and Social Movements* (Los Angeles: University of California Press, 1993), 289–97.

9. Mignolo, *The Darker Side of Western Modernity*, 286.

10. In Greek tragedy *moira* (generally, "fate" or "destiny," but more specifically one's own "portion" granted by the universe in compensation for an individual's actions) and *nemein*, from which derives *nomos* and meaning the process of distribution or allotment itself, are simply two dimensions of how time unfolds. We see this relationship in a close reading of certain Greek tragedies. The *nomos* (in English "law" in the sense of "right," or in German *Recht*) of the state, as Julian Etxabe points out, is secondary to the justification of one's moral or "judicial" decisions, which eventually become enshrined as a legal code or set of precedents. See Julian Etxabe, "Antigone's *Nomos*," *Animus: The Canadian Journal of Philosophy and Humanities* 13 (2009): 61. The "force of law" in Derrida's sense and the "founding" deeds of the tragic hero are consolidated in this sense. This interpretation of *nomos*, which begins to emerge with Sophocles and is cited significantly in Aristotle's *Rhetoric*, separates law from *physis*, or "nature" as what both action and its consequences are essentially embedded. See William Allan, "Tragedy and the Early Greek Philosophical Tradition," in Justina Gregory, ed., *A Companion to Greek Tragedy* (Malden, MA: Blackwell, 2005), 79. Hence, the laws of the *polis*, or the realm of *nomos* as accepted precedent and practice, constitute the sense of what Hegel would later term the "world spirit" acting through "great men."

8. THE END OF THE POLITICAL

1. Hannah Arendt, *Was ist Politik?* (Munich: Piper, 1993), 126.
2. Ibid., 39.
3. Ibid., 81.
4. Hannah Arendt, *On Violence* (New York: Harcourt Brace, 1969), 51.

5. See Andrew Benjamin, *Walter Benjamin and the Architecture of Modernity* (Melbourne: re.press, 2009), 85.

6. See Hannah Arendt, *The Origins of Totalitarianism* (New York: Harcourt, 1973).

7. Richard John Neuhaus, *The Naked Public Square: Religion and Democracy in America* (Grand Rapids MI: Eerdmans, 1984).

8. Claude Lefort, "The Permanence of the Theological-Political," in Hent DeVries and Lawrence Sullivan, eds., *Political Theologies: Public Religions in a Post-Secular World* (New York: Fordham University Press, 2006), 150. See also Annika Thiem, "Schmittian Shadows and Contemporary Theological-Political Constellations," *Social Research: An International Quarterly* 80 (2013): 1–32; Hugues Poltier, *Claude Lefort: La Découverte du Politique* (Paris: Michalon, 1997).

9. Lefort, "The Permanence of the Theological-Political," 151.

10. Ibid., 152.

11. Ibid., 159.

12. See Charles Taylor, *A Secular Age* (Cambridge: Harvard University Press, 2009). Taylor understands the advent of secularity and modernity as a shift from hierarchical and "mediated" access to the plenitude of power radiated by the kingly sovereign. In such a world "human agents are embedded in society, society in the cosmos, and the cosmos incorporates the divine" (ibid., 152). In the secular world, by contrast, mediation gives way to what he calls the "buffered self" where reality is now contained wholly within the independent, *sovereign* subject.

13. Lefort, "The Permanence of the Theological-Political," 162.

14. Ibid., 161.

15. Claude Lefort, "Politics and Human Rights," in John B. Thompson, ed., *The Political Forms of Modern Society: Bureaucracy, Democracy, and Totalitarianism* (Cambridge: MIT Press, 1986), 260.

16. Adam Smith, *The Theory of the Moral Sentiments* (Edinburgh: A. Millar, 1774), 203.

17. Leo Strauss and Joseph Cropsey, *History of Political Philosophy*, 3d ed. (Chicago: University of Chicago Press, 1987), 648.

9. GOD, THE STATE, AND REVOLUTION

1. Alain Badiou, *Metapolitics,* trans. Joan Copjec (New York: Verso, 2005).

2. Ibid., 145.

3. Ibid., 149.

4. Michael Walzer, *The Revolution of the Saints: A Study in the Origin of Radical Politics* (Cambridge: Harvard University Press, 1965), 317.

5. Ibid., 302.

6. Karl Marx and Friedrick Engels, *The German Ideology* (New York: International, 1970), 47.

7. See Max Weber, *Political Writings*, trans. Ronald Speirs (New York: Cambridge University Press), 1994.

8. John Milbank, *Theology and Social Theory: Beyond Secular Reason* (Malden, MA: Blackwell, 1991), 381.

9. Ibid., 381.

10. G. W. F. Hegel, *Philosophy of Right*, book 3, 258.

11. Augustine, *City of God*, trans. Henry Bettenson (New York: Penguin, 1972), XIX, 21, 881.

12. Ibid., II, 27, 85.

13. Ibid., XIV, 28, 593.

14. Ibid., XXII, 30, 1090.

15. Badiou, *Metapolitics*, 146.

16. Alain Badiou, *Logics of Worlds*, trans. Alberto Toscano (New York: Continuum, 2009), 65.

Index

Marxism, xi, 79, 96, 130, 142, 145, 155,
160; Baudrillard and, 87, 89; Ben-
jamin and, 143; class consciousness
of, 150; collapse of, 6, 92; dialectical
materialism of, 77, 87, 143; Hegel
and, 22; neo-Marxism, 59, 109
Mass media, 81
Materialism, 89, 155, 160; dialectical, 77,
87, 143; historical, xi, 92
Mathesis universalis, 91
Mauss, Marcel, 101
McLuhan, Marshall, 87
McPherson, C. B., 4–6
Mediacracy, 81, 87
Mediation, 188*n*12
Meier, Heinrich, 171*n*4
Memory, as representation, 43
Merleau-Ponty, Maurice, 54
Metaphysics, xii, 45, 70–71, 95
Metapolitics (Badiou), 156, 170
Mexico, 136
Microspherology, 121
Middle East, 7
Mignolo, Walter, 92, 118, 125, 134–36,
138, 154
Milbank, John, 163–64, 169
Militants, 170
Mimesis, 62–66
Mind (*Sinne*), 42
Modernism, ix, 3, 46, 51
Modernity, 3, 134, 143, 150, 188*n*12
Moira, 137, 187*n*10
Mondrian, Piet, 46
Money, 74–75; counterfeit, 98–102
Monotheism, 81, 113–15, 117, 119, 123, 136
Monotheistic imperative, 117
Montesquieu, 155
Moral-Christian metaphysics, xii
Morales, Evo, 136
Moses (biblical figure), 119
Les Mots et les choses (Foucault), 4
Mueller, Otto, 51
Multitudinism, 110

Music, 47; atonal, 177*n*14
Mutatis mutandis, 25
Myth, constitutive force and, 56–60
Myth of Er, 15

Nancy, Jean-Luc, 109, 112–13
Napoleonic wars, 105
Nationalism: ethnic, 114; postnational-
ism, xiii, 110–13
National Socialism, 7, 51, 81
Natural law theory, 4
Natural orders, 159
Nazism, 7, 34, 38, 54–56, 63, 139
Negri, Antonio, 110, 112
Neoconservatism, 7
Neo-Kantianism, 11, 105
Neoliberalism, 22, 113, 120–21
Neo-Marxism, 59, 109
Neuhaus, Richard John, 144
New atheists, x
New harmony, 47, 48
Newton, Isaac, 26, 43, 100
New World, 155
New York Times, 8
Nichomachean Ethics (Aristotle), 61
Nietzsche, Friedrich, xv, 7, 121, 141, 157;
Christianity and, 72, 80; crisis of
representation and, 8–9; death of
God and, xiv, 32, 79, 138; Derrida
and, 16; expressionism and, 51–53;
genealogy and, xi–xiii, 10–13, 52–53,
60–61, 71–72, 76; Hegel and, 41–42;
inner event and, 176*n*4; metaphysics
and, 70; political theology and, xii;
poststructuralism and, 14; *ressentiment* and, x, 80, 83–85, 182*n*4; Sloterdijk and, 83; transvaluation and, 50;
truthfulness and, 21; will to power
and, 12, 16, 35, 42–45, 78
Nietzsche and Philosophy (Deleuze),
44, 86
Nihilism, 8–9, 14, 79, 169
9/11 terrorist attacks, 113

INSURRECTIONS: CRITICAL STUDIES IN
RELIGION, POLITICS, AND CULTURE

After the Death of God, John D. Caputo and Gianni Vattimo, edited by Jeffrey W. Robbins

The Politics of Postsecular Religion: Mourning Secular Futures, Ananda Abeysekara

Nietzsche and Levinas: "After the Death of a Certain God," edited by Jill Stauffer and Bettina Bergo

Strange Wonder: The Closure of Metaphysics and the Opening of Awe, Mary-Jane Rubenstein

Religion and the Specter of the West: Sikhism, India, Postcoloniality, and the Politics of Translation, Arvind Mandair

Plasticity at the Dusk of Writing: Dialectic, Destruction, Deconstruction, Catherine Malabou

Anatheism: Returning to God After God, Richard Kearney

Rage and Time: A Psychopolitical Investigation, Peter Sloterdijk

Radical Political Theology: Religion and Politics After Liberalism, Clayton Crockett

Radical Democracy and Political Theology, Jeffrey W. Robbins

Hegel and the Infinite: Religion, Politics, and Dialectic, edited by Slavoj Žižek, Clayton Crockett, and Creston Davis

What Does a Jew Want? On Binationalism and Other Specters, Udi Aloni

A Radical Philosophy of Saint Paul, Stanislas Breton, edited by Ward Blanton, translated by Joseph N. Ballan

Hermeneutic Communism: From Heidegger to Marx, Gianni Vattimo and Santiago Zabala

Deleuze Beyond Badiou: Ontology, Multiplicity, and Event, Clayton Crockett

Self and Emotional Life: Philosophy, Psychoanalysis, and Neuroscience, Adrian Johnston and Catherine Malabou

The Incident at Antioch: A Tragedy in Three Acts / L'Incident d'Antioche: Tragédie en trois actes, Alain Badiou, translated by Susan Spitzer

Philosophical Temperaments: From Plato to Foucault, Peter Sloterdijk